AMERICAN ENGLISH IDIOMATIC EXPRESSIONS
IN 52 WEEKS

D0395669

American English Idiomatic Expressions in

52 Weeks

An Easy Way to Understand English Expressions and Improve Speaking

John Holleman

The Chinese University Press

American English Idiomatic Expressions in 52 Weeks:
An Easy Way to Understand English Expressions and
Improve Speaking
   John Holleman

© **The Chinese University of Hong Kong**, 2006

ISBN 962–996–281–0

THE CHINESE UNIVERSITY PRESS
The Chinese University of Hong Kong
SHA TIN, N.T., HONG KONG
Fax: +852 2603 6692
      +852 2603 7355
E-mail: cup@cuhk.edu.hk
Web-site: www.chineseupress.com

Printed in Hong Kong

Contents

The majority of *English as a Second Language* (ESL) students face major difficulties learning English idioms. Non-native speakers often find themselves at a loss to understand the full meaning of English language conversations because, in many cases, these discussions contain a large number of idioms. This challenge is found in a variety of settings where English is used, including business meetings, workplace discussions and casual conversations among native English speakers. As English language learners work to improve their conversational proficiency, they soon realize that the number of idioms used in spoken English is staggering.

As 2nd language learners discover immediately as they interact with native English speakers, expressions involving idioms can be a serious challenge in understanding the dynamics of a conversation. Being able to comprehend the meaning of these commonly used phrases is essential to capturing the substance of a conversation. Most importantly, being able to use idioms in a discussion increases a person's *confidence* in their overall communicative proficiency in spoken English. This competence in oral communication means that the English language learner has the ability to use English in a variety of situations and under different circumstances. Being able to *confidently* participate in an English conversation about current events, business, work or family is very important for the non-native speaker in his or her efforts to increase their oral proficiency. Therefore, the ability to understand and use English language idioms in conversation is vitally important in developing confidence in the real world use of the language.

The use of idioms is a challenge for English language learners because, compared to standard vocabulary acquisition, understanding these expressions is not clear by simply referring to a dictionary. To assist the 2nd language learner in understanding the meaning of idioms, this week-by-week calendar of English language idioms should be used to systematically learn these expressions found in common usage among native English speakers.

Idiom Classification

Consisting of 3,243 different English idioms, this weekly calendar offers the 2nd language learner a structured method by which they can learn idioms in an efficient and organized manner. A unique classification system consisting of

32 separate categories is used to assist language learners in this book. The purpose of the classification system is to break down the large number of idioms into a study strategy that is both *manageable* and *productive* for the learner. Grouping idioms into easy-to-understand categories is an effective learning tool to assist the English language learner in acquiring an understanding of these distinctive expressions.

The classification system created was intended to be intuitive, practical and simple for ESL learners by placing idioms into functional and direct categories. These 32 functional categories include:

1. *Achievement* — the act or process of accomplishing or completing something
2. *Agree / Approval* — to accept or share an understanding of something
3. *Authority* — referring to the power to influence, obey or judge
4. *Bad / Negative* — something unfavorable or unpleasant
5. *Business Action* — relating to commercial or work activity to generate profit
6. *Communication* — the process of sending and receiving information through speaking, behavior or writing
7. *Completeness* — the extent of wholeness or having enough of something
8. *Consequence* — the effects or result of an action or circumstance
9. *Different* — not the same
10. *Disagree* — to have a different opinion or reaction to something
11. *Emotion* — a natural feeling such as joy, sadness, happiness, love or hate
12. *End* — the conclusion of something
13. *Entertainment* — something that delights or provides amusement
14. *Error* — something that differs from the correct or usual process
15. *Failure* — not succeeding in something
16. *Health* — the condition of wellness for someone's body or mind
17. *Importance* — to be valuable or significant
18. *Location* — relating to where something is positioned or situated
19. *Money* — something relating to currency or a measure of wealth
20. *Movement* — involving motion or a change in something's position
21. *Ownership* — concerning the possession of something
22. *Personal Description* — referring to traits, features or attributes of a person
23. *Plan / Prepare* — concerning the process involved in accomplishing an activity
24. *Quantity* — relating to the amount of something
25. *Relationship* — referring to a connection between people including romance, friendship or hostility
26. *Satisfaction* — involving enjoyment and contentment in circumstances

27. ***Service*** — concerning assistance or being helpful
28. ***Similar*** — referring to the extent that something is alike or related
29. ***Superior*** — someone or something being better
30. ***Time*** — relating to a time period
31. ***Understand*** — referring to knowing and comprehending something
32. ***Work*** — relating to a job, employment or occupations

Directions for Use

Readers are encouraged to use this book on a daily basis to learn American idiomatic expressions. It is expected that, if reviewed systematically on a daily basis, readers will be able to learn the meaning of the expressions accompanied by a sample sentence, demonstrating how it may be used. The 60 to 65 different idioms are presented each week, with most chapters divided into 32 distinct categories to help readers organize, in their minds, how to group the expressions.

This week-by-week calendar method is best used by readers to carry out a 52-week plan to recognize the meaning of the idioms. Authentic examples of sentence usage are provided for each of the 3,243 idioms, showing how the expressions are used in current, everyday American English.

Week 1

✍ Achievement

a going concern — an ongoing enterprise
USAGE: Jacob has *a going concern* that has been profitable for over two years.

above and beyond the call of duty — to do more than is typically expected
USAGE: The manager went *above and beyond the call of duty* when he worked overtime.

ahead of the curve — predicting future progress
USAGE: Susan was *ahead of the curve* when it came to understanding how globalization would change China.

at the top of his/her game — performing at the highest level
USAGE: As one of the top athletes in the city, he is *at the top of his game*.

✍ Agree / Approval

about that — To approve of. Also about it. Note: often pronounced "bout that" or "bout it."
USAGE: I'm so not *about that*. / You want to leave now? I'm *about it*. / Whatever you want to do, I'm *about it*.

add up — seems reasonable
USAGE: The things he said about his boss don't really *add up*.

✍ Authority

above board — appropriate; not secret
USAGE: The managers were *above board* in stating they were uncertain about what happen with the new regulations.

at will — when desired; free to act
USAGE: The soldiers were directed to open fire *at will*.

✍ Bad / Negative

(a) bitter pill — a troublesome experience or situation
USAGE: It was *a bitter pill* for the employees to take, knowing that they might lose their jobs.

✍ Business Action

according to Hoyle — by the rules; correct method
USAGE: *According to Hoyle*, new members may not speak during the first meeting.

✍ Communication

a picture is worth a thousand words — a picture is easier to understand than something written
USAGE: When I saw her standing there feeling depressed, it was *a picture worth a thousand words*!

a piece of my mind — criticism
USAGE: I was really frustrated with the circumstances we found ourselves in, so I told her what I believed and gave her *a piece of my mind*.

actions speak louder than words — a person's behavior communicates more than words spoken
USAGE: The father's care shown to the child demonstrated his *actions spoke louder than words*.

add fuel to the fire — increasing the tension of a problem situation
USAGE: When John argued he didn't believe in punishing the children and he didn't support his wife, he realized he was *adding fuel to the fire*.

add insult to injury — saying or doing something bad to an existing difficult situation
USAGE: When the boss told his employees they were incompetent workers, he was *adding insult to injury*.

air one's dirty laundry/linen in public — communicating something distressing in public that should be kept private or secret
USAGE: The party at the office became uncomfortable when the supervisor began to *air his children's dirty laundry in public*.

all eyes — watching very closely
USAGE: Horace was *all eyes* when the beautiful lady walked into the room with her drink.

all joking aside — to be serious or sober; businesslike
USAGE: Concerned about their money, John told Mary, that ***all joking aside***
   he was serious about changing jobs.

✍ Completeness

as far as — to the extent that
USAGE: ***As far as*** I know, Jim did not receive the job promotion.

as long as — on the condition that
USAGE: ***As long as*** you refill the gas tank, you can borrow my car for the
   trip.

✍ Consequence

a bum rap — underserved blame
USAGE: When Kathy told Jim he was uncaring, it was really ***a bum rap***.

all hell broke loose — significant conflict and confusion
USAGE: When the opposing team won the soccer game, ***all hell broke loose***
   in the stadium.

all's well that ends well — a positive ending
USAGE: Even though there was conflict between the teachers, they resolved
   their conflict, so, ***all's well that ends well***!

an eye for an eye — an equal revenge; retaliation
USAGE: Punishment in the ancient world was sometimes based upon ***an eye***
   for an eye.

✍ Different

duke's mixture — an odd combination
USAGE: The recipe for the stew was a ***duke's mixture***.

✍ Disagree

an axe to grind — a disagreement to argue about
USAGE: Henry was arguing forcefully with the other workers and it seemed
   he had ***an axe to grind*** with the company.

at cross purposes — having opposing, conflicting goals
USAGE: The leaders were ***at cross purposes*** about the design of the project
   and were arguing about what to do.

✍ Emotion

all fired up — excited; motivated
USAGE: The workers were **all fired up** about the pay increase and their future at the company.

all shook up — upset; nervous; afraid; concerned
USAGE: When he discovered the bus accident occurred on the street, James was **all shook up**.

an attitude — a disagreeable attitude; typically angry or agitated
USAGE: She was in a bad mood and upset. She had **an attitude** about working with the rest of the crew.

an even keel — balance; steadfastness; self-control
USAGE: It was important for the surgeon to maintain **an even keel** as he completed the operation.

✍ End

come to a head — the conclusion; climax
USAGE: The conflict between the workers and the supervisor **came to a head** when the boss dismissed the two workers.

✍ Entertainment

a barnburner — an exciting competitive game
USAGE: The World Cup match was a close game; **a real barnburner** to watch!

✍ Error

a lot of bunk — intentional incorrect information; lies
USAGE: When Pam's ex-husband was talking about her to others, she realized it was probably **a lot of bunk**.

all wet — mistaken; an error
USAGE: Mary is **all wet** if she says that the investment requires no money.

✍ Failure

all washed up — failure; falling short
USAGE: John said he felt his life was **all washed up** because of his continued unemployment.

✍ Health

a bun in the oven — pregnancy
USAGE: The women at the office party look at Mary and said, "You've got *a bun in the oven*" and asked her when the baby would be born.

✍ Importance

as a rule — usually; customarily
USAGE: *As a rule*, I exercise at 6 AM each day.

✍ Location

as the crow flies — most direct and shortest distance between two places
USAGE: The main office complex is located about five miles south of town, *as the crow flies*.

✍ Money

ante up — to pay money; contribute
USAGE: As John prepared to purchase the food, the store cashier said, "*Ante up!*"

✍ Movement

at a good clip — fast; moving rapidly
USAGE: He was traveling *at a good clip* as he drove down the road.

blow this joint — leave; depart
USAGE: Bill said, "Let's *blow this joint*," as they walk out of the store.

bump and grind — to move or dance in a sexually provocative manner
USAGE: Steve and Cathy were *bumping and grinding* while they danced at the party.

✍ Ownership

bird in the hand is worth two in the bush — having one now is better than the possibility of many in the future
USAGE: I reminded him that a *bird in the hand is worth two in the bush* when he said he wished to quit his job and work for a larger company.

✍ Personal Description

a big shot — believed to be an important person
USAGE: Richard believed he was *a big shot* because he was rich and familiar with the leadership.

a big wheel — believed to be an important person
USAGE: Steve acted like *a big wheel* because his friend was the chief executive officer.

a big wig — believed to be an important person
USAGE: Thinking she was better than others, Susan wanted to be treated like *a big wig*.

✍ Plan / Prepare

all eggs in one basket — relying on only one plan
USAGE: Investing his lifetime savings into the business start-up, George put *all his eggs in one basket*.

all set — ready to proceed
USAGE: The teacher asked the students, "Are you *all set* and ready to take the examination?"

all's fair in love and war — anything is acceptable in certain circumstances
USAGE: Knowing it was an opportunity of a lifetime to meet the actress, John said he had to miss class to meet her, saying to his friends, *"all's fair in love and war."*

✍ Quantity

all the marbles — the top prize
USAGE: Susan designed the award winning experiment and won the top prize of $10,000; she took home *all the marbles*.

✍ Relationship

a crush on — sudden feeling of attraction or love
USAGE: James had *a romantic crush on* the new girl at the University.

absence makes the heart grow fonder — when people are apart they like each other more
USAGE: Henry had been away from Mary for 6 months. Missing her a great deal, Henry would say to his roommate, *"absence makes the heart grow fonder."*

ace — a close, trusted friend
USAGE: John used to be my number one *ace* until he tried to take my job.

✍ Satisfaction

a bite to eat — to eat a meal
USAGE: Robert and James decided to get *a bite to eat* after class.

a chicken in every pot — enough food supply for a group of people
USAGE: The company president gave a lecture on prosperity and encouraged
   the audience by saying there would be *a chicken in every pot*.

bed down — to rest; go to sleep
USAGE: Steven told the others he was very sleepy and he wanted to *bed down*
   for the night.

✍ Service

at someone's beck and call — always available to help somebody
USAGE: Mary is always *at her children's beck and call* when they return
   home to visit.

✍ Similar

a level playing field — where everyone has an equal opportunity
USAGE: Providing education for all children allows for *a level playing field*
   for all people.

✍ Superior

ace in the hole — a talent or skill that is not obvious
USAGE: John's *ace in the hole* is that he is an expert in creating an attractive
   website.

✍ Time

a month of Sundays — a very long time
USAGE: It had been *a month of Sundays* since Frederick visited the beach.

about time — something that should have happened earlier in time
USAGE: It is *about time* that you got a job!

about to do something — at the point of doing something

USAGE: The manager was ***about to leave*** the office when the phone rang.

ahead of time — early; sooner
USAGE: We started the class ***ahead of time*** so we could have enough time for questions.

✍ Understand

as plain as day — (1) apparent; evident; obvious; (2) clear to see
USAGE (1): The solution facing Bob and Mary was ***as plain as day***.
USAGE (2): Susan could see the directions on the machine ***as plain as day***.

as plain as the nose on your face — (1) clear to see; evident; obvious; (2) easy to see
USAGE (1): It's ***as plain as the nose on your face*** that you will be awarded the contract for the job!
USAGE (2): Mary said the mouse was in the house, behind the door, ***as plain as the nose on your face***.

✍ Work

at the wheel — driving a vehicle
USAGE: Investigating the accident, the police asked the passengers who was ***at the wheel*** when the car was hit.

Week 2

✍ Achievement

bag — to attain
USAGE: I *bagged* the car that I had been searching for.

beat someone to the punch — do something before others do it
USAGE: Robert *beat the others to the punch* and arrived at the meeting first.

behind the curve — a poor performance
USAGE: John was *behind the curve* when he took the admission exam. The other students were better prepared.

bend over backwards to do something — try very hard; a good effort
USAGE: Robert said he would *bend over backwards to help* Mary get a promotion at the company.

bite off more than one can chew — try to do more than one is able to do
USAGE: I think I *bit off more than I can chew* by taking on the new assignment.

✍ Agree / Approval

all right — acceptable; okay; satisfactory
USAGE: She said it would be *all right* if I wanted to smoke a cigarette.

all that — superior; better
USAGE: Because Mary scored highest on the examination, she thinks she's *all that* and more!

✍ Authority

big cheese — a supervisor; boss; chief
USAGE: To complain about the unacceptable service at the restaurant, you should go see the *big cheese*, the manager.

big wigs — important and influential persons
USAGE: The employees appealed to the *big wigs* at the company in an effort
to get some help and improve their work conditions.

✍ Bad / Negative

(a) black mark — a bad reflection on a name or record
USAGE: Since she didn't score high on the examination, she believed that she
had a *black mark* on her school record.

brush with the law — an experience with the police because of breaking the
law
USAGE: Joe had a *brush with the law* when he was young but now he is a
respectable adult with a good job.

✍ Business Action

all in all — in summary; after considering all things
USAGE: We had a few problems in determining the course of action but, *all
in all*, the meeting was successful and a decision was made.

✍ Communication

armed to the teeth — ready to argue; prepared to fight
USAGE: The negotiators for the players were ready to fight for their position;
they were *armed to the teeth*.

as a matter of fact — statement of fact
USAGE: George told the other researchers that, *as a matter of fact*, it was vital
for the advancement of science to conduct the experiment.

ask for the moon — request for more than needed
USAGE: As a negotiation tactic for a salary increase, the employees *asked for
the moon* but expected much less.

bare your soul — disclose personal experiences
USAGE: *Baring his soul*, Steven told his friends that he was nervous following
the ending of his marriage and finalization of his divorce.

(a) bare-faced lie — an intentional or planned lie
USAGE: It is a *bare-faced lie* when Steve said he never visits the store; I know
he goes there each day!

✍ Completeness

as well as — in addition to
USAGE: Please bring your swimming suit *as well as* your towel when we go to the beach.

✍ Consequence

at a loss for words — not able to provide a response
USAGE: When he asked why he wanted to buy a new house, he was *at a loss for words*.

baptism by fire — unpleasant introduction to a situation
USAGE: When discovering she had to meet a sales quota during the first month to keep her job, it was a *baptism by fire* for Susan.

bark up the wrong tree — having incorrect explanation for something
USAGE: When Steve began accusing Mary of ignoring the children, she angrily replied, "if you're calling me a bad parent, you're *barking up the wrong tree*."

✍ Different

far cry — something very different
USAGE: What Michael said to my friend is a *far cry* from what he told me last month.

✍ Disagree

at loggerheads — having a conflict; opposing each other
USAGE: We have been *at loggerheads* over their plans to build a new plant at a new location.

at odds — in disagreement
USAGE: He has been *at odds* with his wife over how to discipline their children.

✍ Emotion

at my wit's end — very nervous
USAGE: Very upset and nervous about not having enough money to finish the project, John said, "I'm *at my wit's end*."

bad taste in my mouth — a feeling that something is not good

USAGE: When I left the meeting I had a ***bad taste in my mouth*** about what might happen next.

beside one's self — very upset or excited about something
USAGE: He was ***beside himself*** with happiness at winning the contest.

bide one's time — patiently wait for an opportunity to occur
USAGE: He is ***biding his time*** as he waits to become leader of his class at the university.

bite the bullet — face a difficult situation
USAGE: I have decided to ***bite the bullet*** and work on repaying the debt.

✎ End

head off — block; stop; prevent
USAGE: The managers were able to ***head off*** a work stoppage by negotiating with the workers.

✎ Entertainment

a barrel of laughs — Something or somebody who is humorus
USAGE: The film was ***a barrel of laughs*** because the jokes were hilarious!

a nail-biter — something with suspense
USAGE: The soccer match was ***a nail-biter*** until the final seconds of the game.

✎ Error

at fault — to be blame for something
USAGE: James admitted that he was ***at fault*** in the automobile accident.

✎ Failure

bail out — leave or abandon
USAGE: Are you ***bailing out*** on the situation when they need you most?

beyond the pale — not acceptable behavior
USAGE: What Jack is doing to his friends is wrong and ***beyond the pale*** for right behavior.

✎ Health

catch a cold — become sick with a cold

USAGE: I *caught a cold* because of the rain and the cold weather.

✍ Importance

at face value — matter of fact; significance
USAGE: Michael took James *at face value* when he said he would not support the request.

bank on — be sure of; count on; to have confidence in
USAGE: You can *bank on* Mike to show up and assist with the workload.

✍ Location

at bay — keep away at a distance
USAGE: The Prime Minister kept the television reporters *at bay* because he didn't want to answer the controversial questions.

✍ Money

ballpark figure — approximate amount; usually money
USAGE: The *ballpark figure* that Bob agreed to pay for the house would be $100,000 in US Dollars.

✍ Movement

catch a ride — to obtain a ride with someone
USAGE: To get to work each day, James must *catch a ride* with his co-workers.

chomping at the bit — ready; eager to go
USAGE: The young children were *chomping at the bit* to visit the toy store.

collecting dust — idle; not used for a while
USAGE: The car had been *collecting dust*, sitting in the garage for several weeks.

✍ Personal Description

a bimbo — a silly, simple girl
USAGE: She was *a bimbo* with her crazy plan to get rich overnight.

a blank look — a person not understanding or confused
USAGE: Unlike others in the room, John had *a blank look* on his face when he didn't understand the joke.

a cheap drunk — someone who gets drunk with a small amount of alcohol
USAGE: They said Anthony was *a cheap drunk* because one glass of wine would make him feel a little intoxicated.

a go-getter — a hard worker
USAGE: Jim worked very hard at the office and the managers considered him *a go-getter*.

✍ Plan / Prepare

back to square one — return to the first step
USAGE: If we don't succeed in winning on the final try, it's *back to square one*.

back yourself into a corner — to be in a tough position with not many options
USAGE: When Bill quit his job without having another, he *backed himself into a corner*.

✍ Quantity

and a half — an extraordinary amount
USAGE: Robert said to his friends, "I'm really sick; I've got a stomach ache *and a half*."

✍ Relationship

all the world's a stage — everyone in the world working together
USAGE: Realizing that world peace depends upon everyone working together, the Prime Minister said, "*all the world's a stage*" and we're all part of the solution.

along for the ride — to accompany someone
USAGE: John was just *along for the ride* and didn't do much work on the project.

✍ Satisfaction

(a) bed of roses — a pleasant situation; good circumstances
USAGE: Because they had much money, John's life was a *bed of roses*.

better off — To improve one's situation or circumstance
USAGE: He would be *better off* if he returned to graduate school to complete his MBA degree.

blue sky — good opportunity
USAGE: After the hectic beginning of the new company, Bill told his employees that from then on, it was *blue sky*!

bottoms up — to finish a drink
USAGE: As Tom left the restaurant, he raised his glass to take his last drink and said, "*bottoms up*."

✍ Service

attend to someone — take care or deal with someone
USAGE: The nurse *attended to several patients* that were waiting in the lobby of the clinic.

✍ Similar

across the board — applies to several different situations
USAGE: The increase in the monetary exchange rate affected companies *across the board* in China.

✍ Time

all along — all the time
USAGE: I knew *all along* that Mary would not be hired for the job.

all at once — suddenly; without warning
USAGE: *All at once*, the children jumped when they saw the snake.

all day long — the whole day
USAGE: Robert had been waiting for the postage mail to arrive *all day long*.

✍ Understand

bee in one's bonnet — an obsession; something that continually occupies one's thoughts
USAGE: Michael has a *bee in his bonnet* over where to build his dream house.

blow my cover — to have real identity revealed
USAGE: Jim *blew the cover* of the policeman when he walked up to his car and called his name.

blow the lid off — disclose the truth

USAGE: The police *blew the lid off* the scandal by revealing the building owners were associated with the fire.

boggle your mind — to confuse; to be confounded
USAGE: The investment plan presented by the business group *boggled Robert's mind* and astounded him with the growth potential.

✍ Achievement

bounce back — to try again
USAGE: After failing in her first try, Susan ***bounced back*** and succeeded in her second attempt.

break fresh ground — deal with something in a new way
USAGE: The researchers were able to ***break fresh ground*** in their search for a cancer cure.

break the bank — win much money at a casino
USAGE: Winning at the poker table, William ***broke the bank*** at the casino.

✍ Agree / Approval

and how — agree very much
USAGE: Like all kids, my daughter really loves sweet candy, ***and how***!

apple of one's eye — one's favorite
USAGE: His youngest daughter is a beautiful child and the ***apple of his eye***.

✍ Authority

bigger fish to fry — more important people to meet or do business with
USAGE: Not wanting to spend time visiting with people without money to invest, John said that he wanted ***bigger fish to fry***.

✍ Bad / Negative

burn down — burn completely (usually used for buildings)
USAGE: The neighbor's house ***burnt down*** completely as a result of a fire that started in the kitchen.

burn up — burn completely (things not buildings)
USAGE: The business inventory of supplies ***burned up*** in the fire.

✍ Business Action

an arm and a leg — (cost) a large amount of money
USAGE: Vincent's new car must have cost him *an arm and a leg* because it
  had many nice features.

✍ Communication

(a) bawling out — to be strongly disciplined
USAGE: The teacher gave the boys a real *bawling out* when they would not
  stop bothering the other students.

beat a dead horse — continue to ask when nothing will result
USAGE: When William kept asking for a refund and the store owner refused,
  he knew he was *beating a dead horse*.

beat around the bush — speak indirectly or ambiguously
USAGE: They asked him to stop *beating around the bush* and give them their
  final decision.

beg your pardon — asked to be excused or not offended
USAGE: "I *beg your pardon*," said Jim as he stood up. "I would like to stand
  for a while."

beside the point — not relevant to the subject discussed
USAGE: John told them what they were discussing was *beside the point* and
  not related to the issue at hand.

blow it out of proportion — to exaggerate
USAGE: Mary *blew it out of proportion* when she said John was "an angry
  young man."

✍ Completeness

at the end of one's rope — at the limit of one's ability to cope
USAGE: I am *at the end of my rope* about what to do about how to raise my
  children.

✍ Consequence

bear the brunt — take the blame
USAGE: James said he would *bear the brunt* of the blame since he was the
  president of the company.

(a) beehive of activity — a place that is very busy

USAGE: The store was a *beehive of activity* when the customers heard about the discounts.

between a rock and a hard place — making a difficult choice between problem options

USAGE: If I told the truth, I would lose my job. Therefore, I was *between a rock and a hard place*.

✎ Different

fish out of water — someone who does not fit in

USAGE: Since he did not know how to play golf, he was like a *fish out of water* at the golf course.

✎ Disagree

beg to differ — a difference of opinion

USAGE: When William explained the reasons the company went bankrupt, George said, "*I beg to differ.*"

bone of contention — a reason for quarrels; the subject of a fight

USAGE: How to deal with punishing the children was a major *bone of contention* in their marriage.

✎ Emotion

blow me down — to be surprised

USAGE: John said, "*Blow me down*; I cannot believe she actually said she would marry Harry."

blow me over — to be surprised

USAGE: Informed that she would receive a large salary increase, Susan said, "Well, *blow me over!*"

blow up — to become very angry

USAGE: George *blew up* at his wife when she wrecked his car.

blue in the face — very angry or upset

USAGE: I argued with him until I became *blue in the face*.

boiling mad — very upset; angry

USAGE: After being insulted by his employee, Horace was *boiling mad* and left the room.

✍ End

hold up — check; stop; delay
USAGE: The Beijing traffic was ***held up*** for over three hours because of several car accidents.

✍ Entertainment

chick flick — films of interest to females; related to romance
USAGE: My girlfriend and her friends always want to watch ***chick flick*** films that deal with love stories

✍ Error

bet on the wrong horse — misjudge a coming event; misread the future
USAGE: John ***bet on the wrong horse*** because he invested his money into a typewriter company that went bankrupt.

✍ Failure

bite the big one — to die or get killed
USAGE: Jim has horrible eating habits, smokes and never exercises. Therefore, I think he will ***bite the big one*** soon.

bite the dust — be killed; break down; be defeated
USAGE: Since it is over ten years old, I think my car has finally ***bitten the dust***.

✍ Health

catch one's breath — stop to rest and breath normally
USAGE: After running the race, I took a break to ***catch my breath***.

✍ Importance

big time — in a significant way
USAGE: After James lost his bicycle, he was in trouble ***big-time*** with his parents.

✍ Location

at home — in a person's house
USAGE: Kathy kept her new computer ***at home***.

at your fingertips — easy to locate
USAGE: When he works on his car, Steven likes to keep his tools nearby *at his fingertips*.

✍ Money

bang for your buck — high value for money
USAGE: Vickie realized she got a *bang for her buck* with the extra features on her new computer purchase.

blow a bundle — to spend a large amount of money
USAGE: William *blew a bundle* on his weekend trip to Shanghai.

✍ Movement

creep up on — crawl quietly and slowly
USAGE: The thief *crept up on* the elderly lady on the subway.

dig in   begin eating
USAGE: Let's *dig in* and eat before everything is cold!

down the pike — come into consideration
USAGE: New company policies came *down the pike* to the employees from the manager.

✍ Ownership

come by — to get, obtain, acquire
USAGE: The oldest son *came by* a significant amount of money recently and is now living in the city.

✍ Personal Description

absent-minded — forgetful; careless
USAGE: My mother is very *absent-minded* and often forgets where she leaves her money.

Achilles' heel — a weakness
USAGE: Jim's *Achilles' heel* is that he loves to buy any new computer gadget, even though he doesn't earn enough money.

against the grain — saying or doing something that is unusual
USAGE: What the teacher said to the child's parents about her philosophy of teaching really went *against the grain*.

✍ Plan / Prepare

bag of tricks — set of methods to utilize
USAGE: Having a *bag of tricks*, Joseph had many different persuasive methods to use in the sales presentation.

bar none — in all cases; no exceptions
USAGE: The coach told the players next year's schedule would be the most difficult season ever, *bar none*.

bend the rules — change the rules for an advantage
USAGE: The coach *bent the rules* so Timothy would be eligible for the game, despite his poor grades

✍ Relationship

bad blood — (1) a poor relationship; (2) hostility
USAGE (1): Bill and James had *bad blood* between them due to a history of major conflict.
USAGE (2): There was harshness in the communication between the sisters. There has been *bad blood* between them for a long time.

✍ Satisfaction

breath of fresh air — a positive, pleasant change
USAGE: It was a *breath of fresh air* to have a manager whom listened to me and accepted my recommendations.

bundle up — put on warm clothes
USAGE: Kathy *bundled up* in the winter cold and went for a walk in the park.

call of nature — the need to go to the toilet
USAGE: John answered the *call of nature* and will return to the meeting in a few minutes.

✍ Service

bail someone/something out — to help or rescue
USAGE: The group of wealthy investors decided to *bail out* the troubled business, saving the worker's jobs.

✍ Superior

all the bells and whistles — having many extra features

USAGE: Wendy's new car is well-appointed and has ***all the bells and whistles***.

✍ Time

all in a day's work — part of a regular schedule
USAGE: Dealing with customer complaints is considered ***all in a day's work*** for Michael.

all of a sudden — suddenly; without advance warning
USAGE: ***All of a sudden*** there was a break in the storm and the sun appeared.

all teed up — ready to begin
USAGE: Ready to start the journey, John told the travelers, "We're ***all teed up*** and ready to start the trip!"

✍ Understand

bone up on — to study; to prepare
USAGE: Tom said that he had to ***bone up on*** his statistics to better understand the manufacturing production numbers.

break down — analyze
USAGE. The managers ***broke down*** the cost figures in the budget for further study.

by heart — memorize
USAGE: Steven memorized the famous quote ***by heart***.

can't make heads or tails of something — unable to find meaning
USAGE: Steve was entirely confused by the letter and suggested that he ***couldn't make heads or tails of the message***.

can't see the forest for the trees — unable to judge or understand the whole picture; only looking at small details
USAGE: Kathy has no real understanding of the impact of the economic policies because she ***can't see the forest for the trees***.

catch on — to understand, learn about
USAGE: Peter found it difficult to ***catch on*** at first, but he finally understood how to solve the problem.

clear as a bell — to understand; clarity
USAGE: James indicated he recognized the issues involved in the case as ***clear as a bell***.

✍ Work

back to the grind — return to work; back to work
USAGE: After the celebrations of the holiday, Charles said he had to get ***back to the grind*** and earn a living!

Week 4

✍ Achievement

bring (it) off — to succeed
USAGE: Mary was concerned about being able to ***bring off*** the employee party.

bring (something) on — cause to develop rapidly
USAGE: I believe that what ***brought on*** his angry reaction was the rudeness of the clerk.

brush up on something — review something already learned
USAGE: I'm going to ***brush up on my understanding*** of American English idioms before my trip to New York.

buckle down — work harder
USAGE: Lewis told his sister that he was going to ***buckle down*** and earn more money over the next year.

✍ Agree / Approval

be there or be square — it is appropriate to attend an event
USAGE: When Susan wondered if she should attend the awards ceremony, Cathy said with a smile, "***Be there or be square***!"

beat the rap — have the accusation dropped
USAGE: The suspected thief ***beat the rap*** and was released from jail.

✍ Authority

bring someone into line — urge someone to agree with you
USAGE: Consistently encouraging them, John was able to persuade the group and ***bring them into line***.

✍ Bad / Negative

bury/hide one's head in the sand — refuse to face something or knowing something unpleasant

USAGE: Helen was so behind schedule with her project that she *buried her head in the sand*.

can't stand — cannot tolerate; disapprove
USAGE: Mary acts like she *can't stand* the other people in her work group.

✍ Business Action

back out — withdraw from an agreement or understanding
USAGE: The trade group *backed out* of the deal with the company to import new clothes into the country.

✍ Communication

blow it out your ear — to discard or disregard with disrespect
USAGE: When Peter was trying to explain his position on pricing the new product, Steve responded angrily, "you can *blow it out your ear*."

blurt out — to say or disclose without thinking
USAGE: Susie *blurted out*, "I asked her to do it" without thinking.

body language — body gestures that reflect meaning; non-verbal language
USAGE: Michael's *body language* didn't match his words when he said he would love her forever.

bone to pick — to argue or to find fault; a dispute
USAGE: John had a *bone to pick* with his co-worker for insulting his wife.

break the ice — relax and informally start a conversation
USAGE: The workers were not enjoying the party until the manager *broke the ice*.

✍ Completeness

blow over — die down or calm down
USAGE: The problem created with the false accusation has finally *blown over* and everyone is working again on the project.

✍ Consequence

blessing in disguise — what once was a problem turns into something good
USAGE: Even though Peter didn't get the job offer, it was a *blessing in disguise* because the company was unstable.

brain drain — the loss of intelligent people
USAGE: With many talented workers leaving and moving to another company, the manager said, "we are having a ***brain drain***."

brush with death — to almost die
USAGE: John had a ***brush with death*** when he almost lost control of his car.

✍ Different

fishy — strange; suspicious
USAGE: Something is ***fishy*** with Mark's reason not to participate. Why doesn't he just admit he is sick?

✍ Disagree

change (one's) mind — change one's decision
USAGE: Sally ***changed her mind*** and said she would not go to the theater production tonight.

change of heart — change the way a person feels about something
USAGE: Patricia had a ***change of heart*** and decided to let her child walk to school by himself.

✍ Emotion

break his/her/my heart — to cause a feeling of sadness
USAGE: When Susan divorced Mike, it ***broke his heart*** and he was sad for many months.

bring the house down — generate laughter in the audience
USAGE: The comedian ***brought the house down*** with his funny jokes about the lost bicycle in Beijing.

bring to mind — recall something
USAGE: Her acting performance in the play ***brought to mind*** the great actresses over the past century.

bundle of nerves — feeling anxious; worried
USAGE: When I told Bill he must successfully pass the computer skills test, he was a ***bundle of nerves***.

calm down — to relax
USAGE: She finally ***calmed down*** after hearing the upsetting news.

✍ End

kick the bucket — die
USAGE: The woman who worked in the factory *kicked the bucket* yesterday.

✍ Error

blind leading the blind — someone who doesn't understand something trying
to explain it to others
USAGE: It is like the *blind leading the blind* watching Vincent teaching the
students how to create a webpage.

✍ Failure

bite the hand that feeds you — turn against a friend or helper
USAGE: Betsy is *biting the hand that feeds her* by criticizing her family.

blow it — not succeed at something
USAGE: I tried hard to pass the math examination, but I'm sure I *blew it*.

✍ Health

clean bill of health — the assurance of being healthy
USAGE: The athlete was given a *clean bill of health* before he resumed
training for the World Cup games.

✍ Importance

bottom line — the main issue or point
USAGE: Hubert said the *bottom line* is that the product must be ready to ship
to stores by June.

✍ Location

blow this joint — to leave a location
USAGE: Leaving the restaurant, the young people said in a rush, "Let's *blow
this joint*."

bring up the rear — be at the end of the line or in the last position
USAGE: The runner from Kenya was *bringing up the rear* in the 10K race.

✍ Money

blow your/his/her wad — to spend or deplete all your money

USAGE: Richard *blew his wad* within two days when he traveled to the foreign city.

bring home the bacon — work and earn money for a family
USAGE: He is working hard, *bringing home the bacon* each month.

✐ Movement

duck out — to leave rapidly
USAGE: George *ducked out* of the meeting after he finished his speech to the managers.

faster than a speeding bullet — very fast
USAGE: When discovering they had won the contest, Bob and Mary rushed to the event headquarters *faster than a speeding bullet*.

fits and starts — stop and go
USAGE: The traffic in Shanghai was moving in *fits and starts*. It took forever to arrive at the stadium!

✐ Ownership

come into — receive; get possession of
USAGE: John and Susan *came into* a lot of money through their investment which they donated to charity.

✐ Personal Description

age of majority — age of legal adulthood
USAGE: The dean told the students they would not be able to drink beer until they reached the *age of majority*.

all decked out — dressed up very well
USAGE: Charles *was decked out* in his new clothes.

all ears — eager to listen
USAGE: Steven was *all ears* when he heard the prize was money.

✐ Plan / Prepare

carry through — put a plan into action
USAGE: James *carried through* with his plan to hire the teenagers for the project.

come unglued — lose control; deteriorate
USAGE: The situation *came unglued* when the leader lost influence with the
group members and arguments broke out among the staff.

cross a bridge before one comes to it — think and worry about future events
or problems before they happen
USAGE: Sharon told Ben they shouldn't worry about the problem now. She
urged them to wait and *cross that bridge when they came to it*.

cut and dried — completely decided; prearranged
USAGE: John said the issue was *cut and dried*, that the decision had already
been made.

✍ Quantity

by a country mile — a long distance; a large margin
USAGE: Because he had a fast car along with driving skills, Henry won the
race *by a country mile*.

✍ Relationship

better half — wife or husband
USAGE: Before I agree to go, I need to ask my *better half*.

birds of a feather flock together — people with similar interests stay together
USAGE: *Birds of a feather flock together* was the response Timothy gave
when asked why he liked to spend time with other investment bankers.

✍ Satisfaction

clean slate — having no errors
USAGE: He began employment with a *clean slate* and has never created
problems on the job.

come back — become popular again
USAGE: During the last several years, orchestra music has *come back* into
popularity again.

✍ Service

be my guest — to help oneself; to accept an offer from another
USAGE: When Henry asked if he could join the others at the restaurant, they
responded, "*be our guest*; please join us at 6 PM."

✍ Similar

all things being equal — if nothing changes; stability
USAGE: *All things being equal*, the Chinese economy will improve next year and more workers will be hired.

✍ Time

all the time — continually; on and on
USAGE: Peter asks for money *all the time* but I don't like to give it to him without justification.

around the clock — all the time; 24 hours per day; continuously
USAGE: The store is open *around the clock*, 24 hours per day, 7 days a week.

as usual — most of the time; as is the custom
USAGE: *As usual*, William forgot to return the borrowed CD.

✍ Understand

clear as mud — not clear; not understandable
USAGE: Frustrated and not understanding the directions, Charles said sarcastically, "Yes, that is *clear as mud*."

clear up — solve or explain a problem
USAGE: The technology director at work *cleared up* the problem I was experiencing with my computer at the office.

collect my thoughts — to concentrate or reflect
USAGE: Adam told his parents he wanted to get away from home and *collect his thoughts* about attending college and plans for the future.

come back — return to one's memory
USAGE: After the accident, Teresa reported she couldn't remember the day of the wreck, but her memory was slowly *coming back*.

✍ Work

blue-collar worker — a worker; a laborer
USAGE: Since he works as a carpenter at a construction site, Peter is considered a *blue-collar worker*.

Week 5

✐ **Achievement**

build a better mousetrap — to improve on a product or service
USAGE: Patricia decided she wanted to *build a better mousetrap* when she
created the new way to accept loan applications for the bank.

by hook or by crook — in any way necessary
USAGE: Susan says she will get tickets to the Olympic games *by hook or by
crook*.

carrot and stick — a promise of reward and threat of punishment at same time
(to persuade)
USAGE: The trade negotiators took a *carrot and stick* approach to obtaining
the agreement in which they were seeking.

carry it off — make something happen
USAGE: Timothy and his colleagues were satisfied they had successfully
carried off the plan.

✐ **Agree / Approval**

beauty is in the eye of the beholder — each person determines what is
attractive
USAGE: John said he believed the lady was the most beautiful woman he had
ever seen, while others disagreed. All of them agreed that *beauty is in the
eye of the beholder*!

beauty is only skin deep — a person should not be judged only by physical looks
USAGE: Realizing her looks would fade in the future as she aged, Bill
emphasized *beauty is only skin deep*.

✐ **Authority**

buck stops here — the final responsibility; highest authority
USAGE: The company president reminded his employees that "since the *buck
stops here*, I accept responsibility for our poor performance."

call on — ask someone to participate
USAGE: The teacher *called on* Steven four times to answer questions in the class.

✐ Bad / Negative

cat burglar — a burglar who enters a building by climbing a wall
USAGE: We lost our stereo when a *cat burglar* entered our apartment and stole many of our new electrical appliances.

✐ Business Action

back to the drawing board — go back to start a project or idea from the beginning
USAGE: The boss didn't like the idea so Michael determined the group should go *back to the drawing board*.

✐ Communication

break the news — disclose information
USAGE: Peter was planning to *break the news* to Kathy about his transfer to Zhengzhou City in the Henan Province.

break the silence — talk about; reveal the truth
USAGE: Recognizing the employees should understand the issues involved, Keith *broke the silence* about the poor financial status of the company.

bring up — introduce a subject into a discussion
USAGE: The employees *brought up* the issue to discuss, but the managers didn't want to talk about it.

bunch of malarkey — an untrue account
USAGE: Joseph said he had a fortune hidden under his bed. What a *bunch of malarkey*!

butter someone up — flatter someone
USAGE: Complimenting her dress, William was trying to *butter up* his wife so she would prepare his favorite food dish.

button your lip — be silent; quiet; do not talk
USAGE: Fearful his brother would tell on him, Ben said, "*button your lip* and don't tell Mother I broke the window."

✍ Completeness

by and large — on the whole; considering everything
USAGE: *By and large* we had a profitable year, despite the high rate of national unemployment.

by far — greatly; by a great margin
USAGE: He is *by far* the smartest student enrolled in the university.

✍ Consequence

caught red-handed — caught with evidence
USAGE: William was *caught red-handed* when the police discovered the stolen items in his car.

chickens come home to roost — words or acts come back to cause trouble for a person
USAGE: Recognizing she must take responsibility in her life, Susan said the *chickens have come home to roost* and she must now face up to what she had done.

✍ Different

go through changes — changing circumstances in life
USAGE: Since the divorce was very traumatic for Mary, she had to *go through many difficult changes*.

horse of a different color — something separate and different
USAGE: John told Mary the situation had changed entirely and the issue facing them now was *a horse of a different color*.

✍ Disagree

change (one's) tune — make a change in a person's story, statement or opinions
USAGE: Henry has begun to *change his tune* about the value of college and is now encouraging us to apply to the university.

come between — disrupt the relationship between (two people)
USAGE: The work demands of Steven's job finally *came between* him and his wife, causing serious marital distress.

✍ Emotion

carried away — lose control or judgment due to strong feelings

USAGE: I got a *carried away* and started screaming during the soccer game.

castles in the air — daydreaming about the future
USAGE: Sally was unrealistic in her plans, building *castles in the air*!

chicken out — stop doing something because of fear
USAGE: He *chickened out* of parachuting from the airplane.

climb the wall — so bored, resulting in anxiousness and frustration
USAGE: Vickie began to *climb the wall* when she was told she would have to
wait overnight for the tickets.

close to home — near to someone's personal feelings, wishes or interests
USAGE: What was said about her mother hit *close to home* because she
became very silent.

✍ End

kick the habit — stop a bad habit like smoking or taking drugs
USAGE: James has been trying to *kick his smoking habit* for about 10
years.

✍ Failure

botch it — to ruin; failure
USAGE: Bobby *botched it* when he tried to repair the computer without
having the necessary technology skills.

buckle under — to stop trying
USAGE: Susan tried to succeed at the new job, but she just *buckled under*
pressure and quit.

✍ Health

come down with — become sick with or catch a cold
USAGE: Horace *came down with* a headache and was unable to attend the
dinner.

✍ Importance

bring home the importance — make someone fully realize something
USAGE: Steve stressed the necessity of exercise to *bring home the importance*
of taking care of oneself

✍ Location

coast is clear — no danger is in sight; no one can see you
USAGE: When the *coast was clear*, John crossed the busy highway.

come back — return to the place you are now
USAGE: Teresa *came back* to Beijing from the countryside.

✍ Money

broke — without money
USAGE: James spent all of his money on the foreign trip and now he is *broke*.

burn a hole in one's pocket — money that a person wants to spend quickly
USAGE: Henry was paid today and, based on his plans for the weekend, the money was *burning a hole in his pocket*.

✍ Movement

flew the coop — to leave; to depart
USAGE: Realizing the police were searching for him, Michael *flew the coop* yesterday.

floor it — push down the gas pedal in a car; go faster
USAGE: Wanting to get to the hospital fast in his new sports car, James *floored it*.

full steam ahead — with full power
USAGE: The conductor gave the order for the train to move *full steam ahead*.

✍ Personal Description

all spruced up — dressed up very nice
USAGE: Wearing his finest clothes to the meeting, Kevin was *all spruced up*.

all talk and no action — a person who does not do what is said
USAGE: Since George is *all talk and no action*, he cannot be relied on to follow through.

all there — reasonable; usually used in negative way
USAGE: She's talking to herself! She's not *all-there*.

✍ Plan / Prepare

cut corners — economize
USAGE: The managers were opposed to ***cutting corners*** in order to save money.

cut out — eliminate
USAGE: John was successful ***cutting out*** carbohydrates in his diet.

dance to a different tune — talk or act differently (usually better) because things have changed
USAGE: When he discovered the payoff would be much higher than expected, Chuck was ***dancing to a different tune***.

✍ Quantity

by leaps and bounds — by large amounts
USAGE: His bank account increased ***by leaps and bounds*** because of successful returns on the investment.

✍ Relationship

blood is thicker than water — biological relationships are stronger than marriage ties
USAGE: Saying "***blood is thicker than water***," Steven said he would support his father over the desires of his wife, Mary.

break up (with someone) — stop a relationship
USAGE: Helen ***broke up*** with her boyfriend, James, last June.

✍ Satisfaction

come in handy — prove to be useful
USAGE: I think the variety of tools will ***come in handy*** to fix the car engine.

come into fashion — become fashionable
USAGE: Robert says although wide neckties have ***come into fashion*** again, he doesn't like them and will never wear them.

come off — be successful
USAGE: The meeting between the two managers ***came off*** without any problems, so the employees were happy.

✍ Service

best interests at heart — considerate of another person
USAGE: When James criticized the students about the results of their exams, he had their *best interests at heart*.

✍ Similar

bitten by the same bug — sharing a similar interest
USAGE: William and Elaine were *bitten by the same bug* because they shared the same interest in riding horses.

✍ Time

as yet — until now; up to the present
USAGE: *As yet*, Susan has not told me about her plans to start a new company.

at first — at the beginning
USAGE: *At first* she didn't want to attend the game with her friends but later she changed her mind.

at first blush — when first seen; without careful study
USAGE: *At first blush*, William seemed like a solid addition to the work team, but later we had problems with his work habits.

✍ Understand

come to one's senses — begin to think clearly or act sensibly
USAGE: John *came to his senses* and decided to buy a more reasonably priced apartment rather than take out a large loan for a very expensive one.

(a) crash course — an intensive learning experience
USAGE: Michael undertook a *crash course* on repairing his desktop printer.

dawn on — become clear
USAGE: It *dawned on* Henry why his wife was angry at the situation.

do a double take — look again in surprise at something
USAGE: Barbara *did a double take* when she saw her husband having lunch with another woman.

✍ Work

burn the candle at both ends — work or play too hard without enough rest

USAGE: Busy all summer and exhausted, Carol had been ***burning the candle at both ends***.

✍ Achievement

carry on — continue, keep doing as before
USAGE: Susan *carried on* with planning for the party despite the warning for an oncoming storm.

carry (something) out — put into action; accomplish
USAGE: The beginning of the school year was *carried out* with a minimum of problems with students, teachers and parents.

carry the ball — take the most important or difficult part in an action or business
USAGE: The employees ended up *carrying the ball* on increasing production at the manufacturing plant.

carry the day — win or be successful
USAGE: Charley's outstanding achievement on the field *carried the day* for the team.

✍ Agree / Approval

blow one's own horn — praise oneself
USAGE: Robert is always *blowing his own horn* about his contributions to his company.

bridge the gap — to negotiate between two or more parties
USAGE: Trying to negotiate the differences between John and Mary, the marriage counselor tried to *bridge the gap* by identifying similar beliefs.

✍ Authority

call the shots — be in charge; give orders
USAGE: Mr. Jones was named president and is now *calling the shots* and in control of the company.

✍ Bad / Negative

catch-22 — a situation where the desired outcome will be bad; a no-win situation
USAGE: Michael said it was a *catch-22* situation where if he went to the office while sick there would be problems but if he didn't show up there would be more problems.

cave in — to weaken and be forced to give up or concede
USAGE: The teacher finally *caved in* to the student's request to change the date of the examination.

✍ Business Action

boot out — make someone leave
USAGE: John was *booted out* of the office party for bringing liquor to the workplace.

✍ Communication

by the way — incidentally; in connection with
USAGE: *By the way*, could you please bring me a glass of water when you return?

by word of mouth — information spread person by person
USAGE: The gossip circulated *by word of mouth* among employees about the work stoppage at the manufacturing plant.

call a spade a spade — speak bluntly, directly
USAGE: Jim was *calling a spade a spade* when he began to criticize his associate for being irresponsible.

call on — visit someone
USAGE: I plan to *call on* the new client when I'm in Paris next month.

call someone's bluff — challenge someone to prove what they say is true
USAGE: Brian decided to *call her bluff* and asked for the results of the research.

call up — telephone
USAGE: Charles indicated he would *call up* Susan's parents when he arrived in town.

✎ Completeness

by the skin of one's teeth — by a very small margin; barely
USAGE: Tony won the 10K run *by the skin of his teeth*.

✎ Consequence

cold spell/snap — a sudden short period of cold weather
USAGE: The school was warm inside despite the *cold snap* outside.

crying shame — a sad or unfortunate situation
USAGE: Susan believed it was a *crying shame* the students were prevented
  from attending the performance.

damned if you do and damned if you don't — you receive blame if you do
  it and receive blame if you do not
USAGE: Bill realized he had a dilemma concerning the employee pay raise
  and whichever way he responded, he was *damned if he did and damned if
  he didn't*.

dead heat — a race that ends in a tie
USAGE: The 10K run between the runners was so close that it ended in a *dead
  heat*.

✎ Different

kooky — strange; out of the ordinary
USAGE: Because the building design was extremely unique, many observers
  believed it was a *kooky* plan.

✎ Disagree

come to blows — begin to fight
USAGE: The teenage boys almost *came to blows* when they argued about
  which team was better.

cut down to size — prove that someone is not as good as he or she thinks
USAGE: Kevin *cut him down to size* when he implied that Bob cheated on the
  examination.

✎ Emotion

come alive — brighten up and become active
USAGE: Kathy *came alive* when Bill walked into the room.

come down to earth — stop imagining or dreaming; think and behave as usual
USAGE: Realizing the challenges he faced in starting the business, Henry *came down to earth* and worked hard to obtain the bank loan.

come to — begin or learn to do or feel something
USAGE: While Susan didn't like Alice at first, she spent more time with her and has *come to* accept her.

come to grief — encounter disappointment
USAGE: John *came to grief* over his decision to dismiss the two senior workers from the staff.

come to grips with — struggle (successfully) with an idea or problem
USAGE: Darren has finally been able to *come to grips with* the death of his father.

✍ End

kill off — kill or destroy
USAGE: The pesticide has *killed off* most of the unwanted insects.

✍ Entertainment

crack a joke — tell a joke
USAGE: Everyone thought Wendy was a lot of fun at the party because she was *cracking jokes*.

✍ Failure

burn one's bridges behind one — do something that makes going back impossible
USAGE: When Robert left his job in anger, he *burned his bridges behind him* and is now unable to work in the banking business.

cast pearls before swine — waste something valuable on someone who doesn't appreciate it
USAGE: Since Martha doesn't value fine art, giving her the sculpture was like *casting pearls before swine*.

✍ Health

come to — to regain consciousness
USAGE: Ellen *came to* several hours after her fall off the steps.

✍ Importance

bring new facts to light — discover and make new facts known
USAGE: The employees were able to ***bring new facts to light*** in the negotiation of a new wage standard.

✍ Location

come from — be a native of a place
USAGE: Many of the workers at the plant ***come from*** the South.

cut across — cross or go through something instead of going around
USAGE: We wanted to cut across the highway because we were in a hurry to ***cut across*** the street.

✍ Money

cash cow — a good source of money; very profitable
USAGE: Jim's new store is a ***cash cow***. I think he is highly profitable with his business.

cash in — exchange something for money
USAGE: John decided to ***cash in*** the credit slip because he needed some money to pay bills.

✍ Movement

get along — leave; proceed
USAGE: Since its getting late, I should be ***getting along*** now.

get around — go to different places; move about
USAGE: Robert really ***gets around***. He has visited almost every nation on the African continent.

get away — succeed in leaving; escape
USAGE: Barbara was able to ***get away*** from the office and meet James for lunch.

✍ Personal Description

all thumbs — have difficulty fixing things or working with one's hands; clumsy
USAGE: Not being very coordinated, John is ***all thumbs*** when it comes to fixing things around the house.

ask for trouble — behave in a way that trouble is likely
USAGE: William is *asking for trouble* if he is again absent for work.

asleep at the switch — not alert to a task or opportunity
USAGE: I think he was *asleep at the switch*. He didn't realize it was his duty to warn the passengers of the unscheduled train stop.

✍ Quantity

chock full — very full
USAGE: The store was *chock full* of fresh vegetables from the countryside.

✍ Relationship

bring up — raise or care for a child
USAGE: My parents *brought up* six children on a limited income.

bury the hatchet — stop quarreling and become friendly with someone
USAGE: Since they were getting older, Horace wanted to *bury the hatchet* with his brother and cultivate a better relationship.

✍ Satisfaction

come up roses — do well
USAGE: John felt his life was *coming up roses* because his business was succeeding.

cup of tea — something one enjoys; special interest
USAGE: Martha told her she didn't want to go to the opera because it wasn't her *cup of tea*.

✍ Service

do someone good — be good or beneficial for someone
USAGE: Jim suggested it would *do Robert good* to take a vacation.

✍ Superior

beat the pants off — to win by a large margin
USAGE: Our national team *beat the pants off* their team by a score of 12 to 2 in the World Cup Finals.

✍ Time

at last — finally; after a long time
USAGE: He had been waiting many years for a job offer from the company but *at last* it came.

at the crack of dawn — first thing in the morning
USAGE: Tina regularly exercises *at the crack of dawn*.

at the drop of a hat — very quickly
USAGE: Needing to arrive at the theater immediately, Steve left the office *at the drop of a hat*.

✍ Understand

does not know if one is coming or going — not knowing; confused what to do
USAGE: Looking confused, the new employee *didn't seem to know if he was coming or going*.

does not know the first thing about something — lacking basic knowledge about something
USAGE: I don't have much confidence in Bill's ability. He *doesn't know the first thing about* repairing cars.

doesn't add up — does not figure; is not logical
USAGE: Confused, the workers looked at each other and said, "that doesn't make sense; it *doesn't add up*."

down pat — understood; memorized
USAGE: Haley had her assignment *down pat* because she had been studying all week.

✍ Work

burn the midnight oil — study until very late at night
USAGE: John and Mary *burned the midnight oil* during the last two nights to finish the project.

✍ Achievement

carry the torch — show loyalty to a cause or a person
USAGE: A loyal supporter, Fred has been ***carrying the torch*** for the increasing membership for a long time.

carry your weight — to do one's share of the work
USAGE: A hard worker, Steven certainly ***carried his weight*** to advance the group's cause.

catch (someone) red-handed — find someone in the middle of doing something wrong
USAGE: The police ***caught the thief red-handed*** with the stolen merchandise.

catch up with (someone/something) — be even with someone (in a race or in schoolwork etc.)
USAGE: Because he worked slowly on the project, Jim needed to ***catch up with*** on completing the task.

✍ Agree / Approval

clear the air — calm down and remove a misunderstanding
USAGE: Bill and Peter took a break, excused themselves from the group and went outside to discuss their differences and ***clear the air***.

✍ Authority

come down hard on — rebuke or punish severely
USAGE: The company has been ***coming down very hard on*** employees that steal equipment from their offices.

✍ Bad / Negative

chips are down — the time when facing a significant obstacle
USAGE: When the ***chips were down***, Jim's friends were nearby and very supportive.

✍ Business Action

business as usual — normal or ordinary circumstances
USAGE: Since Thomas was familiar with the process of filing a complaint, the remainder of the day was *business as usual*.

✍ Communication

card up one's sleeve — a plan or argument kept back to be produced if needed
USAGE: Jim seemed to have a *card up his sleeve* as he looked shrewdly around the room.

care of someone — send something to one person at the address of another person
USAGE: Mary sent the package to him in *care of* Steven's office.

case in point — an example that proves something or helps to make something clear
USAGE: What James said was *case in point* about making sure that we have security at the store.

cat gets one's tongue — can't talk
USAGE: The little boy seemed uneasy and didn't want to talk. Yes, a *cat has got his tongue*.

catch one's eye — attract one's attention
USAGE: Sally tried to *catch his eye* and signal her approval but he didn't notice.

chew out (someone) — scold roughly
USAGE: The manager *chewed out* the employee for leaving his work post without permission.

✍ Completeness

carry over — save for another time
USAGE: We plan to *carry over* the money into budget to next year's budget.

✍ Consequence

dickens of a time — a difficult task or situation
USAGE: Peter had a *dickens of a time* getting the students to do their homework.

don't count your chickens before they hatch — be patient; wait until results happen before celebrating success
USAGE: When Charles said he wanted to buy a new car because he believed his investment would be profitable, Wendy said, "*Don't count your chickens before they hatch*."

double-edged sword — something that can both help and hurt
USAGE: William's new job was a *double-edged sword*. On the one hand, it provided more money but the travel involved hurt his marriage.

✍ Different

make over — make something look different; change the style of
USAGE: Susan decided she wanted a hair *make over* to make her look young.

✍ Disagree

dead set against something — determined not to do something
USAGE: John was *dead set against* his company expanding operations into Japan.

dirty look — a look that shows dislike or disapproval
USAGE: His teacher gave him a *dirty look* when he said the class was meaningless.

✍ Emotion

conk out — fall asleep quickly with great fatigue
USAGE: William was so tired that he *conked out* in the chair and fell asleep.

cool as a cucumber — very calm and brave; not worried or anxious
USAGE: The teenager was as *cool as a cucumber* when she described the conditions of the accident.

crack a smile — let a smile show on one's face
USAGE: In an angry mood, Kathy never *cracked a smile* during the whole class.

crack up — burst into laughter
USAGE: Not able to control his laughter, Joseph *cracked up* when he described what the woman said.

creeps — a strong feeling of fear or disgust
USAGE: I get the *creeps* when I see snakes.

✍ End

kill the goose that laid the golden egg — spoil something that is good or profitable
USAGE: Leaving as the head of a highly profitable company, John *killed the goose that laid the golden egg*.

✍ Failure

cast the first stone — be the first to blame someone
USAGE: Realizing he was not perfect, Henry didn't want to be the one to *cast the first stone* by criticizing the other men.

come a cropper — to fail
USAGE: I think Mike has *come a cropper* in trying to build the house and that's why he is so frustrated.

✍ Health

dead as a doornail — clearly dead
USAGE: Recognizing the rabbit was shot many times, the observers agreed that it was *dead as a doornail*.

✍ Location

dead ahead — exactly in front; before
USAGE: There was a police road block *dead ahead* so we slowed down and prepared to stop.

dead center — exact middle
USAGE: John was driving down the *dead center* of the street and was a danger to the oncoming traffic.

✍ Money

cash in on — see and profit by a chance
USAGE: Many Beijing businesses *cashed in on* their city hosting the 2008 Olympics.

✍ Movement

get away from it all — go on a holiday
USAGE: To relax for the holiday, they traveled to Europe to *get away from it all*.

get back — return
USAGE: Susan and Dave *got back* from the countryside last night.

get behind — go slow while doing something; be late
USAGE: Thomas was absent from class and, therefore, *got behind* in submitting the homework.

✍ Personal Description

at heart — basically; fundamentally
USAGE: Jim is a very nice person *at heart* although many people dislike him because of his bad temper.

babe in arms — a baby; a child
USAGE: Steven was just a *babe in arms* when we traveled abroad to France.

babe in the woods — someone who cannot defend themselves
USAGE: Vincent is a *babe in the woods* when he is with those tough businessmen.

✍ Plan / Prepare

draw up — put in writing
USAGE: The managers worked with the negotiators to *draw up* the new production plan.

ducks in a row — to be organized
USAGE: The manager said, "I have to get my *ducks in a row* before we can begin the new production process."

Dutch treat — where each person pays their own way,
USAGE: When John takes Vickie out on a date, it is always a *Dutch treat* as she pays for her own.

easy as pie — very easy; effortless
USAGE: As William was completing his calculus assignment for school, he said that it was *easy as pie*.

✍ Quantity

coals to Newcastle — bring something of which there is plenty
USAGE: Bringing food to the downtown market was like bringing *coals to Newcastle*.

✍ Relationship

call for someone — come and get someone
USAGE: Jim telephoned and *called for* Mark to go with him.

catch on — become popular
USAGE: Wireless internet usage has begun to *catch on* among many people across the country.

✍ Satisfaction

deck out — dressed very well
USAGE: The ladies were *decked out* in beautiful clothes for the party.

do one's thing — do what is enjoyable
USAGE: Steven is an outdoorsman and considers taking long walks in the countryside *doing his thing*.

✍ Service

fall back on something/someone — turn to for help when something else has failed
USAGE: Wendy *fell back on* her savings she had in the bank when she lost her job.

✍ Superior

blow away — to defeat
USAGE: Before the tennis match began, Bill urged James to *blow away* the competition.

✍ Time

at this point in time — at present; currently
USAGE: *At this point in time*, John indicated he was fearful of the weather condition.

before you can say Jack Robinson — very quickly
USAGE: *Before you could say Jack Robinson*, Bill was in the kitchen preparing breakfast.

✍ Understand

draw a blank — unable to answer

USAGE: He *drew a blank* when he tried to answer his wife's question about the missing furniture.

dying to know — wants to know very urgently
USAGE: James is *dying to know* the new girl's opinion of him.

ear to the ground — pay attention to the way things are going or the way people feel and think
USAGE: Henry has his *ear to the ground* concerning rumors about the new company.

earful — scolding; a lot of information (often critical)
USAGE: William gave his son an *earful* when he failed to arrive on time.

✍ Work

bust my butt — work hard
USAGE: Timothy walked in and said, "I'm exhausted because I *busted my butt* today at work."

Week 8

✍ Achievement

catch-as-catch-can — in any way possible
USAGE: Because the power lines went down throughout the city, all the
  neighbors prepared meals in a ***catch-as-catch-can*** way.

chalk up — record
USAGE: The team ***chalked up*** a five game winning streak.

charge of something — be responsible for an activity or group of people
USAGE: Peter was in ***charge of security*** for the teenager's party.

claim to fame — what causes a person to be famous
USAGE: The athlete's ***claim to fame*** was that he had played in the World Cup
  Finals.

✍ Agree / Approval

close ranks — come together for fighting; unite and work together
USAGE: The students ***closed ranks*** to complete the project before the deadline
  passed.

come to terms — reach an agreement
USAGE: Jim ***came to terms*** with the bank regarding the interest rate on the
  loan.

✍ Authority

crack down on — enforce laws or rules strictly
USAGE: The police decided to ***crack down on*** people driving too fast.

✍ Bad / Negative

clip someone's wings — limit one's activities or possibilities
USAGE: The parents ***clipped John's wings*** because he failed to arrive home
  on-time.

come down — a lowering in status, income, influence or energy
USAGE: Because he lost his job, it was a real *come down* for Peter in terms of popularity with the girls.

✍ Business Action

buy a pig in a poke — buy something without seeing it or knowing if it will be satisfactory
USAGE: Bill advised Mike he shouldn't buy the car without first driving it. Bill said, "it's like *buying a pig in a poke*."

✍ Communication

chew the fat — chat
USAGE: The two old men were smoking and *chewing the fat* in front of the store.

chime in — join in (a song or conversation)
USAGE: While the others were discussing the game, Bill *chimed in* and started complaining about the outside heat.

clam up — stop talking
USAGE: When the manager walked into the room, Peter *clammed up* and looked down at his desk.

come again — please repeat; please say that again
USAGE: Trying to hear the speaker over the crowd, Jack said, "*come again*, I couldn't hear because of the crowd."

come clean — tell the truth
USAGE: Recognizing what he had done was wrong, James was urged to *come clean* and tell his wife the truth.

✍ Completeness

come full circle — completely opposite from one's starting point
USAGE: The team has *come full circle* in its winning percentage since the start of the season.

✍ Consequence

drop like flies — dying or failing in large numbers
USAGE: When the government workers sprayed the insecticide on the plants, the insects started *dropping like flies*.

every cloud has a silver lining — even a bad thing can have a positive aspect
USAGE: Even though Susan did not get the job, it worked out well because she ended up starting her own business. Therefore, *every cloud has a silver lining*!

face the music — accept the consequences of something
USAGE: Due to the increased demands from senior management, Michael will have to *face the music* at some point.

fall through the cracks — to be overlooked
USAGE: The poor people *fell through the cracks* because they didn't have anyone advocating for them.

✍ Different

make room for someone/something — arrange space for
USAGE: Jack cleaned out the front room to *make room for* the new baby's bedroom.

✍ Disagree

dish out — treat or criticize roughly
USAGE: While Timothy finds it easy to *dish out* criticism to others, he doesn't like to hear criticism about himself.

do in — (1) to ruin, destroy; (2) to make tired, exhaust
USAGE (1): Driving the car recklessly, Tom *did in* the new car within the first year.
USAGE (2): After a long time on the treadmill, John was really *done in*.

✍ Emotion

crocodile tears — a show of sorrow that is not really felt
USAGE: While Susan acted sorry for insulting Harry, I believe her sorrow were just *crocodile tears*.

cross one's heart and hope to die — promise that what you are saying is true
USAGE: Saying, "*Cross my heart and hope to die*," Mike promised he would help Kathy with her homework next week.

cross one's mind — think of; occur to someone
USAGE: Harry said it had *crossed his mind* he should go ahead and make the deposit in the bank.

cross to bear/carry — something you must do or continue with even though you are suffering
USAGE: Realizing I was involved in a fatal car accident that killed a child is a *cross to bear*.

✍ End

knock it off — stop doing something; quit
USAGE: Bill told the others to *knock it off* because he was tired of hearing them complain.

✍ Failure

come to nothing — end in failure
USAGE: All their efforts to negotiate a settlement resulted in failure and *came to nothing*.

cook one's goose — ruin one's chances
USAGE: Susan really *cooked her own goose* when she insulted the manager during the interview.

✍ Health

dead to the world — fast asleep
USAGE: Staying awake all night to finish the assignment, Steven was *dead to the world* when he returned to his apartment.

✍ Importance

fat of the land — have the best of everything, especially without having to work for it
USAGE: Tired of living in the crowded city, John moved to the mountains to live off the *fat of the land*.

✍ Location

double back — turn back from where you are going or have been
USAGE: Our group decided to *double back* so we could pick up Robert and Tim at their house.

down the tubes — gone or lost
USAGE: You should succeed in your school work, or your hopes for a good job will go *down the tubes*.

✍ Money

cash on the barrelhead — money paid when something is bought
USAGE: The settlement was a cash deal and Michael was expected to pay *cash on the barrelhead*.

caught short — not having enough of something when you need it (usually money)
USAGE: Since he lost his job last month, John was *caught short* and couldn't pay last month's utility bill.

✍ Movement

get cracking — hurry up; start moving fast; get started
USAGE: Barbara realized she would need to *get cracking* on completing the project if she wanted to finish by the end of the week.

get off — come down from or out of (a bus or train etc.)
USAGE: The tour group decided to *get off* the subway at the next stop.

get off one's butt — get busy; start working
USAGE: Frustrated by his 25 year old son not working, John said, "you need to *get off your butt* and get a job."

✍ Ownership

get hold of (something) — get possession of
USAGE: Needing to get to the game, Mary asked Bob to *get hold of* a car to drive to the stadium.

✍ Personal Description

back on one's feet — return to good financial or physical health
USAGE: Mary is *back on her feet* after losing a lot of money in the poor investment.

(a) bar fly — a person who visits bars frequently
USAGE: Wendy is a *bar fly*! She goes to the bar almost every night.

(a) bar star — a person who is popular at bars
USAGE: Peter is considered a *bar star* by the others because everyone who frequents the bar thinks he is funny!

✍ Plan / Prepare

end in itself — a purpose or goal one wants for itself alone and not as a way to something else
USAGE: For many people, working is an *end in itself* and the money earned is not as important as the fulfillment of completing a project.

end up — finish; finally do something
USAGE: Charlie *ended up* taking a taxi home after missing the last subway train last evening.

every trick in the book — every method known
USAGE: To convince prospective customers to buy the product, William knows *every trick in the book*.

✍ Quantity

dime a dozen — common, easy to get and of little value
USAGE: Old comic books are a *dime a dozen* if you look on the Internet.

✍ Relationship

cheat on (someone) — be unfaithful to someone
USAGE: Robert was discovered *cheating on his wife* which led to the end of their marriage.

cheek by jowl — side by side; in close intimacy
USAGE: A very close couple, Bob and Martha always sit *cheek by jowl* at the movies.

✍ Satisfaction

do with — benefit from
USAGE: Robert said to his wife, "I've had a tough day at work so I could *do with* a cold beer."

do your own thing — doing what one wants; prefers
USAGE: Wanting to *do his own thing*, Tony enjoyed painting scenes of the riverside.

down one's alley — suited to one's tastes and abilities
USAGE: Wood carving is a hobby that is right *down his alley*.

✍ Service

get behind (a person/an idea) — support; help
USAGE: The supporters of the issue *got behind* the leadership seeking to change the policy.

✍ Similar

dead ringer — very similar or equal
USAGE: William was a *dead ringer* for the film star! With the beard, he looks just like him!

✍ Superior

blow out of the water — to be defeated
USAGE: If you try to debate him on the accuracy of the issues, he'll *blow you out of the water*.

✍ Time

brand new — absolutely new
USAGE: John very much wanted to purchase the *brand-new* car.

buy time — obtain additional time
USAGE: Brian delayed the opening of the store so he could *buy some extra time*.

by and by — before long
USAGE: Barbara predicted that *by and by* they will understand the need to buy the house.

✍ Understand

eyes glaze over — to express disbelief
USAGE: When told he would inherit a fortune, Michael's *eyes glazed over*.

face up to — accept something that is not easy
USAGE: You must *face up to* the fact that you will not get the book published without changing the title.

facts of life — what one should know about sex, marriage and birth
USAGE: The father sat down with his son to talk about the *facts of life*.

figure on — depend on; be sure about

USAGE: You can *figure on* an increase in the unemployment rate as a result of the new policy.

✍ Work

(as) busy as a beaver — very busy; active
USAGE: Working around the clock to finish the project for her boss, she was *busy as a beaver*.

Week 9

✍ **Achievement**

come a long way — make great progress
USAGE: Jeremy has *come a long way* in his struggle to learn English.

come across — find something or meet someone by chance
USAGE: She *came across* an amazing story on the history of the World Cup in the magazine.

come along — make progress; thrive
USAGE: Jeremy's pursuit of developing conversational English skill is *coming along* very well.

come hell or high water — no matter what happens
USAGE: He said, "*Come hell or high water* I'm going to the game."

✍ **Agree / Approval**

damn skippy — a phrase indicating approval, excitement, or support
USAGE: Steve said enthusiastically to his wife, "*Damn skippy*, you look great!"

damn straight — a phrase indicating approval, excitement, or support
USAGE: When John was asked if he still wanted to go on vacation, he said, "*Damn straight* I'm going to the beach."

✍ **Authority**

crack the whip — try to make someone work hard or obey by threatening them
USAGE: Vincent knew he would have to *crack the whip* to get his son to complete the chores around the house.

✍ **Bad / Negative**

copycat — someone who copies another person's work or their actions

USAGE: The teenage girls are often *copycats* as they imitate pop singers in their dress.

count one's chickens before they're hatched — assume that something will be successful before it is certain
USAGE: James warned him not to *count his chickens before they're hatched* when Henry discussed his plans for potential profits.

✍ Business Action

calculated risk — an action that may fail but has a good chance to succeed
USAGE: The business group took a *calculated risk* when they opened the new restaurant.

✍ Communication

come on strong — overwhelm with excessively strong language or personality
USAGE: Carol informed Bill that he *came on too strong* when he talked with the girls.

come out with — say; make known
USAGE: The leaders emerged from the meeting and *came out with* exciting news.

come to light — be discovered; become known
USAGE: It *came to light* from the newspaper investigation that the private property was stolen.

come to the point — be direct
USAGE: His speech was interesting but he never really *came to the point*.

(a) common thread — an idea that is shared by more than one person or a group
USAGE: The police revealed there was a *common thread* among all the crimes committed.

common touch — a friendly manner with everyone
USAGE: The new boss has a nice *common touch* among all the employees.

✍ Completeness

count out — leave something out of a plan; exclude
USAGE: Please *count me out* of your plans to go skiing for the weekend.

✍ Consequence

for goodness sake — for the good of everyone considered
USAGE: Betty reminded the group, "*For goodness sake*, let's finish the job before it's too late."

for heaven's sake — for the good of everyone considered
USAGE: Henry said to his wife, "*For heaven's sake*, we must start saving money for the children's school tuition."

from the frying pan into the fire — from bad to worse
USAGE: When the bills started to arrive after the failed surgery, Jim felt his life was like going *from the frying pan into the fire* since he had lost his job.

✍ Different

neither fish nor fowl — something that does not belong to a definite group
USAGE: Uncertain about how to classify the film, Jim finally concluded it was *neither fish nor fowl*.

✍ Disagree

don't give me any of your lip — do not talk back; do not argue
USAGE: When the teenager argued with the policeman, the officer said, "*don't give me any of your lip*."

✍ Emotion

cry out for — need something badly; be lacking
USAGE: The poverty of the small town *cried out for* the development of business activity to stimulate the economy.

cry over spilt milk — cry or complain about something that has already happened
USAGE: Charles suggested the young man shouldn't *cry over spilt milk*. He reminded him that a person can't change the past.

cry your eyes out — cry very much
USAGE: Upset over her father's death, Susan *cried her eyes out* all day.

deadpan — with an expressionless or emotionless face
USAGE: The manager had a *deadpan* expression when he informed the employees the plant would close.

devil-may-care — unworried; not caring what happens
USAGE: Tony exhibited a ***devil-may-care*** attitude about what might happen if he lost his job.

✍ **End**

lay off — stop using or taking (drugs or cigarettes)
USAGE: I was told by my doctor to ***lay off*** smoking or I would be very sick in the future.

✍ **Failure**

cop out — avoid doing something that you were planning to do
USAGE: Jane ***copped out*** from her earlier plan to study with the other students.

cry uncle — admit defeat or that one has lost
USAGE: Tony finally had to ***cry uncle*** when the other teenager knocked him against the tree during the brawl.

✍ **Health**

down the hatch — to swallow; to eat or drink
USAGE: While standing at the bar and holding up the beer mug, John said, "***Down the hatch***" and consumed the drink.

✍ **Importance**

for all the world — for anything; for any price
USAGE: Peter indicated that, ***for all the world***, he would have tried to rescue the children from the burning fire.

✍ **Location**

drop back — move or step backwards; retreat
USAGE: During the long walk up the hiking trail, he ***dropped back*** and allowed the children to catch up.

eat out — eat in a restaurant
USAGE: Bob and Dorothy decided to ***eat out*** at the French restaurant last evening.

✍ **Money**

chicken feed — a small amount of money

USAGE: Vickie realized she had sold her car for ***chicken feed*** because she needed the money fast.

chip in — contribute or pay jointly
USAGE: The boys ***chipped in*** and bought a large pizza to share.

✍ Movement

get off the ground — make a successful beginning; go ahead
USAGE: While it was a great plan on paper, Bill's new business enterprise never really ***got off the ground***.

get on in years — to advance in age
USAGE: He is ***getting on in years*** and is not very healthy.

get one's rear in gear — hurry up; get going
USAGE: Harry howled for Peter to ***get his rear in gear*** so they could catch the subway in time.

✍ Personal Description

bark is worse than one's bite — someone isn't as bad as they sound
USAGE: Since he does a lot of talking, Bill's ***bark is worse than his bite***.

(a) basket case — someone who is nervous
USAGE: Susie was a ***basket case*** after worrying about earning enough money to pay the bills.

✍ Plan / Prepare

fiddle around — tinker, do something in an unplanned way
USAGE: I tried ***fiddling around*** with the computer printer for awhile but it still wouldn't work.

fine-toothed comb — very carefully
USAGE: Trying to find her lost contact lens, Betty went over the bedroom floor with a ***fine-toothed comb***.

✍ Quantity

drop in the bucket — small amount
USAGE: The donations collected for the earthquake relief effort was only a ***drop in the bucket*** compared to what is needed.

✍ Relationship

chip off the old block — person who looks or acts like one of his parents
USAGE: Since he looks just like his father, Alan is a *chip off the old block*.

cog in the machine — one who is not important but only a small part of a large organization
USAGE: Because the employees didn't believe they were valued at the company, they felt like *cogs in a machine*.

✍ Satisfaction

ease off — reduce in severity or pressure; relax
USAGE: The boss asked the manager to *ease off* his excessive demands to increase production rates because employees were complaining.

easy come, easy go — something that you get easily can be lost easily
USAGE: Betty isn't very nice to the boys at school. It seems that, when it comes to boys, her attitude is *easy come, easy go*.

eat you out of house and home — eat all of a person's food
USAGE: Inviting members of the team to dinner, Fred felt the hungry athletes would *eat him out of house and home*.

✍ Service

give me a lift — to provide a ride
USAGE: Peter asked Susan if he could *give her a lift* to the metro station.

✍ Similar

different strokes for different folks — people have different preferences
USAGE: When Lisa said she liked opera more than popular music, John remarked, "*different strokes for different folks*!"

✍ Time

by fits and starts — irregularly; with many stops and starts
USAGE: *By fits and starts*, the team finally was able to prevail and win the championship.

call it a day — end work for the day
USAGE: After a hard 11 hour day at work, John decided to *call it a day*.

cliffhanger — situation where the outcome is uncertain until the very end
USAGE: This year's Super Bowl was a really exciting *cliffhanger*, a game to remember!

✍ Understand

figure out — try to understand or solve
USAGE: Peter studied several books and finally *figured out* how to create web pages.

fleeting glance — a quick look
USAGE: Martha got a *fleeting glance* of the Prime Minister as he left the ceremony.

flip-flop — change ideas on an issue
USAGE: The manager was torn on the situation and did a *flip-flop* on the issue.

float your boat — to interest a person
USAGE: While Charles didn't like symphonic music, he knew many of his friends did like classical music. Many times Charles said, "Whatever *floats their boat*."

✍ Work

by the sweat of one's brow — by hard work
USAGE: Adam worked *by the sweat of his brow* to purchase the land.

Week 10

✍ Achievement

come into one's own — be able to perform or work well because of good circumstances
USAGE: When he turned 22 years old, Tommy *came into his own* as a serious and businesslike professional.

come to pass — to happen, occur
USAGE: It *came to pass* that John became a highly motivated student of history.

come up with — produce or find a thought, idea or answer
USAGE: The plant manager asked the staff to *come up with* a new manufacturing schedule.

cook up — invent, plan and put something together
USAGE: Frustrated, Susan looked at Joe and angrily said, "I know you *cooked up* this problem."

✍ Agree / Approval

even so — nevertheless; however
USAGE: Harry studies for his classes but *even so*, his grades have always been below average.

fair-haired boy — someone who is favored
USAGE: As the youngest head of a Fortune 500 multinational company, James was considered the *fair-haired boy* of the business world.

✍ Authority

fall into line — go and stand properly in a row (like soldiers)
USAGE: The students were forced to *fall into line* as they waited for the doors to open.

✍ Bad / Negative

crash the gate — enter without a ticket or without paying or with no invitation
USAGE: Hundreds of rowdy teenagers who didn't have concert tickets *crashed the gate* of the event.

deep water — serious trouble or difficulty
USAGE: If the accusations of improper actions are proved, Thomas will be in *deep water*.

✍ Business Action

corner the market — be the main provider or supplier
USAGE: The American government was concerned that a software company would potentially *corner the market* on operating system software.

✍ Communication

cool one's heels — be kept waiting because of another's rudeness
USAGE: Angry and upset at her, Jim *cooled his heels* for an hour before she agreed to talk with him.

cop a plea — plead guilty to a crime in order to get a lesser penalty
USAGE: Bill was encouraged to *cop a plea* when the evidence against him was shown to be compelling.

cramp one's style — limit one's talk, expression or action
USAGE: Not wanting to work in a building without windows, it *cramped his style*.

cry wolf — warn of danger that is not there
USAGE: Since he had been known for *crying wolf*, the teacher confronted him about what they thought was another false alarm.

cut both ways — serve both sides of an argument
USAGE: The discussion concerning the controversy *cut both ways* and required careful consideration.

✍ Completeness

cover one's tracks — hide or not say where one has been or what one has done
USAGE: When Keith hid the treasure in the field, he tried to *cover his tracks* but it was possible to see where he had walked.

✍ Consequence

get deeper in — to cause more trouble
USAGE: When William lied to the police, he *got deeper in* trouble with the law.

go downhill — failure; to get worse
USAGE: After John was released from jail for drunken driving, his reputation *went downhill*.

gone to the dogs — not well maintained
USAGE: The condition of Jack's store had *gone to the dogs* since he failed to maintain its outside appearance.

✍ Different

neither here nor there — not relevant to the thing being discussed; off the subject
USAGE: What Bob was arguing about, according to James, was *neither here nor there*.

✍ Disagree

don't have a cow — do not become angry
USAGE: When Robert started to get upset, after the meeting Martha insisted, *"Don't have a cow."*

double-cross — deceive; promise one thing and do another
USAGE: Bart attempted to *double-cross* his business partner but was caught and sent to prison.

✍ Emotion

down in the dumps — unhappy
USAGE: After she was offended by the bus driver, Betty was *down in the dumps* for the rest of the day.

drive someone up a wall — irritate or annoy someone greatly
USAGE: Gloria bluntly told Robert that his constant complaining was *driving her up a wall*.

drive you/me crazy — to be bothered by someone
USAGE: When asked about the loud teenagers, Charles remarked, "they just *drive me crazy*."

drive you/me nuts — to be bothered by someone
USAGE: When asked about receiving unsolicited email messages, Jeffrey remarked, "they just *drive me nuts*."

(as) drunk as a skunk — very intoxicated with alcoholic drink
USAGE: Because James had consumed an entire bottle of wine by himself, he was *drunk as a skunk*.

✍ End

lay to rest — get rid of; put away permanently; stop
USAGE: The plant managers worked hard to *lay to rest* rumors about changes happening at the manufacturing plant.

✍ Failure

dead duck — person or thing in a hopeless situation or condition
USAGE: Once Jacob disclosed private information to a competitor business, he came to be regarded as a *dead duck* in the industry.

✍ Health

feeling his oats — feeling strong and playful with energy
USAGE: Acting in a self-important way and with confidence, John was *feeling his oats* tonight.

✍ Importance

for better or worse — depending on how one looks at a matter
USAGE: *For better or worse*, he has decided to divorce his wife and move to the country.

✍ Location

elbow room — space (enough to be comfortable)
USAGE: John and Vickie moved to the countryside to have a little *elbow room*.

✍ Money

chunk of change — a large amount of money
USAGE: The car that Steven bought cost a *chunk of change*.

✍ Movement

get out from under — escape a situation that one doesn't like
USAGE: Tony said he wanted to *get out from under* his boss always keeping him late at work.

get out of the way — no longer be an obstacle
USAGE: Jimmy *got out of the way* just as the truck passed.

✍ Personal Description

be real — to be truthful
USAGE: John confronted him and said, "Fred, *be real*; don't lie to us."

be straight up — to be truthful
USAGE: Fred responded to John by saying, "I'll *be straight-up* with you and tell you what's really happening with the project."

✍ Plan / Prepare

follow in one's footsteps/tracks — follow someone's example; follow someone exactly
USAGE: Stanley is *following in his father's footsteps* and is training to be a police officer.

✍ Relationship

count on — depend on
USAGE: You can absolutely *count on* David to do what is ethical.

✍ Satisfaction

fair and square — honestly; just; straightforward
USAGE: The team from the Henan Province won the game *fair and square* despite complaints from the other team.

fair game — a likely object of aggressive interest
USAGE: The local company was considered *fair game* as a takeover by several international companies.

✍ Service

give one's right arm — give something of great value

USAGE: John has often said he would *give his right arm* to send his son and daughter to the university.

✍ Time

cold turkey — to stop using an addictive substance abruptly
USAGE: For his health welfare, Thomas stopped smoking cigarettes *cold turkey*.

✍ Understand

fly on the wall — able to hear and see something not intended
USAGE: I would like to be a *fly on the wall* tonight and listen to the plans of the teenagers.

food for thought — something worth thinking about
USAGE: Mary had *food for thought* with her recommendations for implementing the changes.

for certain — without doubt; certainly; surely
USAGE: It is *for certain* that Jimmy will not be playing in the championship game next week.

✍ Work

call it quits — stop; finish
USAGE: Tired of 12 hour workdays in a corporate environment, Henry *called it quits* and started teaching.

Week 11

✍ Achievement

cut the mustard — reach the required standard
USAGE: William doesn't *cut the mustard* and will not be added to the team as a full member

dash off — do or finish quickly; leave quickly
USAGE: Wanting to communicate with him soon, Betty *dashed off* a letter to him in 10 minutes

✍ Agree / Approval

fall for — begin to like very much; begin to love
USAGE: Joseph was highly attracted to and *fell for* the young lady he met at the restaurant.

✍ Authority

firm hand — to be disciplined
USAGE: Because he wanted to have a quiet classroom, the teacher had a *firm hand* in keeping order among the students.

✍ Bad / Negative

dirty laundry — personal problems
USAGE: Bill was very embarrassed for the public to see his *dirty laundry* in the newspaper.

do a job on — do harm to; make ugly or useless
USAGE: Really angry at Charles, Tina *did a job on* him by criticizing him and spreading rumors that damaged his reputation.

✍ Communication

cut (someone) off — stop someone from saying something; disconnect someone on the phone

USAGE: Helen tried to tell him about the risk associated with the investment, but he *cut her off* before she had a chance.

dead giveaway — an obvious signal
USAGE: When David walked in with a gift box it was a *dead giveaway* that he had a gift to present.

do a number on — to deceive
USAGE: Sally *did a number on* her teacher when she denied talking in class.

double-talk — talk that appears to have meaning but does not; evasive language
USAGE: While John tried to explain his reasons for not attending the meeting, the group members knew it was *double-talk* and he was being evasive.

down and dirty — rude; not polite
USAGE: Betty answered very angrily, giving Susan a *down and dirty* response.

✐ Completeness

cover up — hide something wrong or bad
USAGE: The suspected thief attempted to *cover up* evidence that would associate him with the crime.

✐ Consequence

had his/her bell rung — to be hit hard
USAGE: Falling off his bicycle, Jim hit the ground hard and really *had his bell rung*.

hard row to hoe — a challenging or hard task
USAGE: Peter had a *hard row to hoe* during the last several months as he went through cancer treatment.

✐ Disagree

draw fire — (1) receive criticism or argument; (2) be a target; attract or provoke shooting
USAGE (1): The leaders *drew fire* from the crowd when they announced there would not be a prize awarded for the competition.
USAGE (2): The police *drew fire* when they cornered the criminal suspects in the building.

✍ Emotion

dwell on — think about or talk about something all the time
USAGE: Betsy became depressed when she *dwelled on* the tragedy that occurred in her hometown.

eat one's heart out — feeling a negative emotion (anger, jealousy, worry)
USAGE: Robert was *eating his heart out* over losing his home in the fire.

eating someone — bothering or worrying someone
USAGE: Realizing that Bob was in a bad mood, Wendy didn't know what was *eating him*.

end of one's rope — the last of one's ability or ideas about how to proceed or do something
USAGE: Phillip felt at the *end of his rope* about how to save his business from failure.

✍ Failure

dead end — the closed end of a road or an impasse in a situation
USAGE: Driving through the countryside, Peter had to turn back because the highway hit a *dead end*.

✍ Health

glassy eyed — dazed
USAGE: John was confused and *glassy-eyed* because he had been awake continuously for 36 hours.

✍ Location

exit stage left — to leave; to depart
USAGE: After her dance exhibition, the performer did an *exit stage left*.

✍ Money

cost a pretty penny — expensive
USAGE: The new luxury car *cost Bill a pretty penny*.

✍ Movement

get over something — overcome a difficulty; recover from an illness or shock

USAGE: The last six months were very difficult for Stanley in ***getting over the death of his mother***.

get the ball rolling — start something
USAGE: So they could finish the project, Phillip told the crew members, "let's ***get the ball rolling*** and start working."

✍ Personal Description

beat — tired
USAGE: After running on the treadmill for one hour, Deanna was ***beat***.

(a) bee in her bonnet — angry; emotionally upset
USAGE: Frances had a ***bee in her bonnet*** because of what Betty said about her husband.

✍ Plan / Prepare

follow suit — do as someone else has done; follow someone's example
USAGE: Caroline ***followed suit*** of her supervisor and began arriving to work at 7 AM each morning.

follow through — continue or finish an action that one has started
USAGE: While James said he would help in the community clean-up project, he never ***followed through*** with his offer.

✍ Relationship

cozy up (to someone) — try to be friendly to someone; may be insincere
USAGE: Mary remarked that Peter had been trying to ***cozy up*** to her.

✍ Satisfaction

fall into my lap — receive without asking
USAGE: The job offer ***fell into my lap*** because I had not applied for consideration.

feast your eyes on — to look at and enjoy
USAGE: John enjoyed ***feasting his eyes on*** the beautiful paintings on display at the museum.

✍ Service

give out — give to people; distribute

USAGE: We *gave out* coupons for free drinks to visitors at the stadium.

✍ Time

crack of dawn — daybreak; early in the morning
USAGE: For the best fishing, we arrived at the lake before the *crack of dawn*.

crop up — appear or happen unexpectedly
USAGE: Phillip indicated he would be at the meeting unless something urgent
    crops up that would prevent him from attending.

✍ Understand

for shizzle — for sure; for certain
USAGE: Excited about the competition, Tom said, "I'll go to the soccer game
    for shizzle."

for sure — without doubt; certainly; surely
USAGE: Barbara encouraged her teammates by saying, "we'll win the game
    for sure."

for that matter — about that; with regard to that
USAGE: *For that matter*, I'm not really concerned about getting the loan.

✍ Work

clear the decks — clear away things and prepare for action
USAGE: The employees *cleared the decks* and began work on packing up the
    supplies.

Week 12

✍ Achievement

dig a little deeper — try harder
USAGE: Encouraging him to work hard on his grades, the teacher remarked that James needed to *dig a little deeper*.

dish out — serve food from a large bowl or plate
USAGE: As the party was beginning, the host began to *dish out* the food to the guests.

do one's best — try to do something as well as you can
USAGE: I tried to *do my best* on the university entrance exam.

✍ Agree / Approval

fall over oneself — be extremely eager to do something or please someone
USAGE: The students *fell over themselves* in an effort to please their teacher.

✍ Authority

hand over — give possession to someone
USAGE: The citizens *handed over* to the police the criminal suspects hiding in the empty house.

head honcho — the supervisor; the boss
USAGE: Charles told the workers they would need to check with the *head honcho* if they wanted a pay raise.

✍ Bad / Negative

do time — spend time in prison
USAGE: Stanley was *doing time* in jail when I first heard about him.

✍ Communication

down on (someone) — be critical of someone; angry at

USAGE: Karen was really *down on* Betty but I don't know the reason.

drag in — insist on bringing another subject into a discussion
USAGE: He always *drags in* unrelated excuses when we try to discuss his poor job performance.

draw (someone) into — make a person talk or tell something
USAGE: She was shy but we tried to *draw her into* the conversation.

drive at — try or want to say something
USAGE: I don't know what he was *driving at* with his remarks.

drop a hint — casually state a hint or suggestion
USAGE: Bill *dropped a hint* that he wanted to transfer to a new department.

drop (someone) a line — write a note, email or letter to someone
USAGE: Barbara promised she would *drop me a line* when she arrives in Singapore.

✐ Completeness

day and night — continually
USAGE: Brian worked *day and night* to finish the budget proposal before the deadline.

✐ Consequence

have it coming — deserve a punishment
USAGE: The convicted prisoner *had it coming* to him after being found guilty of the crime.

✐ Different

new blood — fresh energy or power; something or someone that gives new life or vigor to something
USAGE: The new management staff injected *new blood* into the operations of the company.

✐ Emotion

fall in love with — begin to love someone
USAGE: I *fell in love with* Karen the first time I saw her in the park.

feel like a million dollars — feel wonderful
USAGE: I *felt like a million dollars* after my work-out this morning.

feel sorry for — pity
USAGE: Jim *felt sorry for* William when his wife left him for another man.

feel up to (do something) — feel able (healthy enough or rested enough) to do something
USAGE: John suggested that he didn't *feel up to* taking the flight to Shanghai.

✍ Failure

dig your own grave — cause a person's own failure
USAGE: When Peter didn't finish the assignment, Charles remarked, "don't you know you're *digging your own grave?*"

✍ Importance

hats off — a tribute
USAGE: Recognizing the achievements of the employees, Bill said, "*Hats off* to all of you for reducing production costs."

✍ Location

fall back — move back; go back
USAGE: Steven *fell back* from the rest of the runners about half way into the 10K race.

✍ Money

cost an arm and a leg — expensive
USAGE: A beautiful new dress, it *cost Susan an arm and a leg*.

cough up — give unwillingly, usually money
USAGE: John *coughed up* enough money to pay the food bill.

✍ Movement

get the show on the road — start working on something or move on
USAGE: Jane urged the group to *get the show on the road* and begin working on the project.

get up — get out of bed; get to one's feet

USAGE: I decided to ***get up*** early today so I could resume writing the report.

✎ Personal Description

behind someone's back — without someone's knowledge
USAGE: Mike was angry because the teenagers borrowed the car ***behind his back***.

✎ Plan / Prepare

follow up — make an action more successful by doing something more
USAGE: Peter ***followed up*** his phone call with Barbara with a personal visit.

for all — in spite of; even with
USAGE: ***For all*** the effort dedicated to increasing awareness among the people, the involvement level is still very low.

✎ Satisfaction

fend for yourself — take care of oneself
USAGE: Henry was told by his parents that after graduation from the University he would have to ***fend for himself***.

fill one's shoes — substitute satisfactorily for
USAGE: Although he is a good professor, Dr. Jones is unable to ***fill the shoes*** of Professor Smith.

✎ Service

give someone a hand — help someone with something
USAGE: Please ***give Peter a hand*** as he moves the piano to the ground floor.

✎ Time

down the line — straight ahead; in the future
USAGE: The new management indicated there would be many changes at the company ***down the line*** in the next several months.

down to the wire — nearing a deadline; running out of time
USAGE: The group worked on the project ***down to the wire*** and completed it satisfactorily.

✍ Understand

fresh pair of eyes — a new reader who has not seen the writing
USAGE: The boss wanted Francis to proofread the report because a *fresh pair of eyes* might find errors to be corrected.

from A to Z — know everything about something
USAGE: He knows all things about wine *from A to Z*.

get a fix on something — have an understanding of a situation
USAGE: John was finally able to *get a fix on the situation* and develop a solution to the problem.

✐ Achievement

do one's bit/part — share in a group project by contributing one's time and effort
USAGE: Cleaning up the kitchen, Clayton **did his bit** for keeping the house clean.

do something rash — take drastic action (usually without thinking)
USAGE: He is extremely angry, so I hope he doesn't **do anything rash**.

do the honors — perform the duty of a host (when serving a drink etc.)
USAGE: Shelley asked her husband if he would **do the honors** and pour the guests a glass of wine.

✐ Agree / Approval

fence sitter — someone who supports both sides of an argument
USAGE: Since it was a controversial issue, Jim was a **fence sitter** because of his uncertainty.

✐ Authority

head up — be at the head of (a group); a leader
USAGE: The Dean **headed up** a group of faculty members going overseas to promote educational exchange.

✐ Bad / Negative

dog-eat-dog — ready or willing to fight and hurt others to get what you want
USAGE: Joseph reminded the students it is a **dog-eat-dog** world in the world of corporate advertising.

dog's life — a difficult life
USAGE: People who avoid improving their skills throughout their career have a **dog's life**.

✍ Communication

drop by — to visit someone or somewhere
USAGE: The manager *dropped by* the bar for a drink.

drop in — make a short or unplanned visit
USAGE: I decided to *drop in* and visit Mary after work.

drown out — make so much noise that it is impossible to hear
USAGE: The game's announcer was *drowned out* by the cheering fans.

eat one's words — admit being wrong in something one has said; retract one's statement
USAGE: Jimmy was forced to *eat his words* after his wife proved what he said was inaccurate.

face time — a period of time during which one is talking with someone face-to-face
USAGE: Rather than communicating through a video conference, Robert wanted to get *face time* with the others.

✍ Completeness

day in and day out — regularly; all the time
USAGE: Joe goes to the deli every morning, *day in and day out* and never gets tired of it.

✍ Consequence

havoc strikes — problems occur
USAGE: When the employment rate went down significantly, *havoc struck* the stock market.

heads or tails — to choose something based on probability
USAGE: Unable to choose which restaurant to eat at, Bob and Mary decided to flip a coin for *heads or tails*.

✍ Disagree

drop dead! — expression of anger
USAGE: After Henry insulted Susan, she told him to *drop dead* and never return.

✍ Emotion

fit to be tied — very angry or upset
USAGE: Outraged, Sharon was *fit to be tied* when she heard that her purse had been stolen.

flare up — become suddenly angry
USAGE: Bill's temper *flared up* when he saw the teenagers break the window and run away.

flash a smile — to smile
USAGE: William *flashed a smile* at the audience when he accepted the award.

flip one's lid — become very excited; lose one's temper
USAGE: He really *flipped his lid* when I told him how much I paid for the car.

✍ Failure

do out of — cause to lose by trickery or cheating
USAGE: He was worried that his cousins would try to *do him out of* his inheritance.

✍ Health

grub — food; a meal
USAGE: Henry said to Tom, "Let's go get some *grub*."

✍ Location

far and wide — everywhere; in all directions
USAGE: Tim looked *far and wide* for the DVD but couldn't find it.

✍ Money

deep pockets — wealthy
USAGE: Bill knew the potential investors had *deep pockets* and an interest in the project

✍ Movement

give chase — chase or run after someone or something
USAGE: The police *gave chase* to the fugitive prisoner.

give free rein to — allow to move about or to do something with freedom

USAGE: Patty was ***given free rein to*** design the fund-raising project.

✍ Personal Description

behind the times — old fashioned
USAGE: My brother is out of date and a little ***behind the times***.

big dog — the best at something
USAGE: Michael is an outstanding player and considered the ***big dog*** of the team!

✍ Plan / Prepare

for love or money — by any means
USAGE: We were unable to get him to parachute from the plane ***for love or money***.

for the world — under any conditions
USAGE: I wouldn't want to live in the city ***for the world***.

✍ Relationship

dance with the one who brought you — being loyal to the person who has helped
USAGE: The politician realized that he needed to support his base and ***dance with the one who brought him***.

✍ Satisfaction

fill the bill — be suitable for what is required
USAGE: Knowing it would serve the purpose, Susan remarked, "the plan will ***fill the bill*** for us."

find your voice — discover a person's own style or purpose
USAGE: Charles ***found his voice*** in the cause and determined to donate his time to help the homeless.

✍ Service

give someone one's word — make a promise or assurance
USAGE: He ***gave me his word*** that he would try his hardest to complete the project.

✍ Time

drag it out — take a long time to finish
USAGE: The actor ***dragged out*** his performance to fit the time needs of the production.

drag on — pass very slowly; make longer
USAGE: The professor's speech seemed to ***drag on*** so finally we decided to leave the lecture early.

✍ Understand

get a grip — to comprehend
USAGE: John suggested he needed to ***get a grip*** on how long-term inflation would affect the economy.

get a load of — take a good look at; see something
USAGE: ***Get a load of*** the guy over there with the four big dogs.

get across — explain; make something understood
USAGE: Peter was successful in ***getting across*** his point about the urgency of nations dealing with terrorism.

✍ Work

clip joint — a business where customers are overcharged
USAGE: They went into a ***clip joint*** near the bus station and had to pay a lot of money for poor entertainment.

Week 14

✍ Achievement

do the trick — work well; achieve a good result
USAGE: Stanley believed the purchase of new equipment should ***do the trick*** and solve the problem.

do with — be acquainted, involved or associated with
USAGE: Leslie didn't have anything to ***do with*** the problems associated with the gathering.

do without — manage without something
USAGE: If there is not enough money, we'll have to ***do without*** some conveniences.

do wonders — produce excellent results
USAGE: If you begin to exercise it will ***do wonders*** for your health.

✍ Agree / Approval

fish for a compliment — hinting for a complement
USAGE: Showing off his new shoes, Henry was ***fishing for a compliment***.

flattery will get you nowhere — saying nice things will not help a situation
USAGE: When Tom complimented Mary on her new dress, she said, "Thanks, but ***flattery will get you nowhere***."

✍ Authority

high handed — bossy; depending on force
USAGE: The supervisor always takes a ***high-handed*** approach when dealing with his employees.

✍ Bad / Negative

don't borrow trouble — don't seek out trouble

USAGE: When Carl suggested he was considering a divorce, Michael said, "***Don't borrow trouble*** and keep your marriage together."

doozy — something strange
USAGE: The bizarre shoes were a ***doozy***!

fall on — meet (troubles)
USAGE: The town had ***fallen on*** hard times before the new computer company moved in and created many jobs.

✍ Communication

fall on deaf ears — talk to people who will not listen
USAGE: The advice given by the leaders ***fell on deaf ears*** because the students didn't want to listen.

fast talker — clever talker who convinces others easily
USAGE: John warned us that Bill is a ***fast talker*** and, therefore, we should be careful not to believe everything he says.

feel out — talk or act carefully with someone and find out what he thinks
USAGE: I will try and ***feel out*** my boss this weekend and see what he thinks about the possibility of your promotion.

fill (someone) in — tell someone the details
USAGE: Henry will ***fill you in*** about the plans for expansion.

fill out — write down the facts that are asked for (in a report etc.)
USAGE: We were asked to ***fill out*** the application forms before we interviewed for the job.

✍ Completeness

deep-six — throw away; dispose of
USAGE: I decided to ***deep-six*** the old VHS tapes since the current standard is DVD format.

✍ Consequence

hell of a time — a very difficult time
USAGE: Tony had a ***hell of a time*** putting the equipment in the truck.

hell to pay — difficult consequences

USAGE: The manager knew there would be ***hell to pay*** if sales didn't reach the estimated predictions.

hit bottom — be at the very lowest; not be able to go any lower
USAGE: The economy ***hit bottom*** last year but is finally starting to improve.

✍ Different

new broom sweeps clean — a new person or group makes many changes
USAGE: Like a ***new broom sweeps clean***, the new leadership at the company put into place significant changes.

✍ Disagree

falling-out — argument; disagreement; quarrel
USAGE: Harry and Thomas had a ***falling-out*** several months ago and haven't spoken since.

fight fire with fire — fight with the same weapon used by the enemy
USAGE: Recognizing it was necessary to make his point, John used statistics to ***fight fire with fire***.

✍ Emotion

flip out — go insane; go out of one's mind; become very angry
USAGE: Martha ***flipped out*** when she heard I had sold her car.

fly off the handle — become angry
USAGE: William really ***flew off the handle*** when he saw the cost for traveling to Australia.

flying high — very happy; joyful
USAGE: When she found out she had won a car in a contest, Wendy was ***flying high***.

foam at the mouth — be very angry
USAGE: He was ***foaming at the mouth*** when told a dent was in his car.

footloose and fancy free — carefree
USAGE: As a single girl and recent university graduate, Susan was ***footloose and fancy free*** in her mood.

for crying out loud — to exhibit surprise or anger

USAGE: Peter told her, "*for crying out loud*, don't waste your time with the unimportant details."

✍ Error

break down — stop working because of mechanical failure
USAGE: The car *broke down* on an isolated country road.

✍ Failure

down and out — (1) have no money; (2) poor and unfortunate
USAGE (1): Unable to find a job, Steven was *down and out* and concerned about the welfare of his family.
USAGE (2): *Down and out*, Steven was homeless and didn't have any money.

✍ Importance

last but not least — in the last place but not the least important
USAGE: *Last but not least*, Peter walked to the front of the class to pick up his report card.

✍ Location

flag a cab — to find a taxi or cab
USAGE: Rather than wait for the subway train, we *flagged a cab* to get downtown faster.

✍ Money

draw in one's horns — spend less money
USAGE: Not doing well financially, the company needed to *draw in their horns* for awhile.

drop a bundle — lose money through a gambling loss
USAGE: Martha was furious with Tom because he *dropped a bundle* at the casino.

✍ Movement

give ground — move back; retreat; stop opposing someone
USAGE: Thomas didn't *give any ground* on his plan to introduce environmental regulation to the government.

give in — give someone his own way; stop opposing someone
USAGE: The government *gave in* to the citizens' demand for more security from terrorism.

✍ Ownership

get rid of something — dispose; sell or destroy something
USAGE: Having purchased a new television, Bill had to *get rid of the old one*.

✍ Personal Description

birthday suit — completely naked; no clothes on
USAGE: Joking to her son, Mary said, "As a baby, I've seen you in your *birthday suit*."

✍ Plan / Prepare

free hand — great freedom to do something
USAGE: We had a *free hand* in designing the new sports facility for the institute.

from scratch — from the very beginning
USAGE: Because he was resourceful, Ben wanted to build the house *from scratch*.

✍ Quantity

enough is enough — a sufficient amount; time to stop
USAGE: As the server kept putting food on his plate, Steven remarked, *"enough is enough."*

✍ Relationship

drop him/her like a hot potato — stop associating with another person
USAGE: Vickie warned Nancy that if he finds out you're dating another guy, he'll *drop you like a hot potato*.

✍ Satisfaction

fine-tune — cause something to run smoothly
USAGE: Working hard to improve the performance of his car, John *fine-tuned* the engine.

fit as a fiddle — in good athletic condition or health
USAGE: Even though Betty's grandfather is 92 years old, he is *fit as a fiddle*.

fit like a glove — fit perfectly
USAGE: The new pair of jeans he bought *fit like a glove*.

✍ Service

give someone the benefit of the doubt — believe someone is innocent rather
than guilty when you are not sure
USAGE: While John *gave him the benefit of the doubt*, I still think he is a liar.

✍ Similar

fair play — justice; equal and right action
USAGE: The manager believed in *fair play* when dealing with issues related
to employee wages.

✍ Time

drag one's feet/heels — act slowly or reluctantly
USAGE: Mary criticized James for *dragging his feet* about beginning the
home renovation project.

draw first blood — be first to attack
USAGE: Our team *drew first blood* in the soccer match by scoring the first
goal.

every dog has his day — everyone will have his chance or turn; everyone will
get what he deserves
USAGE: Reminding Joe he should be patient, Steven said, "Remember, *every
dog has his day*."

✍ Understand

get along — manage
USAGE: Very economical, Becky is able to *get along* on very little money.

get at — to make understandable
USAGE: Confused, Charles didn't know what Tim was trying to *get at* during
the meeting.

get it through one's head — understand; believe

USAGE: Peter finally ***got it through his head*** that he can't get a job without making an effort.

get mixed up — become confused
USAGE: The manager apologized to the employees for ***getting*** the dates of the holidays ***mixed up***.

✍ Work

close up shop — to close one's place of business for the night
USAGE: It was 5 PM, so William told the staff he was going to ***close up shop***.

Week 15

✍ Achievement

dodge a bullet — avoid a misfortune, failure or loss
USAGE: When John didn't lose his job when many others did, he realized he *dodged the bullet*.

double up — share a room or home with someone
USAGE: To save costs, the manager asked employees to *double up* in hotel rooms when traveling on business.

dress up — put on one's best clothes
USAGE: Harry *dressed up* when he dined with Susan at dinner.

✍ Agree / Approval

give a damn — to care or not care about something
USAGE: Phillip said angrily, "I don't *give a damn* about what she says about me."

✍ Authority

hold down — keep in obedience; keep control of
USAGE: The police officers were successful in *holding down* the prison riot.

✍ Bad / Negative

faulty — of extremely poor quality
USAGE: Repeatedly breaking down, the newly purchased air conditioner unit was *faulty*.

fed up with — disgusted or bored with someone or something
USAGE: Highly frustrated, Michael was getting *fed up with* the constant demands of his boss.

✍ Communication

find one's tongue — be able to give a reply
USAGE: When insulted by the store clerk, Bill *found his tongue* with a forceful reply.

find out — learn; discover
USAGE: Susan was angry at me because she *found out* I dropped the class.

fish for — try to get or to find out (something) by hinting at it
USAGE: On many days Joe would *fish for* information since he knew my wife was the manager's secretary.

flap your gums — to talk
USAGE: James was standing there *flapping his gums* about last night's game.

flea in one's ear — an annoying hint; an idea or answer that is not welcome
USAGE: I put a *flea in his ear* about making sure he returns my car.

✍ Completeness

die down — come slowly to an end; grow weaker
USAGE: When the sound of the crowd outside *died down* we were able to continue our conversation.

✍ Consequence

hit the jackpot — be very lucky or successful
USAGE: Unexpectedly successful, Tom *hit the jackpot* with the investment into the wireless Internet business.

hit the nail on the head — make a correct guess or analysis
USAGE: Linda *hit the nail on the head* when she suggested the others weren't interested in the project.

hit the spot — refresh or satisfy
USAGE: Drinking a cold glass of water following the 10K run really *hit the spot*.

✍ Different

new deal — a complete change; a fresh start; another chance
USAGE: He was given a *new deal* by the team although the previous year he was not very good.

✍ Disagree

fight tooth and nail — fight fiercely
USAGE: Mary was *fighting tooth and nail* to get nominated for the award.

fix his/her/your wagon — to hurt someone
USAGE: He makes me furious! I'll *fix his wagon* by making sure he gets a penalty.

✍ Emotion

for dear life — as though afraid of losing one's life
USAGE: The hiker held on to the tree *for dear life* as he waited for the safety crew to rescue him.

frame of mind (good/bad) — one's mental state
USAGE: Tom made sure his boss was in a good *frame of mind* before he asked for a salary increase.

freak out — become angry or lose control of oneself
USAGE: William *freaked out* when he found out a thief broke into his house.

frightened to death — very afraid
USAGE: When he saw the smoke coming from behind the door, George was *frightened to death*.

from the bottom of one's heart — with great feeling; sincerely
USAGE: Scott expressed his appreciation, thanking him *from the bottom of his heart* for raising money to help with his daughter's surgery.

✍ Entertainment

first run — movie shown for the first time
USAGE: Each week there is usually at least one *first run* movie released for viewing.

✍ Error

bull in a china shop — someone who is clumsy
USAGE: Bumping into the shelf, James was like a *bull in a china shop*.

✍ Failure

down the drain — wasted or lost

USAGE: Spending a lot of money on the project, some people thought Thomas was throwing money *down the drain*.

✍ Location

get lost! — go away
USAGE: The older sister told her younger brother to *get lost* so she could finish her homework.

give a wide berth to — keep away from; keep a safe distance from
USAGE: John remarked that he always *gives a wide berth* to his wife when she is angry.

✍ Money

face value — value or price printed on a stamp/bond/paper money etc.
USAGE: Timothy gave him the *face value* printed on the used stamps, although they were much more valuable.

fat cat — wealthy person
USAGE: Very wealthy, Steven is a *fat cat* and spends a lot of money traveling around the world.

✍ Movement

give off — send out; let out; put forth
USAGE: The box of the old food in the closet was beginning to *give off* a bad smell.

✍ Ownership

give away — give something to someone
USAGE: Michael *gave away* his new bicycle to a poor teenager in the countryside.

✍ Personal Description

bleeding heart — one who seeks sympathy for others
USAGE: Compassionate towards poor people, John is a *bleeding heart* and interested in programs to help the homeless.

born with a silver spoon in one's mouth — born rich; provided from birth with everything needed

USAGE: Because his parents were wealthy, Peter was ***born with a silver spoon in his mouth*** and has never worked in his life.

(a) budding genius — an extraordinary smart child
USAGE: Able to do mathematical calculations in her mind, the young child was believed to be a ***budding genius***.

✐ Plan / Prepare

front — a cover-up, disguise, deception
USAGE: Henry pretended to be a school teacher as a ***front*** for an illegal drug operation.

gathering dust — not being used
USAGE: The bicycles were in the outside building, ***gathering dust*** for many months

get down to — get started on
USAGE: Phillip said, "let's ***get down to*** business so we can go home early."

✐ Quantity

everything but the kitchen sink — a very large variety; almost everything
USAGE: Taking almost everything with her on the trip, Karen had ***everything but the kitchen sink***.

✐ Relationship

fair-weather friend — a person who is a friend only when one is successful
USAGE: James said Ralph was only a ***fair-weather friend*** and you wouldn't be able to rely on him when needed.

✐ Satisfaction

foot in the door — an opening or opportunity
USAGE: Working hard to market the new product, Peter realized a great opportunity by getting a ***foot in the door*** with the new company.

get a break — get an opportunity or good deal
USAGE: I ***got a break*** when I succeeded in obtaining an interview for the job!

get by — satisfy needs or demands (usually related to money)

USAGE: Betty is able to *get by* on the salary because her rent doesn't cost much.

✍ Service

give someone the green light — give permission to go ahead with a project
USAGE: The boss *gave Jonathan the green light* to begin negotiating for the sales contract.

✍ Similar

fair shake — honest treatment
USAGE: The employees didn't believe they were given a *fair shake* regarding their request for a wage increase.

✍ Superior

blow you out of the water — to defeat
USAGE: If you try to beat Elaine at the board game, she will *blow you out of the water*.

✍ Time

every other — alternate; every second one
USAGE: John and Mary try to visit her parents in the country every other Saturday.

every so often — occasionally
USAGE: William would take the dog for a walk *every so often*.

fall out of use — no longer used
USAGE: The use of dot-matrix printers has *fallen out of use* over the last few years.

✍ Understand

get through to — be understood by; make (someone) understand
USAGE: I tried to get Susan to understand the reasons for my decision, but I couldn't really *get through to* her.

get to the bottom of — find out the real cause
USAGE: The police are working hard to *get to the bottom of* the criminal investigation.

get to the heart of — understand the most important thing about something
USAGE: Jimmy's father talked with him for over one hour in order to *get to the heart of* the matter.

get wise to something/somebody — learn about something kept secret
USAGE: Timothy finally *got wise to* the fact they were stealing money out of his wallet.

✍ Work

every walk of life — all occupations
USAGE: It was a very diverse gathering with people from *every walk of life* attending.

Week 16

✍ **Achievement**

drive a hard bargain — conclude a bargain without making any concessions
USAGE: A tough businessman, Bart **drives a hard bargain** with his deals.

drum up — invent, encourage by making an effort
USAGE: John was able to **drum up** a lot of business on his recent trip.

duck soup — easy; effortless
USAGE: When asked about the difficulty of the examination, Bill said, "it was **duck soup** and not at all hard."

early bird catches the worm — a person who gets up early in the morning has the best chance of success
USAGE: She always gets to work early in the morning because she knows the **early bird catches the worm**.

✍ **Agree / Approval**

give a hoot — to care or not care about something
USAGE: Robert doesn't seem to **give a hoot** about finishing the project on time.

✍ **Authority**

hold the purse strings — control the spending
USAGE: John remarked, "around our house, my wife **holds the purse strings** to our budget!"

✍ **Bad / Negative**

find fault with — criticize
USAGE: Very frustrated with his supervisor, Thomas said he was always **finding fault with** his work.

fly in the ointment — a small thing that spoils enjoyment

USAGE: While Ted was satisfied with the construction project, he admitted that a *fly in the ointment* was the lack of enough parking spaces.

✍ Communication

for the asking — by asking; on request
USAGE: You can get a free ticket to the concert *for the asking* from the music store.

get a word in — find a chance to say something when others are talking
USAGE: Terry was frustrated that she couldn't *get a word in* while talking to Fred.

get a word in edgewise — manage to break into a conversation
USAGE: Since Terry couldn't *get a word in edgewise*, she left the meeting.

get down to brass tacks — begin discussing the essential matters immediately
USAGE: Tom suggested they needed to *get down to brass tacks* and solve the problem.

get hold of (someone) — find a person so you can speak with him or her
USAGE: I tried to telephone Henry but I couldn't *get hold of him*.

✍ Completeness

die off — die one after another until the number is small
USAGE: Since many animals on the endangered species list have *died off*, scientists are working hard to eliminate this trend.

die out — die or disappear slowly until all gone
USAGE: Pre-historic animals *died out* over 10 million years ago.

✍ Consequence

hit-and-run — striking suddenly and leaving quickly
USAGE: The drunk driver was arrested for a *hit-and-run* accident that resulted in the death of a pedestrian.

hot potato — a situation likely to cause trouble to the person handling it
USAGE: The issue of a pay increase is a *hot potato* that management must address.

hot water — trouble

USAGE: Bob has been in ***hot water*** with his wife since he failed to come home last Saturday night.

✍ Different

odds and ends — various items
USAGE: Barbara's hobby was making craft items from ***odds and ends*** around the house.

✍ Disagree

for the birds — uninteresting; something you don't like
USAGE: Susan agreed that spending the holiday cleaning her house was really *for the birds*.

✍ Emotion

from the heart — sincerely; honestly
USAGE: Peter gave Rebecca a poem he wrote straight *from the heart*.

full of beans — in high spirits; energetic
USAGE: She seems to be *full of beans* today because she couldn't sit still. She must be excited about something.

funny bone — sense of humor
USAGE: The movie was hilarious and it really tickled my *funny bone*.

gee whiz — used as an exclamation to show surprise or other strong feelings
USAGE: Charles excitingly asked, "***Gee whiz*** are we really going to attend the soccer match tomorrow?"

✍ End

lay up — take out of active service; put in a boat dock or a garage
USAGE: The weather was getting cold and rough, so Tony decided to ***lay up*** the boat for the winter season.

✍ Entertainment

flick — movie
USAGE: Robert and Mary remarked that the film was a good *flick*.

✍ Error

butter fingers — not able to grasp or hold onto
USAGE: Betty remarked, "You've got *butter fingers*" when Bill accidentally
 let the radio fall out of the boat into the lake.

✍ Failure

drop by the wayside — give up or fail before the finish
USAGE: During the 10K run, several runners *dropped by the wayside*.

drop out (of school) — quit school or a course of some kind
USAGE: Peter was really frustrated in his failure to understand calculus, so he
 dropped out of school after 2 months.

✍ Health

hale and hearty — in very good health; well and strong
USAGE: My father is very robust in shape! He's a real *hale and hearty* fellow.

✍ Location

hang around — pass time or stay someplace without a real purpose or aim
USAGE: The children were relaxing and *hanging around* the house on the
 weekend.

✍ Money

flat broke — have no money
USAGE: Bill remarked that he was *flat broke* and unable to pay the bill.

foot the bill — pay
USAGE: Cheryl was thankful her father was willing to *foot the bill* for the new
 car.

✍ Movement

give someone an inch and they will take a mile — if you give someone a
 little they will want more and more
USAGE: Phillip stressed I shouldn't lend Bob any money because if I *gave
 him an inch he would take a mile*.

give someone the slip — escape from someone
USAGE: The criminal suspects *gave the police the slip*.

✍ Ownership

have dibs on — demand a share of something or be in line to use something
USAGE: I *have dibs on* the antique car if it is put up for sale.

✍ Personal Description

butt of the joke — the object of humor; the subject of a joke
USAGE: Henry felt like he was the *butt of the joke* because the others were
  laughing at him.

cool under pressure — clear thinking; calm while experiencing pressure
USAGE: Wendy was *cool under pressure* while facing the heavy demands of
  the project.

✍ Plan / Prepare

get one's feet wet — begin; do something for the first time
USAGE: John managed to *get his feet wet* in writing short stories and now
  writes best selling books.

get ready — prepare yourself
USAGE: Susan had to wake up and *get ready* for work.

get set — get ready to start
USAGE: The race officials instructed the runners to *get set* for the beginning
  of the race.

✍ Quantity

fall off — decrease
USAGE: The government officials reported that the number of unemployed
  workers had *fallen off* recently.

✍ Relationship

fall in with — become associated with a bad group of people
USAGE: Enrolling in the new school, Peter *fell in with* a bad group of
  friends.

falling out — a disagreement; a break in relationship
USAGE: John and Steve had a *falling out* because they had a disagreement
  over money.

✍ Satisfaction

get it all together — be in full control and possession of one's mental faculties
USAGE: Harold finally *got it all together* and applied for the job at the University.

get off easy — escape a worse punishment
USAGE: The convicted robber *got off easy* because he received only a one year sentence.

get to — have a chance to; be able to
USAGE: Joe didn't *get to* see Nancy while in New York City.

✍ Service

give someone their due — give someone the credit they deserve
USAGE: Brian suggested we needed to *give him his due*. He made a fortune in construction.

✍ Superior

cream of the crop — best of the group; the top choice
USAGE: The soccer team was made up of *cream of the crop* players.

✍ Time

first come, first served — the person who comes first will have his turn first
USAGE: The clerk announced, *"first come, first served"* as he walked up to the first customer in the store.

firsthand — directly
USAGE: William learned *firsthand* from Susan the upsetting news about the robbery.

for good — permanently
USAGE: Joseph will be moving to Chicago *for good*.

✍ Understand

give it the once over — examine something quickly
USAGE: Steven *gave the contract a once over* and immediately signed it.

give pause to — cause one to stop and think

USAGE: The high rate of crime in many cities really *gives a person pause to* think about their personal safety.

go figure — hard to understand
USAGE: Helen told me she hated me, and then she smiled. *Go figure*!

go in circles — to be confused
USAGE: Very confused, Joe was *going in circles* trying to figure out what happen to his investment.

Week 17

✍ **Achievement**

easy does it — carefully do something without sudden movements
USAGE: As they started moving the large piano, John reminded the workers, *"Easy does it."*

egg (someone) on — urge or push someone to do something
USAGE: Ted was *egging his friend on* to jump into the lake.

eke out — earn with difficulty
USAGE: Phillip was barely able to *eke out* a living on the small wage he earned.

elbow grease — effort and strength to clean something
USAGE: Kenneth put a lot of *elbow grease* into cleaning the old house.

✍ **Agree / Approval**

give an inch — to compromise
USAGE: The negotiations were stalled and, finally, representatives from management *gave an inch* and agreed to discuss the possibility of a pay raise.

✍ **Authority**

hold the reins — be the most influential person
USAGE: A real authority at his company, Brian has been *holding the reins* in his organization for many years.

✍ **Bad / Negative**

fly-by-night — unreliable (business)
USAGE: Joe didn't want to do business with the company because he believed it was a *fly-by-night* operation.

foul up — ruin or spoil by stupid mistake; go wrong

USAGE: Because there was confusion on the travel tour packages, the plans for the trip were all *fouled up*.

✎ Business Action

cut back — use fewer; use less
USAGE: Because of budget limitations, we had to *cut back* on food served at the party.

✎ Communication

get in touch with someone — contact someone
USAGE: Richard said he will *get in touch with Bill* when he is in Los Angeles next month.

get off your soap box — do not preach or moralize
USAGE: When Steven told Martha to stop criticizing the others, she angrily replied, "*Get off your soap box*."

get one's own way — cause people to do what you want
USAGE: Jane is impressed with John because he often succeeds in *getting his own way* when negotiating with others.

get the message — understand clearly what is meant
USAGE: Betsy was frustrated because she repeatedly advised Fred on the process, but she didn't think he *got the message*.

get what's coming to one — receive the good or bad that one deserves
USAGE: The convicted criminal *got what was coming to him* when he was sent to prison for three years.

✎ Completeness

do away with — put an end to; stop; get rid of
USAGE: The business decided to *do away with* the practice of accepting discount coupons.

✎ Consequence

if worse comes to worse — if the worse possible thing happens
USAGE: *If worse comes to worse* we can cancel our trip and go next year.

in a bind — in trouble

USAGE: They will really be *in a bind* if they can't sell their house by next month.

in a hole — in some trouble; in an embarrassing or difficult position
USAGE: He is really *in a hole* now that he has problems both at work and at home.

✍ Different

off and on — intermittently; at times
USAGE: The car's engine was making an unusual noise *off and on* as they started to drive.

✍ Disagree

free-for-all — a fight without rules
USAGE: The boys engaged in a *free-for-all* fight behind the store.

✍ Emotion

get a grip on oneself — take control of one's feelings
USAGE: Trying to calm James down, Susan advised him to *get a grip on himself* and not worry.

get a kick out of — enjoy
USAGE: Charles *got a kick out of* seeing his children perform in the school musical production.

get a laugh — cause to laugh
USAGE: Carol could always *get a laugh* when Robert told his stories.

get a rise out of someone — tease, have fun with someone by making him or her angry
USAGE: We *got a rise out of Peter* when we left the door open and the dogs rushed through the house.

✍ Entertainment

groove — to dance
USAGE: It was amusing to watch James dance and *groove* to the music.

✍ Error

call off — cancel

USAGE: The championship game was *called off* because of the intense storm.

✍ Failure

eat away — rot; erode; destroy
USAGE: The insects had been *eating away* at the vegetation throughout the growing season.

✍ Health

hard as nails — physically very fit and strong; rough; stern
USAGE: The supervisor was *hard as nails* in his approach to lazy workers.

✍ Importance

let (something) go — pay no attention to; neglect
USAGE: Several of the ladies commented that Judy had *let her dress and appearance go* after her husband's death.

✍ Location

hang back — stay some distance behind; unwilling to do something
USAGE: Sometimes Larry is hesitant and *hangs back* when help is needed in his department.

hang up — (1) place a telephone receiver back on the telephone and break the connection; (2) place on a hook, peg or hangar
USAGE (1): After Kathy *hung up* the telephone she left to go to work.
USAGE (2): The visitors were asked to *hang up* their coats as they entered the building.

✍ Money

for a song — for very little money
USAGE: Always looking for a good deal, Peter bought the car *for a song*.

fork out — pay
USAGE: Because it's expensive to repair foreign cars, Henry had to *fork out* a lot of money to fix his car.

✍ Movement

go around — go from one place or person to another

USAGE: We decided to *go around* from one store to another to find a good present.

go around in circles — without getting anywhere; uselessly
USAGE: Brian has been *going around in circles* for weeks now and still hasn't made any progress on the project.

✍ Personal Description

crackpot — a person with ideas that don't make sense
USAGE: Scott insisted that she is a *crackpot* and impossible to predict.

crazy like a fox — smart while appearing ignorant, playing stupid
USAGE: Tom said she is *crazy like a fox*. He believes she wants us to think she's dense.

curiosity killed the cat — being too nosy may lead a person into trouble
USAGE: Carla warned Steven against being too nosy. Carla said to him, "Don't ask so many questions. *Curiosity killed the cat*."

✍ Plan / Prepare

get the feel of — become used to or learn about something
USAGE: Bill advised Mary that, as she became familiar with the computer and *got the feel of* the mouse, it would be easier to use.

get with it — pay attention; get busy
USAGE: The boss directed Tim to *get with it* or he might lose his job.

hand down — arrange to give something to someone after one's death
USAGE: My grandfather *handed down* his old wristwatch to my father as a keepsake.

hand to hand — from one person to another and another
USAGE: Old pictures of the family were passed down *hand to hand* from past to present generations.

✍ Quantity

few and far between — not many; rare; few and scattered
USAGE: Restaurants were *few and far between* on the main highway through the mountains.

✍ Relationship

favorite son — a person viewed with pride in hometown because of achievement
USAGE: Jim is our town's *favorite son* because we are so proud of him.

✍ Satisfaction

getup — fancy dress or costume
USAGE: The other women remarked on the unusual *getup* that Mary was
   wearing to the party.

give him/her the eye — to look at another with interest
USAGE: James *gave Cathy the eye* because she was attractive.

give oneself up to — let oneself enjoy; not hold oneself back from
USAGE: She *gave herself up to* enjoy the party although she felt needed at the
   office.

✍ Service

give the devil his due — be fair (even to someone who is bad and who you
   dislike)
USAGE: While John is irritable most of the time, you have to *give the devil his
   due* because he always gets the job done.

✍ Similar

fighting chance — a fair chance
USAGE: Since Peter was able to meet with the manager, he felt he had a
   fighting chance to get the job.

✍ Superior

cut above — better
USAGE: William boasted to the prospective customer, "the quality of our cars
   is a *cut above* the competition."

✍ Time

for keeps — for always; forever
USAGE: The sports star told the young fan he was giving him the signed
   soccer ball *for keeps*.

for once — one time

USAGE: Larry commented, "***For once***, Mary listened to what I said. She usually disregards me."

for the time being — for now, for awhile
USAGE: Lawrence remarked that while he would like to buy a new car, ***for the time being*** he'll keep his current vehicle.

✍ Understand

go over — examine
USAGE: The new manager will ***go over*** the production costs on Friday.

go through — (1) examine or think about carefully; search; (2) experience; suffer; live through
USAGE (1): The police arrived in order to ***go through*** the crime scene.
USAGE (2): Having lived through two destructive earthquakes, Jim has had to ***go through*** difficult times,

got my eye on — interested in; observing
USAGE: Interested in working at the university, Susan said she has ***got her eye on*** the job posting board for available positions.

✍ Work

fool around — spend time playing rather than working; waste time
USAGE: Mark reminded Jim if he would ***fool around*** less, he would be able to finish the project.

✍ Achievement

face down — confront boldly and win; defy
USAGE: The team successfully *faced down* their competitors and won the game.

feather in one's cap — something you achieve and are proud of
USAGE: Achieving the sales increase for the year, it was a *feather in his cap*.

fish or cut bait — taking action instead of only talking about it
USAGE: Instead of only talking about finishing the project, just do it! It's time to *fish or cut bait*!

✍ Agree / Approval

give your word — to promise
USAGE: John urged Mary to keep her promise to attend because she *gave him her word*.

go along — agree; co-operate
USAGE: The boys decided to *go along* with the plan to play ball.

✍ Authority

in charge — in control or authority; responsible
USAGE: Joseph is *in charge of* the sales department at the technology company.

in line — keep within acceptable limits
USAGE: The parents worked hard to keep the children *in line* and appropriately disciplined.

✍ Bad / Negative

four-letter words — obscene words, profanity: such as damn, hell, shit
USAGE: When the soccer coach was shouting at the players, he used a lot of *four-letter words*.

freeze out — keep from sharing something by unfriendly or dishonest treatment
USAGE: Wanting to alienate Harry from the decision making process, they tried to *freeze him out* of the planning process.

from pillar to post — from one problem or thing to another
USAGE: While his parents went *from pillar to post* trying to solve his speech problem, nothing seemed to help.

✍ Business Action

cut down on — use less of something
USAGE: Recently, James has **cut down on** the amount of food he eats so he can lose weight.

✍ Communication

get wind of — hear about something
USAGE: I **got wind of** a product being developed by the company's competitor.

gift of gab — good and convincing at talking
USAGE: Kevin has the **gift of gab** and is the center of action at parties.

give a ribbing — to tease
USAGE: Terry's friends **gave him a ribbing** for losing his keys.

give away — let (a secret) become known
USAGE: He tried to stop Nancy before she accidentally **gave away** their plans to give their son a trip.

give it a rest — to stop talking
USAGE: Tired of hearing him talk, Mary asked Bob to **give it a rest** and be quiet.

give out — to declare
USAGE: Susan **gave out** a loud yell when she saw the mouse run across the room.

give rise to — be the cause of something
USAGE: The production problems at the plant **gave rise to** other issues that had to be solved.

give someone a piece of your mind — scold or become angry with someone
USAGE: Angry with him for not helping, Susan **gave John a piece of her mind**.

✍ Completeness

don't know the half of it — do not know all the facts
USAGE: My wife left and divorced me, Joe said, but you *don't know the half of it*.

✍ Consequence

in a jam — in trouble
USAGE: Thomas is *in a jam* trying to meet increased production requirements combined with a budget cut.

in a pinch — okay when nothing else is available
USAGE: Jack mentioned that he would, *in a pinch*, take advantage of special rules to enable the team to succeed.

in a spot — in some trouble; in an embarrassing or difficult position
USAGE: Sharon is *in a spot* because she lost her job and doesn't have enough money for the rent.

✍ Different

off base — inaccurate
USAGE: Frederick suggested that Bob was really *off base* on his budget estimates.

off center — different from the usual pattern; not quite like most others; odd
USAGE: The sculpture was *off-center* and didn't really fit in with the rest of the art on display.

✍ Disagree

gang up on someone — attack in a group; get together to hurt someone
USAGE: The school teacher firmly disciplined the children who *ganged up on the new student*.

get off my case — to stop criticizing
USAGE: Mary told Robert to *get off her case* and leave her alone.

✍ Emotion

get back at — do something bad to someone who has done something bad
USAGE: Angry at Bill for not emailing her, Angela *got back at* him by not answering his telephone calls.

get cold feet — become afraid at the last minute
USAGE: James *got cold feet* and cancelled his plan to go to France.

get (someone) down — make (someone) unhappy; cause discouragement
USAGE: The long hours that Susan has been working has begun to *get her down*.

get (someone's) goat — annoy someone
USAGE: Frustrated, John said the teenagers had been *getting his goat* recently.

get going — excite, stir up and make angry
USAGE: Once Vincent *gets going*, he will talk about the investment strategy for hours.

get in the swing of things — adapt to a new environment or situation
USAGE: Peter really *got in the swing of things* with the new group.

get on one's high horse — behave with arrogance
USAGE: Robert *got on his high horse* and behaved like he was better than others.

✍ End

on one's/its last leg — at the end of someone/something's strength or usefulness
USAGE: With it breaking down almost every day, I think Jack's old car is *on its last leg*.

✍ Entertainment

happy hour — a time in bars or restaurants when drinks are served at a discount
USAGE: Brian and I stopped at the bar during *happy hour* and had a couple of drinks.

✍ Error

call on the carpet — call someone before an authority to be scolded or reprimanded
USAGE: Peter was *called on the carpet* by his manager for insulting the customer.

✍ Failure

eat crow — admit one is mistaken or defeated

USAGE: Henry was forced to *eat crow* when it was publicized that his predictions were groundless.

eat dirt — accept another's insult or bad treatment; act humble
USAGE: Being insulted by the older boy, Joe felt like he was *eating dirt*.

✍ Location

hang your hat — a place to live
USAGE: Finally having his own house in the middle of the city, Steven had a place he could *hang his hat*.

✍ Money

fork over — hand over; give
USAGE: The thief directed me to *fork over* my wallet immediately or he was going to shoot me.

freeload — accept food and housing at someone else's expense
USAGE: Fred was angry at his brother because he was always *freeloading* from others and avoided finding a job.

✍ Movement

go off — (1) leave; depart; (2) begin to ring or buzz
USAGE (1): He decided to *go off* and have lunch by himself.
USAGE (2): The fire alarm at the school started to *go off* as the students entered the building in the morning.

✍ Ownership

have on — be wearing something
USAGE: What did Mary have on when she attended the party?

✍ Personal Description

curry favor — flatter someone to get help or friendship
USAGE: James worked to *curry favor* with the members of the admissions committee.

cut off one's nose to spite one's face — make things worse for oneself because one is angry at someone else
USAGE: When Peter insulted the neighbors, they called the police and they

arrested him. Peter only then realized he was ***cutting off his nose to spite his face***.

dark horse — little known entrant
USAGE: At first he was a ***dark horse*** entry into the race, but ended up winning the competition.

✍ Plan / Prepare

hard and fast rule — rules that cannot be altered to fit special cases
USAGE: There is no ***hard and fast rule*** about preventing a girl from playing on the national soccer team.

hard pressed — burdened with urgent business
USAGE: Timothy said he was ***hard pressed*** for time and indicated he would like to meet later.

have a shot at — have an opportunity
USAGE: If Wendy obtains investment money, she will ***have a shot at*** starting the business.

have half a mind — feel tempted or inclined to do something
USAGE: Highly frustrated, John said he ***had half a mind*** to go and submit his resignation to the manager.

✍ Quantity

fifth wheel — too many or unnecessary presence
USAGE: John and two other guys were already working on the project, so I felt like a ***fifth wheel***.

✍ Relationship

fix someone up with someone — help someone get a date by arranging a meeting for the two
USAGE: Henry wanted to ***fix my sister up with his friend*** Joseph.

flesh and blood — a close relative
USAGE: I want to help her in every way because, as my sister, she's my ***flesh and blood***.

✍ Satisfaction

go one's own way — go or act the way one wants

USAGE: Tony has decided to *go his own way* and travel throughout the western part of the country.

go over well — be liked; be successful
USAGE: Betty told Karen she believes the party will *go over well* because she's done much preparation.

going for (someone) — in one's favor
USAGE: Amanda should do well in her job search because she has many good things *going for her*.

✐ Superior

drink you under the table — to be able to drink more liquor than another without passing out
USAGE: Henry said, "I'll *drink you under the table* because I can drink 6 cans of beer and still talk straight."

go (someone) one better — do something better than someone else
USAGE: I decided to *go him one better* and buy a larger and more powerful car.

✐ Time

forever and a day — for a very long time
USAGE: John told his wife, Vickie, his love for her would last *forever and a day*.

from day one — from the beginning
USAGE: *From day one*, Kenneth indicated he would do whatever it took to achieve the results.

from now on — from this moment forward
USAGE: *From now on*, Jack said he would stay away from smoking cigarettes.

✐ Understand

hard to swallow — hard to accept
USAGE: Karen told Bob his intimate friendships with women were very upsetting to her and *hard to swallow*.

have it — get or find the answer
USAGE: Becky said, "I think I *have it*. The reason Caroline is leaving is because she is going to deliver a baby."

have it from a good source — hear or get news; understand
USAGE: I *have it from a good source* that the new president will be visiting us tomorrow.

haywire — broken or confused
USAGE: John's plan went *haywire* when his directions were misunderstood.

✍ Work

get axed — to be fired
USAGE: Unable to meet sales expectations, Charles *got axed* by the company.

Week 19

✍ Achievement

fly by the seat of one's pants — do a job instinctively rather than by using concrete information
USAGE: Bill felt like he was *flying by the seat of his pants* when providing childcare for his son.

for all one is worth — as hard as one can
USAGE: Joe told him he would try *for all his worth* to help him gain entry to the game.

force one's hand — make someone do something sooner than planned
USAGE: I *forced his hand* and he informed me of his plans for the upcoming year.

gain ground — go forward; make progress
USAGE: The automobile manufacturer had *gained ground* in its effort to capture a greater share of the market.

✍ Agree / Approval

go through — be allowed; pass; be agreed upon
USAGE: The change of regulation was allowed to *go through* by the commission.

✍ Authority

in the charge of — under the care or supervision of
USAGE: The teenage girl has been *in the charge of* her grandmother since her mother died two years ago.

✍ Bad / Negative

get away with murder — do something very bad without being caught or punished
USAGE: As an unethical manager, Peter *got away with murder* in his supervision of the dishonest accounting at the company.

get away with something — do something one shouldn't and not get caught
   at it
USAGE: The offender *got away with the robbery* and escaped to Mexico.

✍ **Communication**

give someone the eye — look or stare at someone (especially in a cold or
   unfriendly way)
USAGE: The security guard *gave the suspicious looking man the eye* when he
   entered the store.

give to understand — make a person understand by telling him very plainly
   or boldly
USAGE: I was *given to understand* that I could use high speed internet at the
   library free of charge.

give voice to — tell what one feels or thinks
USAGE: He *gave voice to* his sentiments about being free to openly express
   his beliefs.

give-and-take — sharing, giving and receiving back and forth between people
USAGE: As newlyweds, John and Mary recognized it was important to have
   a *give-and-take* approach for a good marriage.

giveaway — an open secret or disclosure
USAGE: Dale's comments were a *giveaway* to the group. Now everyone
   knows he is planning to retire.

glad hand — a friendly handshake; a warm greeting; sometimes not sincere
USAGE: The businessman spent the afternoon *glad handing* the workers at
   the shopping center.

✍ **Completeness**

double-check — check again to be sure something is correct
USAGE: John *double-checked* the departure time of his airline flight.

draw the line — set a limit
USAGE: The teacher *drew the line* at what would be considered acceptable
   behavior by students in the classroom.

✍ **Consequence**

in any case/event — no matter what happens; surely; without fail

USAGE: The manager suggested the products would not be in production this year but *in any case* would begin next year.

in for — unable to avoid; sure to get
USAGE: Robert is *in for* a shock when he discovers that his money will not be available.

in hot water — in trouble
USAGE: The teenager is *in hot water* over breaking the borrowed bicycle.

✍ Different

off the beam — wrong; mistaken
USAGE: The findings James reported about the cost were *off the beam* and immediately corrected by his supervisor.

✍ Disagree

get your goat — to annoy
USAGE: Mary didn't allow him to *get her goat* about the mistake made at the office last week.

✍ Emotion

get on one's nerves — irritate someone
USAGE: His constant fault-finding really *got on Betty's nerves*.

get one's dander up — become or make angry
USAGE: Robert *gets his dander up* when his wife mentions the failure of his business last year.

get out of bed on the wrong side — be in a bad mood
USAGE: In an agitated mood, it's clear that Sharon *got out of the bed on the wrong side* this morning.

get out of hand — lose control
USAGE: The graduation party was starting to *get out of hand* so the hosts stopped the music.

get under one's skin — bother someone; upset someone
USAGE: Elizabeth said John *got under her skin* with his constant complaining and fault-finding of others.

✍ End

one foot in the grave — near death
USAGE: Bill remarked his grandfather has *one foot in the grave* and may not live much longer.

✍ Entertainment

have over — invite someone to your house
USAGE: Carol and Steven told us they will *have us over* when the construction is finished.

✍ Error

can of worms — a complicated situation or problem
USAGE: John realized implementing the recommendations for reform would open up a *can of worms* for the company.

✍ Failure

eat humble pie — admit one's error and apologize
USAGE: Fred had to *eat humble pie* in front of his wife when it was discovered his claims were mistaken.

✍ Health

in a family way — pregnant; going to have a baby
USAGE: Vickie is *in a family way* and is really excited about the expected birth of the baby in January.

✍ Location

head off — get in front of and stop; turn back
USAGE: In pursuit of the crime suspects, the police were successful in *heading them off* on the highway and putting them in jail.

here and there — in various places; go to various places
USAGE: Charles and Rita were *here and there* during their vacation tour of Australia.

✍ Money

from hand to mouth — not having much money; spending money on necessities
USAGE: Frank's family was poor, living *from hand to mouth*.

from rags to riches — from being poor to being wealthy
USAGE: Starting the film company from his basement, Bill went *from rags to riches*.

give an arm and a leg — to give or pay a lot
USAGE: Joseph said he would *give an arm and a leg* to hug his wife.

✐ Movement

good riddance — losing something and happy about it
USAGE: When told the difficult employee had resigned his job, John said, "*Good riddance*!"

✐ Ownership

in common — shared together or equally; in use or ownership by all
USAGE: All the boys in the dormitory had to use the bathroom *in common* with the other residents.

✐ Personal Description

dead tired — very tired; exhausted
USAGE: Peter was *dead tired* after running the 10K race.

deadbeat — a person who never pays his debts
USAGE: Michael was considered a *deadbeat* father because he didn't pay child support to his ex-wife.

doll up — dress in fancy clothes
USAGE: Barbara was *dolled up* in a beautiful dress for the party.

✐ Plan / Prepare

have in mind — intend; plan
USAGE: John asked Susan what she *had in mind* for the celebration of their son's graduation.

✐ Quantity

fifty-fifty — equally; evenly
USAGE: Phillip and Brian agreed to divide the cost of the taxicab on a *fifty-fifty* basis.

✍ Relationship

French kiss — open mouth kiss
USAGE: James and Mary were ***French kissing*** on the park bench.

✍ Satisfaction

going great guns — working out very well
USAGE: Bill's new business was succeeding and ***going great guns*** during the first several months of operation.

good deal — good quality and a cheap price
USAGE: Because of strong competition among computer manufacturers, a customer can get a ***good deal*** on a laptop computer.

good to go — ready
USAGE: Joe told the other students, "We're ***good to go***!"

✍ Service

go about — be busy with; start working on
USAGE: Henry has been ***going about*** his work duties despite the death of his father last week.

✍ Time

from the get go — from the beginning
USAGE: Thomas has been working hard ***from the get go*** on improving his computer programming skills.

from the word go — from the beginning
USAGE: All of the athletes have been practicing their throwing techniques ***from the word go***.

from time to time — occasionally
USAGE: Kelly remarked they enjoy visiting the museum ***from time to time***.

✍ Understand

head in the cloud — daydreaming
USAGE: Mary said that Bob seems distracted much of the time as if his ***head is in the clouds***.

head in the sand — unwilling or unable to see

USAGE: Company management had their *head in the sand* in terms of understanding how plant safety could improve worker productivity.

head is spinning — confused
USAGE: When the supervisor told William he was fired, his *head was spinning*.

helter-skelter — careless; in disorder
USAGE: When the secretary arrived at work, she found the files scattered *helter-skelter* over the office floor.

✍ Work

get the sack — be fired or dismissed from work
USAGE: The manager advised James that unless he improved his productivity, he would *get the sack*.

Week 20

✍ **Achievement**

get after someone — urge someone do something he should but has neglected
USAGE: While he should have done it earlier, I'll *get after Ted* to fix the printer when he returns from vacation.

get ahead — advance or be successful
USAGE. Mary is an extremely hard working accountant and I know she will *get ahead* in her career.

get blood from a stone — something impossible
USAGE: Getting assistance from Peter is like *getting blood from a stone*.

get on with it — continue working or speaking
USAGE: While telling the story, Charles took a break and later said, "OK, let's *get on with it* and I'll finish the story."

get the better of (someone) — win against; beat; defeat
USAGE: In the finals of the championship, Peter *got the better of me* and won the match.

✍ **Agree / Approval**

have it your way — do what you want to do
USAGE: Horace said, "OK, *have it your way*, we'll eat wherever you want."

✍ **Authority**

in the saddle — in command; in control
USAGE: The manager is back *in the saddle* again after being away on a different project for several months.

✍ **Bad / Negative**

give it to — punish; scold
USAGE: Joseph really *gave it to* his son when the school headmaster informed him that he skipped 5 days of school.

give oneself away — show guilt; show one has done wrong
USAGE: While Betty denied any involvement in the misadventure, her nervous laugher *gave her away* and signaled guilt.

✍ Business Action

deliver the goods — to reach success or goal
USAGE: Larry is one of the best managers at the company. He *delivers the goods* when it comes to leadership.

✍ Communication

gloss over — attempt to make what is wrong not important; hide error
USAGE: The executives wanted to *gloss over* the money lost in production last year.

go off half-cocked — speak before being prepared
USAGE: Phillip sometimes *goes off half-cocked* when he is unsure.

go on — talk for a long time
USAGE: Mary was *going on* about her marital problems, yet I had to leave for my meeting.

go without saying — easy to see; self-evident
USAGE: Thomas is a great soccer player, so it *goes without saying* the team will miss him.

grill you — to ask many questions
USAGE: Sometimes my wife *grills me* when I come home late.

✍ Completeness

each and every — every person or thing
USAGE: The teacher told *each and every* student to prepare for the examination.

✍ Consequence

in light of — because of new information
USAGE: *In light of* information about his criminal past, the manager was immediately discharged from the company.

in order to — for the purpose of
USAGE: The university faculty decided to offer the degree online *in order to* serve students at a distance.

in the cards — expected or likely to happen
USAGE: Because of economic pressures, production cutbacks are *in the cards* at the company.

✍ Different

offbeat — non-conventional; different from the usual
USAGE: The foreign film was an *offbeat* comedy popular among students.

✍ Disagree

give (someone) a hard time — to tease someone
USAGE: Susan *gave William a hard time* about his unusually decorated apartment.

give a person hell — to scold
USAGE: Lawrence *gives a person hell* if you talk on a cell phone at work.

✍ Emotion

get up on the wrong side of the bed — in a bad mood
USAGE: Judy said it was clear that Bill *got up on the wrong side of the bed* since he was in a bad mood.

get up the nerve — brave enough to do something
USAGE: Barbara *got up the nerve* to ask Charles about his class grade.

get-up-and-go — possessing enthusiasm
USAGE: Joseph has a lot of *get-up-and-go* and I believe he will be successful in the new job.

gnashing of teeth — suffering and pain
USAGE: History suggests there's been *gnashing of teeth* among the persecuted people.

go ape — become excited and enthusiastic
USAGE: James *went ape* when he understood what the changes would mean for his daily activity.

✍ Entertainment

hit parade — a list of popular songs
USAGE: Bob and Mary have an extensive collection of *hit parade* music.

✍ Failure

fall apart — not working properly
USAGE: The computer equipment purchased from Thomas *fell apart* within two weeks of installation.

✍ Health

keep body and soul together — survive difficult times; keep alive
USAGE: Survivors of the earthquake worked hard to *keep body and soul together* during the disaster itself and the long rebuilding period.

✍ Importance

like a ton of bricks — to impact strongly
USAGE: The news of William's death hit me *like a ton of bricks*.

✍ Location

high and dry — stranded
USAGE: Running out of gas, James was left *high and dry* in the middle of the countryside.

high and low — in every place
USAGE: John reported the rescue team looked *high and low* throughout the town for the missing child.

✍ Money

go broke — to lose all money
USAGE: Because of an unwise investment strategy, Peter *went broke* and was in financial ruin.

go Dutch — individuals each pay for themselves
USAGE: Joe is not generous on his dates. Susan told me he always *goes Dutch* with girls.

✍ Movement

good riddance to bad rubbish — glad that someone or something is no longer present
USAGE: When informed that Susan moved to another city, Robert said, "*Good riddance to bad rubbish*! We never could get along."

✍ Ownership

lay hands on something — to find something
USAGE: Peter told Mary he wanted to show her his website if he could *lay his hands on* a computer connected to the Internet.

✍ Personal Description

done for — ruined; defeated; the end of
USAGE: Disappointed in his team's poor performance during the season, Joe said he believed his coaching career was *done for*.

done with — to complete something
USAGE: Walter was *done with* the project and ready to move on to another task.

do-or-die — absolutely determined to succeed
USAGE: Recognizing the importance of succeeding in the project, John had a *do-or-die* attitude to achieving results.

✍ Plan / Prepare

hit and miss — occasionally succeeding; sometimes failing
USAGE: Charles realized it could be *hit and miss* to reach a settlement on the difficult issues.

hit the books — to prepare and study
USAGE: Bob *hit the books* all week in order to be prepared for the examination.

hold out — extend assistance and help
USAGE: The members of the religious group *held out* their efforts to assist those in poverty.

✍ Quantity

for good measure — adding a bit more than required
USAGE: Tony remarked he wanted to add sugar to the recipe just *for good measure*.

✍ Relationship

get along with someone — to have a good relationship with someone
USAGE: Harry told his wife he found it hard to *get along with his new colleague*.

get even — retaliation
USAGE: Upset at those who insulted him, Robert planned how he could *get even* with them.

✍ Satisfaction

grass is always greener on the other side — a thing that is different seems better
USAGE: Susan has moved to four different cities in the last three years. It seems she's always thinking the *grass is always greener on the other side*.

hang in the balance — uncertain; suspenseful
USAGE: The path of action was *hanging in the balance* depending on decisions made during the negotiation.

hang out — enjoy time spent with friends
USAGE: Bobby enjoyed *hanging out* with his friends at the park.

✍ Similar

fine line — similar, yet subtle difference
USAGE: There is a *fine line* between being funny and rude.

✍ Time

from/go way back — in the past
USAGE: Jeffrey said he has known Bill for a long time and they *go way back*.
USAGE: I know him *from way back*. In fact we went to elementary school together.

full plate — very busy schedule
USAGE: Peter had a *full plate* and couldn't come to the party after work.

✍ Understand

hide/bury one's head in the sand — keep from knowing something unpleasant
USAGE: Wanting to be able to deny any knowledge of things, *James buries his head in the sand* on certain issues.

hit on/upon — to identify option
USAGE: Terry *hit upon* the idea of the group going out to dinner when the seminar was rescheduled.

hit the bull's-eye — identify main point
USAGE: Bill *hit the bull's-eye* when he said sales must increase or everyone
would be out of a job.

hit the high spots — cover the highlights
USAGE: Because of time limitations, Brian could only *hit the high spots* of
the report.

✍ Work

gig — a job assignment
USAGE: Mark was very excited because he had a new *gig* that paid very well.

✍ Achievement

get through — succeed in passing an exam or some ordeal
USAGE: Helen has had a lot of difficulty *getting through* her calculus exams.

get to first base — a good beginning
USAGE: Jane tried to successfully interact with the new boss, but she didn't *get to first base.*

give 110% — to work extra hard
USAGE: The student group *gave 110%* on their effort to complete the project on-time.

give it your best shot — to make the strongest effort
USAGE: The teacher instructed the students to take the examination and *give it their best shot.*

✍ Agree / Approval

(a) hot ticket — something that is popular
USAGE: The concert was *a hot ticket* among the teenagers.

in black and white — something in writing
USAGE: Wanting to make sure it was clearly understood by all, Jack said "Let's get the agreement *in black and white*."

✍ Authority

kangaroo court — self-appointed judge
USAGE: The people in the bar judged Harry as if they were in a *kangaroo court.*

✍ Bad / Negative

give someone enough rope and they will hang themselves — give a person the chance and they may get themselves in trouble

USAGE: Lawrence believed that John would end up damaging his reputation with the job. He said, "If you *give John enough rope he will hang himself*."

✍ Business Action

farm out — retain help from someone else
USAGE: Henry and his colleagues *farmed out* the project to another company having greater expertise in the area.

✍ Communication

hammer out — to agree by negotiation
USAGE: The employees and company management were successful in *hammering out* an agreement.

hand it to (someone) — to offer credit and praise
USAGE: Steven said he had to *hand it to Mary* for achieving so much in her business.

hand you a line — told something false
USAGE: Darren told his sister the taxi driver *handed her a line* and she should be cautious about its accuracy.

hang on — wait on the telephone
USAGE: While talking on the phone, Michael told Susan to *hang on* while he checked his email.

hang on every word — listen carefully to every word
USAGE: When Mr. Smith told them what the test would include, the students would *hang on every word*.

harp on — repeatedly dwell on something
USAGE: Susan would *harp on* her belief that fashion was highly important.

hash it over — to discuss and consider
USAGE: Charles and John *hashed over* the considerations of the proposed deal with an eye to long term profitability.

✍ Completeness

fall behind — failure to keep up
USAGE: Harry *fell behind* in his class assignments and had difficulty catching up.

✍ Consequence

in the clear — free of suspicion
USAGE: After questioning the teenagers about the robbery, the detectives told the boys they were ***in the clear*** and could leave.

in the wake of — as a result of
USAGE: ***In the wake of*** allegations of cheating at the university, the professors established a policy on honesty.

in the wrong — at fault
USAGE: Jimmy knew he was ***in the wrong*** when he made what ended up being a false accusation.

✍ Different

old hat — not current
USAGE: Peter said he didn't like his job because it had become ***old hat*** and old fashioned.

✍ Disagree

give someone the brush-off — to reject someone
USAGE: When Michael asked Susan for a date, she ***gave him the brush-off***.

give the boot — to dismiss
USAGE: If you continue to arrive late to work, your boss will ***give you the boot***.

✍ Emotion

go ballistic — to become upset
USAGE: Charles ***went ballistic*** when he learned he had been replaced by another team member.

go bananas — to become upset
USAGE: John ***went bananas*** when he received the bad news.

go for the jugular — to take strong action against
USAGE: Charles was so angry with William that he ***went for the jugular*** and fired him.

go hog wild — very excited
USAGE: John ***went hog wild*** when he discovered she was awarded the prize.

go into orbit — to become very angry
USAGE: He *went into orbit* when he heard about his wife buying the car without consulting him.

✍ End

over one's dead body — will never happen
USAGE: Committed to his position, Mike said, "She will work at this company *over my dead body*."

✍ Entertainment

horse around — to play or tease
USAGE: Stephen was *horsing around* with another student before the teacher arrived.

✍ Failure

fall flat — to fail
USAGE: John's effort at apologizing *fell flat* and Susan didn't accept his request for forgiveness.

fall from grace — to lose support
USAGE: The once popular manager *fell from grace* with workers at the company.

✍ Health

keep (someone) up — to prevent sleeping
USAGE: The loud music played by the students *kept me up* last night.

✍ Importance

little frog in a big pond — one person in a large group
USAGE: Moving from the countryside to the city, John is now a *little frog in a big pond*.

✍ Location

high seas — the ocean
USAGE: The ship was sailing on the *high seas*.

hit the hay — go to bed

USAGE: Joseph said he wanted to ***hit the hay*** because he had to wake up early
tomorrow.

✍ Money

gravy train — a very profitable enterprise or job
USAGE: Starting the business that became extremely profitable, Mark believed
the enterprise was really a ***gravy train***.

grease one's palm — to secretly pay money for a favor
USAGE: Joe ***greased the palm*** of the waiter to get a table at the elite restaurant.

✍ Movement

greased lightning — move very fast
USAGE: Henry was moving so fast that they called him "***greased lightening***."

grind to a halt — to stop
USAGE: The production line ***ground to a halt*** at the manufacturing plant when
the power went off.

✍ Personal Description

dork — strange or stupid characteristic
USAGE: Jennifer told Mark to quit being a ***dork***!

down-to-earth — sensible; simple
USAGE: She believed Vincent was a very ***down-to-earth*** person.

dressed to kill — wear fancy clothes
USAGE: Karen was ***dressed to kill*** in her beautiful new dress.

✍ Plan / Prepare

hold out for something — to wait or resist for something
USAGE: Knowing he had achieved a large sales increase for the company,
John was ***holding out for a pay increase***.

hold out on — refuse something
USAGE: He is ***holding out on*** me and won't give me the latest sales figures.

hold the fort — maintain security
USAGE: Timothy was ***holding the fort*** at home while his parents were traveling
overseas.

✍ Quantity

gas up — refuel a gas tank
USAGE: Because he was going on a long drive tomorrow, Kevin *gassed up* his car tonight.

✍ Relationship

get off on the wrong foot — make a bad start
USAGE: Rick had difficulty in relating to Bob because he *got off on the wrong foot* with him at the beginning.

get off one's back — to leave someone alone
USAGE: Tom remarked to his friends that he wished his wife would *get off his back* about the repairing items around the house.

give someone the cold shoulder — to be unfriendly to
USAGE: Patricia *gave George the cold shoulder* at the gathering.

✍ Satisfaction

happy as a peacock — very happy
USAGE: Mary was *happy as a peacock* when told her hair was beautiful.

happy camper — content with situation
USAGE: Very satisfied in his job, John said he was a *happy camper* at his company.

has it made — to be successful and happy
USAGE: William *has it made* since he's got a happy family and fulfilling career.

✍ Service

go ahead — begin something
USAGE: John decided to *go ahead* and begin the project.

✍ Superior

far out — excellent
USAGE: The students liked the design and suggested it was *far out*!

✍ Time

get a move on — to hurry up

USAGE: The policeman suggested to the slow-moving crowd that they **get a move on**.

get a wiggle on — to hurry
USAGE: Kevin told the others, "Let's **get a wiggle on** or else we'll be late."

get around to — accomplish a task
USAGE: The building manager finally **got around to** repairing the hole in the wall.

✍ Understand

hold on to — keep; hold tightly
USAGE: It is important to **hold on to** your purse when on the train or you may lose it.

hold water — a credible idea
USAGE: Robert's ideas were not correct and didn't **hold water**.

(a) household name — a familiar name
USAGE: Well known people are **household names** to many individuals.

if the shoe fits, wear it — accept a description if accurate
USAGE: Peter heard someone describe him as lazy and, while he didn't like it, he responded, "*If the shoe fits, wear it*."

✍ Work

girl Friday — an employee who does different jobs in an office
USAGE: Kathy is our **girl Friday**. She does a variety of jobs in the office.

✍ Achievement

go about — be busy with; start working on
USAGE: The team members have been ***going about*** their practice for the upcoming soccer season.

go after — to pursue
USAGE: John wanted to ***go after*** and capture the thief when he heard about the robbery.

go all-out — to do one's best
USAGE: Henry ***went all out*** to win the contract.

go for — to try for
USAGE: William decided to ***go for*** admission at the prestigious university.

go for broke — to risk in the achievement of a goal
USAGE: He gambled on the investment and decided to ***go for broke*** on earning a high profit return.

✍ Agree / Approval

in league with — in secret partnership
USAGE: James and his friends have been ***in league with*** the mayor in trying to persuade the others to participate.

✍ Authority

keep down — keep control of
USAGE: The prison guards were successful in ***keeping down*** the prisoner rebellion.

✍ Bad / Negative

go to rack and ruin — to deteriorate
USAGE: The once beautiful building has ***gone to rack and ruin*** in the last several years.

good for nothing — useless
USAGE: I'll be glad when we sell our ***good-for-nothing*** car.

grody — unappealing; disgusting
USAGE: The kitchen was filthy and ***grody*** with rotten food and trash all around.

✍ Business Action

fast buck — make money easily, sometimes dishonestly
USAGE: Lazy people believe it is possible to make a ***fast buck*** without putting forth much effort.

✍ Communication

have a word with — to talk briefly
USAGE: Bill said he would ***have a word with*** Susan before dinner.

have to do with — to be about a subject
USAGE: I'm told that tonight's lecture ***has to do with*** the history of Africa.

hear from — receive contact from someone
USAGE: I haven't ***heard from*** my former college roommate for over one year.

hear me out — request to be heard
USAGE: Karen pleaded with him, "Please, ***hear me out*** because I want to explain what went wrong."

✍ Completeness

fall by the wayside — to fall behind
USAGE: While James was leading early in the race, he ***fell by the wayside*** towards the end of the race.

✍ Consequence

in view of — in consideration of
USAGE: ***In view of*** last year's problems, we want to be very careful with this year's project.

jump to conclusions — make a quick summary without thinking
USAGE: When Richard saw the new car outside, he ***jumped to the conclusion*** that Mary had bought it.

Katie bar the door — anticipating a disturbance
USAGE: The group of teenagers knocked on the door and appeared to be ready
for trouble. Michael looked at the others and said, "*Katie bar the door*."

✍ Different

on again, off again / off again, on again — uncertain circumstances
USAGE: The plans for the employee picnic were *on again, off again* because
of the stormy weather.

✍ Disagree

go at — to argue
USAGE: When he walked in the room they were *going at* it with a loud
argument.

go at it hammer and tongs — a fierce argument
USAGE: Robert and Stan were *going at it hammer and tongs* concerning the
dispute over money.

✍ Emotion

go off the deep end — exceedingly upset emotionally
USAGE: Extremely upset over the tragic news, we were afraid he would *go off
the deep end*.

go to pieces — exceedingly upset emotionally
USAGE: Richard *went to pieces* when receiving news that his wife had died in
an accident.

go to town — (1) to do with much excitement; (2) work rapidly to finish
USAGE (1): He *went to town* eating the cake.
USAGE (2): Bob and Mary really *went to town* yesterday finishing the project.

good grief!— used to show surprise
USAGE: Stanley said, "*Good grief*! Its almost noon and we're not yet
finished."

✍ End

pan out — to end successfully
USAGE: The teacher encouraged James with his plan, saying, "I hope your
plan for the new business *pans out* favorably."

✍ Failure

fall off the wagon — return to consuming alcoholic drinks
USAGE: Bill *fell off the wagon* after being sober for 6 months.

✍ Location

hit the sack — go to bed
USAGE: Joe said he was sleepy and wanted to *hit the sack*.

hither and thither — to look in all directions
USAGE: Martha looked *hither and thither* for her lost purse.

✍ Money

greenback — money
USAGE: Michael said he needed more *greenbacks* in order to buy the new car.

hand to mouth — having money for only basic expenses
USAGE: Because Jason was very poor, he lived a *hand to mouth* existence.

✍ Movement

hand over fist — at a rapid rate
USAGE: John had a very profitable business that was generating money *hand over fist*.

hang on — continue or persevere
USAGE: Although he was tired of the project, Tim decided to *hang on* and keep working on completing the task.

have a go at — make attempt at doing something
USAGE: Phillip decided to *have a go at* driving the construction vehicle.

✍ Ownership

lay hold of — obtain possession of something
USAGE: Susan told Bill if she could *lay hold of* a DVD player, she would show him the film.

✍ Personal Description

dressed to the nines (teeth) — dressed in fancy clothes

USAGE: Looking terrific in their new dresses, the ladies were ***dressed to the nines*** for the party.

drop your drawers — remove one's pants and underwear
USAGE: At the hospital, the nurse directed John to ***drop his drawers*** so he could change into the hospital gown.

drown one's sorrows — consume alcohol to forget problems
USAGE: Very depressed over his divorce, Bob went to the hotel bar to ***drown his sorrows*** over whiskey.

✍ Plan / Prepare

hold the line — to maintain level
USAGE: The government economists have been working hard to ***hold the line*** on the nation's inflation level.

hold up — lift; raise
USAGE: The teachers advised the students to ***hold up*** their hands when they discovered the answer.

hold your horses — to be restrained
USAGE: When William said he wanted to leave before eating breakfast, Tom reminded him to ***hold his horses***.

hook up — connect; fit together
USAGE: Moving into a new apartment, Richard knew he would need a ***hook up*** to the utility line.

✍ Quantity

give or take — plus or minus a small amount
USAGE: Vickie said the town was located 100 meters away, ***give or take*** a few meters.

✍ Relationship

go out with (someone) — to date someone
USAGE: Wendy was very excited to ***go out with Peter*** on a date.

go steady — date only one person
USAGE: Susan has been ***going steady*** with John for several months and they may set a wedding date.

✍ Satisfaction

have designs on — to want; to envy
USAGE: Susan *had designs on* an attractive ring she saw in the jewelry store.

have it both ways — to want two exclusive options
USAGE: John advised Susan that she *couldn't have it both ways*; she must choose one or the other.

have it made — successful and satisfied
USAGE: Peter *has it made* with his new job at the bank.

✍ Service

go for a spin — take a ride in a car
USAGE: John asked Mary if she wanted to *go for a spin* in his new car.

✍ Superior

fierce — excellent quality
USAGE: Joe told Karen, "Yes, that's one *fierce* cup of coffee you've fixed!"

✍ Time

get in on the ground floor — start at early stage
USAGE: Tommy was able to *get in on the ground floor* of the investment plan.

get (something) over with — conclusion; end
USAGE: Stanley wanted to *get his exercise over with* so he could watch the movie.

get-go — the beginning
USAGE: The teenagers wanted to travel to the coast from the *get-go*.

go on — continue
USAGE: The others wanted to *go on* and meet before the party.

✍ Understand

in a fog/haze — confused and uncertain
USAGE: Richard sometimes seems like he is *in a fog* and doesn't understand the process.

in a world of one's own — disregarding others
USAGE: Patricia behaves as if she is *in a world of her own* and ignores the needs of others.

in check — kept under control
USAGE: The demands of the striking employees were kept *in check* by the managers.

in fact — actually
USAGE: She wants to hire him. *In fact*, she wants him to start work tomorrow!

✍ Work

goof off — play around and not work
USAGE: The students were *goofing off* during class and did not complete any of their assignments.

✍ Achievement

go great guns — accomplishing something rapidly
USAGE: He was *going great guns* in completing the research project by the
deadline.

go into — to do something
USAGE: John is applying to business school to earn his MBA so he can *go into*
private business.

go out of one's way — to be very helpful
USAGE: He *went out of his way* to help me when I visited his company last
spring.

go overboard — to do something in the extreme
USAGE: Tim really *went overboard* when he proposed marriage to Susan. He
rented an entire restaurant for the evening.

✍ Agree / Approval

in one's good books — be highly approved of
USAGE: I'm on my best behavior around her, trying to get *in her good books*.

in point of fact — actually; in reality
USAGE: *In point of fact*, it is essential that we have more money available to
complete the project.

✍ Authority

lead by the nose — to control; to lead
USAGE: In my opinion, it seems like Bill's wife is bossy and *leads him
around by the nose*.

lead the way — to guide
USAGE: Since Jack had experience in starting a business, we wanted him to
lead the way.

✍ Bad / Negative

had the cheek (to do something) — rudeness; impudence
USAGE: Wanda *had the cheek to tell* Susan that she wasn't in the mood to go
to work today.

half-baked — foolish; not sound
USAGE: Fred's plan about starting a hair cutting business for dogs was really
a *half-baked* idea.

handwriting on the wall — a bad sign of future action
USAGE: The company president said the *handwriting was on the wall* and
because of poor sales, employee salaries would be reduced.

✍ Communication

heart-to-heart — intimate communication
USAGE: Steven suggested to Mary they have a *heart-to-heart* talk about their
recent disagreements.

hem and haw — hesitant; evasive
USAGE: When I asked Jack about why he didn't submit the assignment, he
hemmed and hawed about something I couldn't understand.

hold forth — (1) a public speech; (2) make an offer
USAGE (1): John was *holding forth* in a speech why he thought criminals
should be sentenced to longer prison terms.
USAGE (2): The teacher *held forth* a pledge to give the students extra points
for the assignment.

hold one's fire — hold back argument or disagreement
USAGE: Because he realized she would be critical of the plan, he said, "*Hold
your fire* until you have heard the entire plan."

✍ Completeness

fill (something) in — write words into a form
USAGE: The job applicant was directed to *fill in* the employment application
and give it to the manager.

✍ Consequence

keep one's fingers crossed — anticipate good results

USAGE: She asked her friends to **keep their fingers crossed** that she would be offered the job.

kettle of fish — difficult situation
USAGE: Thinking about the difficult situation, Tom looked at Sam and said, "We've got a tough **kettle of fish**."

kick oneself — sorry for; regret
USAGE: Michael was frustrated and **kicked himself** for not asking about the job earlier.

knock one's block off — to hit another person
USAGE: Betty's husband continued to argue and she angrily said, "If you don't be quiet, I feel like **knocking your block off**!"

✍ Disagree

go jump in a lake — quit bothering another
USAGE: After insulting her, Julie angrily replied, "**Go jump in a lake**!"

gun for someone — try to defeat someone
USAGE: My old girlfriend has been **gunning for me** ever since we broke up our relationship.

head-on — opposed to someone in an argument
USAGE: The defense attorney decided to deal with the accusation in a **head-on** manner during the court proceedings.

✍ Emotion

green with envy — envy; desirous
USAGE: Jealous of Mark's new car, Joe was **green with envy**.

guard is down — vulnerable; unguarded
USAGE: Vickie's **guard was down** when they started to criticize her.

gung-ho — enthusiastic; eager; zealous
USAGE: Excited about the new job, Charles was **gung-ho** about completing the assignment.

hair stand on end — become fearful or alarmed
USAGE: When Mary viewed the crime scene, her **hair stood on end** with fear.

ham it up — act funny, add humor and tell jokes
USAGE: Susan likes to *ham it up* when she gives a lecture to make it entertaining.

✍ Error

cancel out — remove or cancel the effect of something
USAGE: The kindness demonstrated by Nancy was *cancelled out* by a rude comment in her speech to the group.

✍ Failure

fall short (of one's expectations) — not as good as expected
USAGE: The author's book *fell short of most readers' expectation*.

fall through — to fail; will not happen
USAGE: My plan to retire in South America *fell through* when my savings were wiped out by poor investments.

✍ Health

knock the living daylights out of someone — hit and make someone unconscious
USAGE: It was a violent fight with the boxer *knocking the living daylights out of his opponent*.

✍ Importance

main drag — the main street in a town
USAGE: The teenagers spend their evenings driving on the city's *main drag*.

✍ Location

hole in the wall — a little-known place to eat or drink
USAGE: Robert and Mary enjoyed going to the *hole in the wall* restaurant because it had great food.

hook-up — a connection
USAGE: The repairman was trying to find the electrical *hook-up* so he could finish the project.

✍ Money

hard up — needing money

USAGE: *Hard up* for cash, Joe asked Timothy if he could borrow some money.

have deep pockets — wealthy
USAGE: After he purchased the luxury car, many people realized that Bill *had deep pockets*.

✍ Movement

head out — to leave or depart
USAGE: Kenneth informed the group it was time for them to *head out* to the theater.

head over heels — falling down; head first
USAGE: When Jack's bicycle hit the curb, he fell *head over heels* on the street.

head start — to start before others
USAGE: In order to get a *head start*, Lisa and Betty got an early start on the drive.

✍ Ownership

lay in — accumulate supply of needed material
USAGE: Hearing predictions of a typhoon, Bob and Mary worked to *lay in* supplies that might be needed.

✍ Personal Description

drugstore cowboy — pretending to be a cowboy
USAGE: Since he was wearing a cowboy hat, James looked like a *drugstore cowboy*.

dumb bunny — a stupid or gullible person
USAGE: John proved he is a *dumb bunny* when he believed the story about dragons.

dweeb — someone who is bookish or overly studious
USAGE: Charles said Sharon is hard to communicate with because she's such a *dweeb*. He said all she thinks about is biology.

✍ Plan / Prepare

hop to it — get started quickly
USAGE: Jacob wanted to *hop to it* and finish the project as soon as possible.

hush up — keep private; usually concealed bad news
USAGE: The managers tried to *hush up* news of the inferior products being made at the company, but the newspaper exposed the story.

hush-hush — keep private; usually concealed bad news
USAGE: When most people found out they were keeping it *hush-hush*, the managers were forced to admit the cover-up.

✍ Quantity

half the battle — part of the work
USAGE: Dale suggested that writing the report was only *half the battle*. The real work, he said, was persuading leaders of the urgency of action.

✍ Relationship

grow on you — favor will increase
USAGE: John told Mary that appreciation of the new house would *grow on her*.

✍ Satisfaction

have one's eye on — has a desire for something
USAGE: Jack *had his eye on* a new car he would like to buy.

head above water — to stay clear of difficulty
USAGE: Kevin works very hard in his job to keep his *head above water*.

high life — a luxurious way of life
USAGE: After receiving a large amount of money from his parents, Peter has been living the *high life*.

✍ Service

go halves — share equally
USAGE: Benjamin and Charles decided to *go halves* on the purchase of a new boat.

✍ Time

golden opportunity — a good and timely chance
USAGE: The family reunion was a *golden opportunity* for the brothers to try to resolve their conflict.

golden years — 65 years old or older
USAGE: John said he was looking forward to retirement and his *golden years*.

hang-up — a delay
USAGE: There was a *hang-up* in the arrival of the ambulance due to traffic congestion.

✍ Understand

in hand — under control
USAGE: The teacher had the misbehaving student *in hand* when the visitor arrived in the classroom.

in memory of — a special reminder of
USAGE: *In memory of* their dead mother, the brothers hired a portrait artist to do a special painting.

in on — told about
USAGE: Karen was finally let *in on* the secret about the missing office equipment.

✍ Work

ground floor — the beginning of a situation
USAGE: William and James were very excited about getting in on the *ground floor* of the investment opportunity.

✍ Achievement

go places — on the way to success
USAGE: With John recently completing his MBA degree, I know he is ***going places***.

go the extra mile — to work extra hard
USAGE: The teacher told him if he would ***go the extra mile*** he could reach the top of his class.

✍ Agree / Approval

in tune — getting along well with others
USAGE: The group has been working together and is ***in tune*** with each other.

jump/get/climb on the bandwagon — join a popular activity
USAGE: The emphasis on fitness means that everyone has ***jumped on the exercise bandwagon***.

✍ Authority

lean on — pressure applied to make a person comply
USAGE: Using a threat of violence, the teenager was ***leaning on*** some of the students to do his homework.

lord it over — to behave as a superior to someone
USAGE: Since he became the boss, he seems to want to ***lord over*** employees that he doesn't even supervise.

✍ Bad / Negative

have the goods on someone — find out true and often bad information about someone
USAGE: Harold suggested that the police ***have the goods on him*** and will immediately talk to the judge.

have two strikes against one — something working against a person
USAGE: John already *has two strikes against him* and missing work again
  will cause major problems.

hell and high water — encounter significant difficulties
USAGE: The rescue workers went through *hell and high water* to get supplies
  to the tsunami survivors.

✍ Communication

hold one's own — defending a position
USAGE: Despite her mild manners, Elizabeth can *hold her own* in a
  disagreement with anyone.

hold one's peace — maintain silence to keep peace
USAGE: The supervisor asked Bill to *hold his peace* around Kevin so that a
  confrontation may be avoided.

hold one's tongue — keep quiet
USAGE: Tom made the decision to *hold his tongue* instead of giving his opinion.

hold something back — keep information to oneself
USAGE: Susan is *holding back* the details of the new construction process
  until the new manager arrives.

horn in on — listen in or interfere
USAGE: Linda *horned in on* the private conversation and, in the process,
  angered the group.

✍ Completeness

flat-out — frankly; openly; directly
USAGE: Victor suggested *flat-out* that he would not attend the meeting.

from stem to stern — completely
USAGE: The police detectives investigated the crime scene *from stem-to-
stern* with exact precision.

✍ Consequence

land on one's feet — come out of a bad situation successfully
USAGE: She succeeded in *landing on her feet* following a very upsetting
  argument with her supervisor.

lay one's cards on the table — successfully come through a bad situation
USAGE: Henry decided to *lay his cards on the table* and tell his wife about the money he lost through a poor investment.

leave hanging (in the air) — undecided or unsettled
USAGE: The resolution of the issue was uncertain and it will be *left hanging in the air* until the next meeting.

✍ Different

on the other hand — looking at the opposite side of a matter
USAGE: There is an encouraging expectation that the economy will be improving, but *on the other hand* there is a grim prediction that government funding will be reduced.

✍ Disagree

hold back — to be restrained
USAGE: William sometimes *holds back* his thoughts in disagreement.

in one's hair — persist in annoying someone
USAGE: Kathy is often annoying and gets *in my hair* with her continual talking.

in spite of — regardless of
USAGE: *In spite of* a high unemployment rate, I found my job in one week.

✍ Emotion

hang by a thread — at risk; depend on a very small thing
USAGE: The outcome of the soccer championship was *hanging by a thread* until the final minute of the game.

hang in (there) — persist; don't give up
USAGE: John urged Nancy to *hang in* there and successfully complete her MBA degree.

hang it! — annoyance or disappointment
USAGE: When hitting and injuring his toe, Bill screamed, "*Hang it*" in pain.

hang-up — a psychological inhibition
USAGE: Wendy has a *hang-up* about insects and is afraid of anything that crawls.

hard feelings — anger or bitterness
USAGE: Carol admitted she had *hard feelings* about the conflict she experienced
  with the others.

✐ Error

change horses in midstream — change plans
USAGE: Recognizing she wanted to *change horses in midstream*, she decided
  to return to the university at age 45 and study nursing.

✐ Failure

fat chance — no chance
USAGE: John admitted it was a *fat chance* that he would be able to obtain the
  loan from the bank.

✐ Health

knocked up — to get pregnant
USAGE: Robert *knocked up* Lisa and they were looking forward to having the
  baby.

✐ Location

hot on your heels — following close behind
USAGE: Chasing the criminal suspects, the police were *hot on their heels*.

in the first place — to begin with
USAGE: John gave reasons why he didn't want to travel. *In the first place*, he
  suggested, he felt unsafe flying in aircraft.

✐ Money

highway robbery — an extremely high price
USAGE: Because the price was too expensive, Robert believed the costs for
  the tickets were *highway robbery*.

in deep — seriously involved
USAGE: Since Richard had borrowed heavily to finance his lifestyle, he was
  in deep with debt.

in kind — to repay with something of equal value
USAGE: Arrangements were made by James to repay the loan *in kind* through
  the use of his truck.

✍ Movement

head-on — front end to front end collision
USAGE: The police were called to a serious *head-on* car crash that killed two
    people.

hedge in — block in; unable to move
USAGE: Tom was *hedged in* among the large crowd at the game and couldn't
    move.

here goes — commitment to do something
USAGE: Hoping that she would accept, Mark said, "*Here goes*, I'm asking her
    to marry me!"

✍ Personal Description

dyed in the wool — a confirmed type
USAGE: Enjoying his heritage, Henry is a *dyed in the wool* traditionalist.

eager beaver — a person willing to help and zealous
USAGE: Sharon is always enthusiastic and an *eager beaver* to get things
    done.

easy-going — relaxed style
USAGE: Martha exhibits an *easy-going* style with people.

✍ Plan / Prepare

in keeping with — consistent with pattern
USAGE: *In keeping with* the tradition of the home team kicking first, John and
    his teammates began the long-awaited game.

in the wind — likely to happen
USAGE: Stanley believes it is *in the wind* that a new manufacturing plant will
    be built in the city.

in the works — in preparation for; being planned
USAGE: According to John, it was *in the works* for a new office tower to be
    constructed.

ins and outs — all the details
USAGE: Vickie was aware of the *ins and outs* of the plan to place computers
    in all the classrooms.

✐ Quantity

hill of beans — small amount
USAGE: The disagreement between the sisters didn't amount to a *hill of beans*.

✐ Relationship

hand in hand — to be together
USAGE: John and Mary worked closely and were always *hand in hand*.

handle with kid gloves — handle with much sensitivity
USAGE: Because Carol is very sensitive, she needs to be *handled with kid gloves* or she gets her feelings hurt.

✐ Satisfaction

high on the hog — to live in luxury
USAGE: When James became rich, he purchased several new cars and lived *high on the hog*.

hit on all cylinders — operating efficiently
USAGE: Because the company was running well, Jim knew the operation was *hitting on all cylinders*.

hit someone between the eyes — make an effective impression on
USAGE: Her motivating speech was so effective that it *hit the audience between the eyes*.

✐ Service

go to bat for — to help someone out
USAGE: The manager assured the workers he would *go to bat for* them in the negotiations for increased pay.

✐ Superior

hand something to someone on a silver platter — give a person something that has not been earned
USAGE: Because Kevin's parents owned a business, he was *handed a great job on a silver platter* and didn't have to try very hard.

✐ Time

here and now — immediately; at present

USAGE: Charles told Susan he wanted the assignment to be completed **here and now**.

high time — right time to do something
USAGE: John suggested it was **high time** to introduce the product to the market.

hold good — continue; endure
USAGE: The rate of admission applications submitted to the university **held good** during the past year.

✍ Understand

in one's mind's eye — in a person's imagination
USAGE: The counselor told Betty, "**In your mind's eye** imagine you are achieving success."

in one's shoes — understand someone else's situation
USAGE: John said it was hard to be **in Bill's shoes** and understand his situation.

in the bag — certain; sure
USAGE: The agreement between the managers and workers was **in the bag**.

in the clear — nothing to limit future action
USAGE: Susan believed the situation had improved and everything was **in the clear** to reach an agreement.

✍ Work

hang out one's shingle — open a professional office
USAGE: Having graduated from medical school, Richard is **hanging out his shingle** and starting his doctor's office.

✍ Achievement

grasp at straws — make a desperate attempt at something
USAGE: She was *grasping at straws* in trying to persuade the others to partner with her on the project.

gun for something — try very hard to get something
USAGE: John had been *gunning to obtain a promotion at work for some time*.

had better — should do something
USAGE: Mary realized she *had better* attend the meeting or she would be penalized.

✍ Agree / Approval

lay it on thick — to praise someone too much
USAGE: In an effort to please her, Larry was *laying it on thick* to Laura at the party.

live up to — act according to
USAGE: Peter is trying very hard to *live up to* his reputation as a smart businessman.

✍ Authority

make oneself felt — use one's authority
USAGE: The manager was able to *make himself felt* by issuing orders to workers at the business.

of age — mark of maturity
USAGE: The parents were pleased as they observed their son come *of age*.

✍ Bad / Negative

hit the bottle — drink alcohol beverages

USAGE: He started to *hit the bottle* after he lost his job and his drinking habits got worse.

hold that over my head — to be reminded of a mistake or error
USAGE: Because he once wrecked a car, she *held it over his head* as a reason he could not drive her car.

hold up — robbery at gunpoint
USAGE: The thief cornered the couple on the street and *held them up* to get their money.

✍ Business Action

feather one's nest — taking advantage of position to help oneself
USAGE: The manager had been *feathering his nest* while working at the company.

✍ Communication

hot air — exaggerated talk
USAGE: Horace is sometimes full of *hot air* when he talks. I think he's just trying to impress others.

how about — inquiring about reaction to something
USAGE: *How about* that new car you drove?

how come — why
USAGE: *How come* you don't use the Internet more?

how's that — repeat what was said
USAGE: *How's that*? Please say that again because I couldn't hear you.

hush up — stop talking, crying, or making noise
USAGE: Little Johnny was told to *hush up* when he started crying.

in a nutshell — briefly; in a few words
USAGE: Bill told the others, "*In a nutshell*, the problem is that we aren't making enough sales."

✍ Completeness

full-fledged — complete; full status
USAGE: Robert was excited because he had become a *full-fledged* member of the team, complete with his own office.

✍ Consequence

leave (someone) holding the bag — getting blamed for something
USAGE: John was *left holding the bag* when his friends gave him the counterfeit
money.

leave in the lurch — abandon or leave alone when needed
USAGE: Steven *left James in the lurch* when he failed to assist him with the
project.

let bygones be bygones — forget about past disagreements, problems
USAGE: Wanting to move beyond their longstanding conflict, Jim and Bob
agreed to *let bygones be bygones* and to work through past disagreements.

✍ Different

on the sly — secretly
USAGE: Since they wanted to avoid the newspaper reporters, James and Betsy
went to the restaurant *on the sly*.

✍ Disagree

jump all over someone — criticize or scold
USAGE: Lisa *jumped all over* her husband Richard when he started describing
the beauty of the other women.

jump down someone's throat — to be angry with someone
USAGE: The boss *jumped down my throat* when he discovered I wrecked the
company car.

✍ Emotion

hate one's guts — intense dislike for someone
USAGE: Furious after losing a job promotion, Lisa angrily said, "I *hate her
guts* because the false accusations about me she made to the boss."

have a ball — enjoy a good time
USAGE: John said he *had a ball* at the celebration and didn't get home until
2 AM.

have a crush on — to be very attracted to someone
USAGE: George said the girl was beautiful and he *had a crush on* her.

have a fit — become extremely upset

USAGE: Lisa became angry and ***had a fit*** when she saw the woman hug her husband.

have a heart — to have compassion
USAGE: John suggested to Mary that she ***have a heart*** when disciplining the children.

✍ End

peter out — decrease gradually
USAGE: The crowd's excitement about winning the game ***petered out*** and everyone soon went home.

✍ Entertainment

idiot box — a television set
USAGE: Lisa told Bill he was spending too much time in front of the ***idiot box***.

✍ Error

close call/shave — an accident almost happening
USAGE: We had a ***close call*** this morning when I almost hit a boy on a bicycle.

✍ Failure

fizzle out — fail after a good start
USAGE: The crowd's excitement began to ***fizzle out*** as the fate of the home team faded.

✍ Health

laid up — limited to bed rest
USAGE: Sick with stomach problems, Robert was ***laid up*** in the bed.

✍ Location

joint — a particular place, location
USAGE: John said, "Come on over to my ***joint*** and we will have a drink."

jumping off place — the beginning place of a trip
USAGE: The group gathered at the crossroads, which was the ***jumping-off place*** for the trip.

lay low — (1) to keep hidden; (2) stay out of sight and action
USAGE (1): The criminal suspects were *laying low* while the police were
  searching throughout the city.
USAGE (2): After the hostility at the meeting, James decided to *lay low* until
  the anger calmed down.

✍ Money

in the black — maintain a profit
USAGE: The established company has been profitable and *in the black* for
  over 15 years.

in the hole — in financial debt
USAGE: Joe is financially distressed because he is constantly *in the hole*.

in the market for — wanting to buy
USAGE: Robert said he was *in the market for* a fuel efficient car.

✍ Movement

here goes nothing — ready to start but may fail
USAGE: After unsuccessfully asking Henry for a loan, Bill thought he would
  try again. When arriving at Henry's office, Bill said, "*Here goes nothing*,
  I'll give it another shot."

high gear — at full speed; much energy
USAGE: Susan has her plan for examination preparation in *high gear*.

hit the deck — to get working or prepared
USAGE: Steven and Joe were ready to *hit the deck* and get the work done.

✍ Ownership

make do with something — substitute one thing for another
USAGE: They discovered there was no sugar in the kitchen but they could
  make do without it.

✍ Personal Description

eat like a bird — eats very little
USAGE: Barbara *eats like a bird*. When we go to a restaurant, she doesn't eat
  most of her food.

eat like a horse — eats very much
USAGE: Thomas has a huge appetite and *eats like a horse*!

eat one's cake and have it too — want to both use and keep something
USAGE: William wants to *eat his cake and have it too*; he wants to earn a lot
of money but doesn't want to do what it takes!

✑ Plan / Prepare

inside out — knowing something very well
USAGE: As an expert in the dynasties of China, William knew the history of
the Henan Province *inside out*.

jam on the brakes — quickly put brakes on to stop car
USAGE: John *jammed on the brakes* to avoid an accident on the crowded city
street.

just so — with great care and preparation
USAGE: Caroline worked on styling her hair so that it looked *just so* for the
evening reception. She looked fabulous!

✑ Quantity

in short supply — not very much
USAGE: Because gasoline was *in short supply*, the government placed
restrictions on the amount each person could purchase.

✑ Relationship

hands are tied — unable to assist
USAGE: While Charles said he would like to help, he went on to say his *hands
were tied* because his job contract would not permit him to assist with the
project.

hands off — leave alone; don't interfere
USAGE: James had a *hands-off* position on the issues being debated by his
sisters.

has a thing going — a romance with someone
USAGE: Jim *has a thing going* with a girl he likes.

✑ Satisfaction

in clover — a carefree and prosperous life

USAGE: Bob and Karen are *in clover* since they moved to the mountains after selling their business to an investment group.

in luck — fortunate
USAGE: Bill suggested we are *in luck* because the restaurant has agreed to stay open later than usual to accommodate our schedule.

in one's element — in an environment that is suited to someone
USAGE: Charles is *in his element* since he is working with computers and information technology.

✍ Service

greasy spoon — an inexpensive restaurant
USAGE: Charles likes to eat at the local restaurant, which he calls a *greasy spoon*.

✍ Superior

hands down — a clear win
USAGE: Everyone agreed that Rebecca won the debate *hands down* over the other competitors.

✍ Time

hold off — to delay
USAGE: The committee decided to *hold off* the meeting with students until next week.

hold on — to wait
USAGE: Angela asked him to *hold on* while she returned to turn off the lights.

hold over — to keep longer
USAGE: Because of popular request, the play was *held over* for one more week.

✍ Understand

in the clouds — impractical and unrealistic
USAGE: Bill's thinking is sometimes *in the clouds* and difficult to understand.

in the dark — no information about something
USAGE: Still waiting to hear from them, Kevin is still *in the dark* about a job offer from the company.

in the swim — active in knowing what is happening
USAGE: Since Carol keeps informed about happenings around the company, she is definitely *in the swim*.

keep a secret — not revealing a secret
USAGE: Bart is *keeping a secret* about the future plans of the company.

keep an eye on something/someone — to watch over
USAGE: Peter asked Elizabeth to *keep an eye on his child* while he went to the meeting.

✍ Work

head-hunting — process of recruiting executive personnel
USAGE: The *head-hunter* called Steven to ask if was interested in interviewing for an executive position.

hire out — offer temporary use of services for money
USAGE: Vincent *hired himself out* as an accountant to companies.

Week 26

✍ Achievement

hang onto — hold onto firmly
USAGE: The players on the team were advised to *hang onto* their caps because of the strong wind.

have a hand in — be partly responsible for something
USAGE: As co-founder, Joseph *had a hand in* building the very profitable business.

have something on the ball — knowledgeable and talented
USAGE: Thomas is resourceful and really *has a lot on the ball*. He is a very creative person.

heavy duty — difficult, demanding task
USAGE: James was required to do *heavy duty* work to rescue the company from bankruptcy.

✍ Agree / Approval

meet someone half-way — try to compromise with someone
USAGE: In efforts to reach an agreement between the two sides, the employees were willing to *meet the managers half-way*.

✍ Authority

on the loose — to be free; not shut in
USAGE: Bill allows his dogs to be *on the loose* in his office building and this annoys many people.

✍ Bad / Negative

in the doghouse — in trouble
USAGE: After insulting his wife, James was *in the doghouse* with her.

in the soup — in trouble

USAGE: He was *in the soup* after a serious miscalculation of costs involved in the project.

✍ Business Action

fence — to sell stolen goods
USAGE: The thief planned on *fencing* the ring that he stole.

✍ Communication

in a word — briefly; to sum up
USAGE: Stanley told the group that, *in a word*, the problem at the company was low employee wages.

in/out of one's shell — withdrawn from others; silent
USAGE: The women urged Jane to come *out of her shell* and confide to them her feelings.

in other words — to say something differently
USAGE: The supervisor emphasized to the employees, "*In other words*, if we don't reduce costs we will be forced to close."

in the air — current; prevalent
USAGE: There was a sense of anticipation and excitement *in the air* about the new project.

in touch — to be in contact
USAGE: Even though John moved to a new city, he wanted to stay *in touch* with his old friends.

✍ Completeness

ghost of a chance — very little chance
USAGE: Mark realized he didn't have a *ghost of a chance* to receive the job promotion.

✍ Consequence

let go — allow something to pass
USAGE: While Susan was offended at his comment, she *let it go*.

let go of — to release
USAGE: Richard accidentally *let go of* the box and it fell to the ground.

let it lay — leave it alone
USAGE: While Stanley was insulted when the others ignored him, his friends urged him to *let it lay* and forget it.

let off — discharge or explode (gun, fireworks)
USAGE: To celebrate the start of the new year, they *let off* firecrackers and sparklers at midnight.

✍ Different

one for the books — something highly unusual
USAGE: Her very unusual comments were strange and *one for the books*!

✍ Disagree

jump on someone — to scold, criticize
USAGE: Vincent *jumped on Joe* when he made the inappropriate comment about the other workers.

look down on someone — regard with a feeling of dominance
USAGE: Believing he was more intelligent than the other employees, Bill *looked down on* their remarks.

✍ Emotion

have a meltdown — to become extremely angry
USAGE: He *had a meltdown* when he realized the computer was infected by a virus.

have a time — (1) have a fun time; (2) have trouble
USAGE (1): The girls agreed they all *had a time* at the celebration last night.
USAGE (2): He *had a time* when his computer crashed while working on the project.

have egg on one's face — to be ashamed, embarrassed
USAGE: After making the rude comment, John realized he *had egg on his face* knowing he had offended the others.

have eyes only for — be exclusively attracted to someone
USAGE: Richard is in love with Susan and *has eyes only for* her.

have had it (with someone/something) — can't endure anymore
USAGE: Frustrated with her behavior, Jim remarked that he's *had it with her* irritating comments.

✍ Error

cross out — draw line through writing
USAGE: He ***crossed out*** the incorrect information on the application and wrote in the correct amount.

✍ Failure

flash in the pan — something once popular and then fails
USAGE: While a crowd-pleaser for a short time, his popularity was a ***flash in the pan***.

get the ax — to be fired
USAGE: Unable to meet expectations on the job, he ***got the ax*** last week.

✍ Health

lap up — eat or drink
USAGE: Extremely hungry, the dogs ***lapped up*** the food.

✍ Location

lay over — to wait before proceeding on
USAGE: The passengers were informed they would have an unexpected ***layover*** in Shanghai on their flight to Los Angeles.

leave behind — to leave something somewhere
USAGE: Connie realized she had ***left behind*** her purse at the restaurant.

lie in state — following death of a noted person, the coffin is viewed by public
USAGE: The Prime Minister ***lay in state*** for three days after his death.

✍ Money

in the red — not make a profit
USAGE: Due to high labor costs, the company has been ***in the red*** for six months.

itching palm — desire for money
USAGE: The corrupt policeman had an ***itching palm*** and suggested we should bribe him.

✍ Movement

hit the dirt — fall to the ground to take cover from gunfire

USAGE: The police yelled to the observers to *hit the dirt* when the criminals began shooting in the public square.

hit the road — to leave in a vehicle
USAGE: John remarked we should *hit the road* at 6 AM in order to complete the drive by tomorrow evening.

hold one's horses — be patient
USAGE: Knowing the others were in a hurry to leave, Peter said, "*Hold your horses*, I'll be ready in a minute!"

✍ Personal Description

every Tom, Dick and Harry — the average person
USAGE: William suggested he didn't want to be the same as *every Tom, Dick and Harry*.

eyes are bigger than one's stomach — wanting more food than one can eat
USAGE: Seeing him put a lot of food on the plate, the mother said, "Your *eyes are bigger than your stomach*! You won't be able to eat all that food."

eyes in the back of one's head — ability to know what is happening all around
USAGE: Almost as if she had *eyes in the back of her head*, the teacher seem to know everything that happened in the classroom.

eyes pop out — very surprised
USAGE: Susan's *eyes popped out* when she saw her name on the list of winners.

✍ Plan / Prepare

just the same — nevertheless; anyway
USAGE: While she was told she didn't need to be present, Martha attended *just the same*.

just what the doctor ordered — what is needed or wanted
USAGE: Tommy remarked that having an extra long lunch break was *just what the doctor ordered* to enable him to catch up on running errands.

keep from — to refrain from
USAGE: She believed strongly in the issue and couldn't *keep from* expressing her opinion.

✍ Quantity

jam-packed — very crowded
USAGE: The subway train was *jam-packed* with students.

✍ Relationship

have an affair — an adulterous sexual relationship
USAGE: Susan is very angry because she discovered her husband was *having an affair*.

✍ Satisfaction

in the same boat — in the same situation
USAGE: Knowing they were all jobless, Joe said, "We're all *in the same boat* now."

inside track — an advantage
USAGE: Barbara believed she had the *inside track* on getting the job promotion at work.

iron out — work out and solve
USAGE: Jim and Bill discussed the problem and *ironed out* their disagreements with the issue.

✍ Service

hand in — to submit
USAGE: The student went to the university to *hand in* his application for admission.

✍ Superior

hang you out to dry — to defeat
USAGE: The coach of the national team told the newspaper reporter that his players would *hang the opposing team out to dry*.

✍ Time

hours on end — seemingly endless
USAGE: The team practiced steadily for *hours on end* but still lost the game.

in a rush — in a hurry
USAGE: Since Richard was *in a rush*, he asked the attendant to work faster.

in advance — ahead of time
USAGE: The students arrived at the museum ***in advance*** of the scheduled time.

in due course — at the right or designated time
USAGE: The professor informed the students they would receive their final grades ***in due course***.

✍ Understand

keep one's own counsel — keep one's ideas private
USAGE: John was careful to ***keep his own counsel*** regarding his plans to sell the business.

keep one's wits about one — stay calm in danger or confusion
USAGE: Despite confusion during the fire, Charles was able to ***keep his wits about him*** and assist in the rescue efforts.

keep under one's hat — not telling anyone; keep secret
USAGE: Keeping secret his holiday plans, Steven ***kept it under his hat***.

Week 27

✍ **Achievement**

hitch one's wagon to a star — follow a great dream or purpose
USAGE: Dreaming of *hitching his wagon to a star*, Don wants to follow his desire to be on the national soccer team.

hold off — keep away, usually by force
USAGE: Steven was able to *hold off* the robber long enough for some bystanders to help.

hold up — to prove true and valid
USAGE: Upon questioning by the police, John's story *held up* and he was released.

in a rut — always doing the same thing
USAGE: Peter and Carol feel they are *in a rut* because they eat at the same restaurant week after week.

✍ **Agree / Approval**

middle of the road — midway between two extreme view points
USAGE: Robert always held moderate beliefs and most people regard him as *middle of the road* in his approach.

✍ **Authority**

over one's head — go to a higher person in authority
USAGE: The manager was angered because one of his employees went *over his head* to the president with a complaint.

pass the buck — shift responsibility to someone else
USAGE: Bill never accepts responsibility for problems at the company. Rather, he always tries to *pass the buck* to someone else.

✍ Bad / Negative

jump bail — accused person does not show at trial and forfeits money paid to secure appearance
USAGE: He *jumped bail* by failing to appear in court today.

kick around — treats others badly
USAGE: I don't like Kathy very much because she is always *kicking other people around*.

✍ Business Action

finger in the pie — part ownership or responsibility
USAGE: Jim is very active in private business and has *his finger in the pie* of several emerging businesses in the city.

✍ Communication

keep in touch — maintain friendships
USAGE: Even though he graduated from college fifteen years ago, John *keeps in touch* with many of his college friends.

keep one's mouth shut — demand silence
USAGE: John angrily told the man to *keep his mouth shut*.

keep quiet — remain silent
USAGE: The librarian advised the students to obey the rules and *keep quiet*.

lash out — verbally attack someone
USAGE: When he said he had intentionally lied about his feelings, Susan angrily *lashed out* at him.

last word — the final say in deciding something
USAGE: She usually has the *last word* when a major decision needs to be made about their family.

✍ Consequence

let (someone) off the hook — excuse someone from task or duty
USAGE: Karen *let him off the hook* even though he didn't complete his part of the job.

let sleeping dogs lie — allow past problems to stay in past

USAGE: His friends urged him to be restrained and *let sleeping dogs lie* and avoid arguing over the past.

✍ Different

out in left field — inaccurate and not the right answer
USAGE: John later realized what he said at the party was *out in left field* and totally wrong.

✍ Disagree

look down one's nose at someone/something — snobbish and overly proud
USAGE: He acts conceited and *looks down his nose at other employees*.

no cigar — not agreed to
USAGE: The two groups were close in reaching an agreement but in the end it was *no cigar*.

✍ Emotion

have it out with someone — angrily discuss something
USAGE: Vincent *had it out with Carol* about a dispute over their family budget.

have one's heart set on something — want something very much
USAGE: Larry's son *has his heart set on getting a new bicycle* for his 13th birthday gift.

have the last laugh — ultimate success despite initial ridicule by others
USAGE: I *had the last laugh* when I achieved my sales goals for the month after the others joked it couldn't be done.

heart goes out to someone — to feel sympathy for others
USAGE: Susan said her *heart went out to* the victims of the earthquake.

heart is in the right place — kindhearted
USAGE: While Bill can be difficult at times, his *heart is in the right place*.

✍ End

put away — put an animal to death
USAGE: The animal doctor had to *put away* our dog because he had an incurable and very painful condition.

✍ Failure

get the worst of — be defeated or beaten, suffer most
USAGE: Jane *got the worst of* the deal when she discovered the diamond she
purchased was a fake.

give oneself up — to surrender
USAGE: The criminal suspects *gave themselves up* to the police after an arrest
warrant was issued.

✍ Health

morning after — a hangover
USAGE: When Tom said he wasn't feeling well, James looked at him and said,
"I think your problem is the *morning after* a late night on the town."

off the wagon — begin to drink alcohol again after stopping for awhile
USAGE: Since we saw him at the bar last night, he probably is *off the wagon*.

✍ Importance

make a difference — cause a change in a situation
USAGE: The managers agreed that it doesn't *make any difference* whether she
attends the meeting.

✍ Location

lie in wait — watch from a concealed position to launch attack or surprise
USAGE: The robbers were *lying in wait* along the road to hold up the travelers.

line up — stand one behind another
USAGE: Because there was a large crowd at the theater, we had to *line up* for
tickets.

✍ Money

jack up — raise prices
USAGE: Because of the fuel shortage, the petrol station *jacked up* their prices.

keep books — keep accounting of the money gained and spent
USAGE: Karen's job was to *keep books* and manage the accounting for the
company.

keep one's head above water — the ability to earn income and pay bills

USAGE: Because he lost his job last month, Rick is having trouble *keeping his head above water*.

✍ Movement

hold still — do not move
USAGE: Mary asked Bob to *hold still* while she trimmed his hair.

in and out — coming in and going out often
USAGE: He's been moving around all day, *in and out* of the office.

✍ Ownership

move in on — to seize control of something
USAGE: Our managers were concerned because the new company was *moving in on* our share of the market.

✍ Personal Description

faded — inebriated; intoxicated
USAGE: Jack drank several beers last night and was pretty *faded*!

faint of heart — timid
USAGE: To assist in the rescue effort and observe the aftermath of the earthquake is not for the *faint of heart*.

feet on the ground — sensible, wise and rational
USAGE: Robert is regarded by most as a reasonable person who has his *feet on the ground*.

few bricks short of a full load — not logical or rational
USAGE: When he started to eat dirt, I knew he was a *few bricks short of a full load*.

✍ Plan / Prepare

keep house — maintain a house; manage housework
USAGE: Wendy has been *keeping house* for her mother while she was recovering from surgery.

keep one's eye on the ball — be watchful and ready to respond
USAGE: Bill advised John he should *keep his eye on the ball* because events can change very fast.

keep track of — maintain a record
USAGE: The manager asked Phillip to **keep track of** travel expenses for the company.

✐ Quantity

leave out — omit; exclude
USAGE: James described what happened at the meeting, but **left out** the details of the conference call.

✐ Relationship

have it in for someone — show ill will or dislike for a person
USAGE: Karen suggested the reason she didn't receive the promotion is because she believes her manager **has it in for her**.

have something on someone — have information or evidence that someone did something wrong
USAGE: The police were questioning the man because they seem to **have something on him**.

✐ Satisfaction

(a) jim dandy — something good, exceptional
USAGE: You should see Bill's new car. It's a **jim dandy**!

keep it real — genuine; to resist the temptation to be fake
USAGE: Robert always has very original ideas and **keeps it real** with his authentic approach.

keep up appearances — outward show of accomplishment or stability
USAGE: Peter worked hard to **keep up appearances** of success despite the fact that he was fired from his job.

✐ Service

hand out — to distribute
USAGE: The manager **handed out** the paychecks to employees.

✐ Similar

nip and tuck — evenly matched competition with lead shifting
USAGE: It was **nip and tuck** whether our company would exceed last year's sales figures. We're working hard to go beyond last year's record!

✍ Superior

have an edge over — have an advantage for dominance
USAGE: Stanley realized his work group *had an edge over* the other group in reaching the company's production goal.

✍ Time

in good time — a little early; before due
USAGE: John told Susan he would get the report to her *in good time* so she could review it before the meeting.

in no time — soon; quickly; immediately
USAGE: Michael told me he would get me the information *in no time* so I could complete the project.

in nothing flat — very quickly
USAGE: Carol finished the assignment *in nothing flat*.

✍ Understand

knock on wood — express hope that something will or will not happen
USAGE: Phillip suggested he would again reach his yearly sales expectations, *knock on wood*.

know it all — a person who acts as if they know all the answers; pretentious
USAGE: He acts bossy around most people and comes across as a *know-it-all*.

knows which side one's bread is buttered on — knows who can help and understand what is good for oneself
USAGE: Shrewd in understanding how things work in the company, Jack has a good relationship with the managers and *knows which side his bread is buttered on*.

lay down the law — direct someone using influence and authority
USAGE: The parents *laid down the law* to their teenager about not skipping school.

✍ Work

hold down a job — maintain employment
USAGE: Because of frequent absenteeism at work, Joe has a hard time *holding down a job*.

✍ Achievement

in arms — armed; ready for conflict
USAGE: The employees were all *in arms* when discovering there would not be salary increases next year.

in case — in the event; in order to be prepared
USAGE: John advised the others that, *in case* of a fire, the alarm will sound throughout the building.

in the groove — performing very well
USAGE: The coach suggests that after several weeks of training, the players are *in the groove* and ready to compete.

irons in the fire — an undertaking in which a person is very busy
USAGE: Karen is extremely busy with many projects. She has many *irons in the fire*.

✍ Agree / Approval

no doubt — surely; most certainly
USAGE: Peter remarked that he will, *no doubt*, apply for the job.

no matter — regardless of
USAGE: *No matter* how much needs to be done, Jimmy said that he will serve.

✍ Authority

pecking order — the way people are ranked in relation to each other
USAGE: The *pecking order* at the company means that John will get first choice of assignments.

pick up — to gather; take to the police station
USAGE: The detectives *picked up* the man for questioning about the robbery.

✍ Bad / Negative

kick up a fuss — make a disturbance
USAGE: The teenagers really *kicked up a fuss* when told the game room would be closed.

knocked off — to be murdered
USAGE: During the robbery, the store employee was *knocked off*.

✍ Communication

lay into — attack with words; verbal combativeness
USAGE: Furious at what she said about him, Kevin said he was prepared to *lay into* Susan when she arrived.

leave alone — do not disturb someone
USAGE: Henry asked the boys to *leave the girls alone* so they could study.

left-handed compliment — an ambiguous compliment that is really an insult
USAGE: Carol gave Bill a *left-handed compliment* about his unusually colored shirt.

let down easy — convey bad news in a kind way
USAGE: Barbara decided she would tell Robert he didn't win the award and do it in a way that would *let him down easy*.

let (someone) have it — hit someone hard
USAGE: She *let Joe have it* when he intentionally insulted her friends at dinner.

let it all hang out — to be very honest, direct and forthright in conversation
USAGE: Very open in his comments to her, Steven *let it all hang out* and said she was the reason he didn't receive the job promotion.

let (someone) know — advise; inform
USAGE: John asked Mary to *let him know* when she wanted to leave.

✍ Completeness

give out — exhaust supply
USAGE: They went on a 2 week camping trip but the food supplies *gave out* after only 8 days.

go out the window — to be abandoned; go out of effect

USAGE: With the new manager hired, the formal dress code has been abandoned and *has gone out the window*.

✍ Consequence

let the chips fall where they may — go ahead without regard to consequences
USAGE: Joe said he was going to proceed with the project and *let the chips fall where they may*.

like water off a duck's back — disregard; without effect
USAGE: When Thomas is criticized, he often regards it *like water off a ducks back*.

live down — act to change reputation
USAGE: Robert is trying to *live down* his reputation as a womanizer.

✍ Different

out of step — (1) inconsistent with someone or policy; (2) out of harmony; not keeping up
USAGE (1): With the ideas he advocates, Steven is *out of step* with the company philosophy.
USAGE (2): Because Dr. Lee wanted to offer classes over the Internet at the school, he was *out of step* with the rest of his colleagues.

✍ Disagree

no deal — not agreed to
USAGE: When asked if he wanted to purchase the car for the negotiated price, Vincent said *no deal*.

no dice — no; certainly not
USAGE: John said, "*No dice*, I can't make you a loan."

✍ Emotion

heart skip a beat — be startled or excited from surprise, joy or fright
USAGE: Carol's *heart skipped a beat* when told that she was the prizewinner in the contest.

heart stands still — be very frightened, distressed or worried
USAGE: Barbara's *heart stood still* when she was told her father had suffered a stroke.

heavy heart — a feeling of sadness, unhappiness or hopelessness
USAGE: William remarked that he had a ***heavy heart*** since the death of his wife.

higher than a kite — intoxicated
USAGE: After a night on the town with his friends, Phillip was ***higher than a kite***.

hit the ceiling — get angry
USAGE: Charles ***hit the ceiling*** when his teenager son told him he had wrecked the car.

✍ End

put down — stop by force, crush
USAGE: The prison guards ***put down*** the rebellion by the prisoners.

✍ Entertainment

live it up — have a good time
USAGE: Joe really ***lives it up*** during business trips.

✍ Error

feed someone a line — deceive
USAGE: Peter was ***feeding the girl a line*** about him being a wealthy software developer.

✍ Failure

give out — fail
USAGE: The car began making a strange noise and finally ***gave out*** on the side of the road.

give up — abandon; stop
USAGE: Scott ***gave up*** on his longstanding goal to write a mystery novel.

✍ Health

on one's feet — recovering from sickness or difficulty
USAGE: Joseph is ***on his feet*** again after being sick for several days.

✍ Importance

make light of — minimize the importance

USAGE: Charles *made light of* my interest in flying and my desire to become a pilot.

✍ Location

live out of a suitcase — spend much time traveling with only possessions being suitcase contents
USAGE: Business professionals often travel and *live out of a suitcase*.

look for — try to find; search for; hunt
USAGE: Mary spent over one hour *looking for* her purse.

look (something) up — search for information in print or on the Internet
USAGE: Susan said she would *look up* the company's website on the Internet.

✍ Money

kick over — pay; contribute
USAGE: Joseph *kicked over* a lot of money for a digital video camera with many features.

kickback — money paid illegally to receive favorable treatment
USAGE: The company executives were convicted and sentenced to prison time for attempting to give a government official a *kickback* from the project.

lay away — save
USAGE: In anticipation of purchasing Jane's birthday gift, Bill tried to *lay away* a few dollars each week.

✍ Movement

in tow — (1) being taken from place to place, along with someone; (2) being pulled
USAGE (1): Barbara was going from shop to shop with her young child *in tow*.
USAGE (2): Peter's car had a trailer *in tow* in which he was hauling away trash.

jazz up — brighten up; add more noise or movement or color
USAGE: With the new paint colors and bright lights installed, the ballroom was *jazzed up*.

✍ Ownership

number one — selfish

USAGE: Richard is selfish and most of the time he is looking out for *number one*.

✍ Personal Description

five o'clock shadow — male facial hair growth toward the end of the day
USAGE: Needing to shave, Jack had grown a *five o'clock shadow*.

free and easy — informal
USAGE: Larry has a casual approach and it is demonstrated by his *free and easy* attitude.

go straight — obey the law
USAGE: While Scott had a criminal history, ten years ago he made the commitment to *go straight* and has been obeying the law ever since.

go to one's head — become conceited
USAGE: It looks as if his promotion has *gone to his head* because he seems arrogant.

✍ Plan / Prepare

keep up with the news — keep informed through news media
USAGE: Wanting to *keep up with the news*, Michael reads two newspapers each day over the Internet.

lay out — plan something
USAGE: The business owners will *lay out* their expansion plans at the morning ceremony.

lay up — store up and save for future use
USAGE: My parents were *laying up* non-perishable food items for possible future emergencies.

✍ Quantity

more and more — an increasing number
USAGE: *More and more* people are using the Internet as a necessary part of their daily lives.

✍ Relationship

hit it off — get along well with someone

USAGE: Steven and Julie *hit it off* and developed an attraction to each other.

in cahoots with — in secret agreement or partnership
USAGE: Management officials and community leaders were *in cahoots with* each other in trying to keep the electricity expenses down.

✍ Satisfaction

keep up with the Joneses — try to be the same as your neighbors
USAGE: Kevin has always been concerned with his image and spends a lot of time thinking about *keeping up with the Joneses*.

kick around — relax
USAGE: Just to relax last Saturday, I stayed home and *kicked around* the house.

kick back — relax and do nothing
USAGE: Lawrence said he wanted to *kick back* over the weekend and read a book

✍ Service

hand-me-down — something given away after another person doesn't need it
USAGE: Timothy has always been ashamed that he had to wear *hand-me-down* clothing from family members.

✍ Similar

on the same wavelength — thinking similarly about something
USAGE: Anthony and Bill have been *on the same wavelength* for months about the need to have Internet access available at the new building.

✍ Superior

one up — having an advantage; being one step ahead
USAGE: The older students admitted they had a *one up* on the younger students since they had completed the project during the previously year.

✍ Time

in one's tracks — abruptly; immediately
USAGE: Joe was stopped *in his tracks* when he saw the wild bear standing in the middle of the road.

in store — ready to happen; waiting
USAGE: While uncertain about the future, Jack said he was ready for whatever might be *in store*.

in the course of — during
USAGE: *In the course of* William's 78 years, he visited 39 countries.

✍ **Understand**

lay eyes on — see; to view
USAGE: Henry said he had never *laid eyes on* a more beautiful woman in his life.

lay it on the line — to say plainly and directly
USAGE: Looking at the budget, James told the other managers he was going to *lay it on the line* about budget cuts next year.

leg to stand on — to use facts or claims to support one's position
USAGE: He didn't have a *leg to stand on* as he tried to justify his reasons for skipping work.

lock the barn door after the horse is stolen — be careful or try to make something safe when it is too late
USAGE: Placing fire extinguishers in the building after a fire is like *locking the barn door after the horse is stolen*.

✍ **Work**

in the line of duty — done or happening as part of a job
USAGE: The soldier was killed *in the line of duty*, defending his country.

jack-of-all-trades — a person who can do many tasks
USAGE: James is a valuable employee because he is a *jack-of-all-trades* around the manufacturing plant.

Week 29

✎ **Achievement**

jump through a hoop — to do whatever one is told to do
USAGE: Lawrence is willing to *jump through hoops* to meet the demands of his supervisor.

keep one's word — fulfill one's promise
USAGE: Susan does not have much credibility because she usually doesn't *keep her word*.

keep the ball rolling — keep up an activity or action
USAGE: The group wanted to *keep the ball rolling* so the project would be completed in time.

kill two birds with one stone — accomplish two things with one action
USAGE: Always busy with a lot of demands, Charles *killed two birds with one stone* by completing his paper while waiting for the train.

✎ **Agree / Approval**

once over — quick examination of someone or something
USAGE: Before purchasing the car, Thomas gave it a *once over*.

pass muster — pass a test or checkup; be good enough
USAGE: John had serious questions if the students would be able to *pass muster* on the examination.

✎ **Authority**

pull rank — use one's authority to get a privilege or favor
USAGE: The manager *pulled rank* on the staff member in charge of transportation so he could get the nicest car for his use.

pull strings — use influence and power informally
USAGE: Joseph *pulled some strings* and got his daughter a job at the company.

✍ Bad / Negative

last straw — the last insult or mistake that results in consequence
USAGE: When Jack was absent from work without informing his boss, it was the *last straw* and he was fired.

last year — outdated; antiquated; out of fashion
USAGE: The university student told his friend, "Your shirt is so *last-year*."

laugh off — do not take seriously
USAGE: He unwisely *laughed off* the recommendations of his boss and, as a result, didn't obtain the promotion.

✍ Business Action

flea market — a place where antiques or used items are sold
USAGE: They purchased an antique telephone they found at the *flea market*. They later discovered the antique phone was very valuable.

✍ Communication

let on — try to make people believe something
USAGE: John tried to *let on* and pretend he didn't know the details of the expansion plans.

let out — reveal; allow to be known
USAGE: The managers *let out* details about the construction plans for the new headquarters.

let the cat out of the bag — to reveal a secret
USAGE: Bill *let the cat out of the bag* about the new product to be introduced to the market.

lip service — support shown by words only and not by action
USAGE: He only gave *lip service* to our request but it wasn't backed up by any action.

little pitchers have big ears — children overhearing things they are not supposed to hear
USAGE: When Lisa saw her son listening in to the conversation from behind the door, she said, "*Little pitchers have big ears*."

✍ Completeness

go the distance — reach completion

USAGE: Richard suggested he was willing to *go the distance* in successfully completing the project.

go the whole hog — make a thorough job of something
USAGE: The employees *went the whole hog* in their efforts to make the new manager's family feel welcomed in their city.

✍ Consequence

long shot — a bet or other risk taken though not likely to succeed
USAGE: Steven realized that while it would be a *long shot* to win the award, he still wanted to complete the project and be considered.

lose ground — go backward; become weaker; not improve
USAGE: The company has been *losing ground* in their efforts to stay competitive in the marketplace with new products.

make one's bed and lie in it — be responsible for what one has done and then accept the consequence
USAGE: Fred told his son that because he had quit his job and now has no money, he *made his bed and now must lie in it*.

✍ Disagree

no go — refuse to agree; certainly not
USAGE: Jimmy suggested it was *no go* for him being able to undertake the project this year.

not for all the tea in China — absolutely not
USAGE: When the salesman repeatedly asked Kevin if he would like to buy the new computer system, he finally said, "No, *not for all the tea in China!*"

✍ Emotion

hit the roof — become very angry; go into a rage
USAGE: William *hit the roof* when he heard there would be budget cuts throughout the company.

hold a grudge — not forgive someone for something
USAGE: Because of past conflict, Bill has *held a grudge* against George for several years.

hold one's breath — stop breathing for a moment when one is excited or nervous

USAGE: At the awards ceremony, Susan nervously **held her breadth** as the winner was announced.

hold up — keep up one's courage or spirits
USAGE: Wendy's hopes for the future were **holding up** well despite her frustration of being unemployed.

holy cat — used to express strong feelings of astonishment, pleasure or anger
USAGE: When Bill saw the bank robber run across the street, he said, "*Holy cat*, let's call the police immediately."

✐ End

put off — postpone
USAGE: The meeting was **put off** because of an emergency that occurred with the manager's family.

✐ Failure

give up the ghost — stop working; die
USAGE: The 12 year old car malfunctioned and **gave up the ghost**. I now must buy another car.

give up the ship — don't stop fighting and hoping
USAGE: The coach talked for a long time to the players and urged them to play hard and not **give up the ship**.

✐ Health

on the wagon — not drinking alcohol
USAGE: Sober and feeling better than ever, Robert has been **on the wagon** for the last 6 months.

✐ Importance

matter — be important
USAGE: Harry remarked to the others that it doesn't **matter** if it rains because it will be held inside.

✐ Location

lose one's way — become lost
USAGE: The first time Henry traveled to Beijing, he **lost his way**.

lover's lane — a road where lovers walk or park in the evening
USAGE: The teenagers sometime go over to the local *lover's lane* on dates.

✍ Money

lay out — spend some money
USAGE: Bill will have to *lay out* a lot of money for his new downtown apartment.

layaway plan — a plan in which one pays some money down and then pays the rest little by little and the store holds the article until the full price has been paid
USAGE: Stanley decided to buy the set of furniture on the store's *layaway plan*.

✍ Movomont

keel over — turn upside down; tip over
USAGE: The boat *keeled over* in the middle of the river but those on board were rescued.

keep pace — go as fast; go at the same rate
USAGE: While it was hard to *keep pace* with the advanced students, David managed.

keep up — (1) keep something in the same good condition; (2) go on; maintain
USAGE (1): She spends a lot of effort *keeping up* the flower garden at her home.
USAGE (2): The manager is working hard to *keep up* the same production level as last month.

✍ Personal Description

good sport — person who loses well
USAGE: Harry is a *good sport* and doesn't complain if he loses a game.

green — be inexperienced or immature
USAGE: James has been out of college only one year so he is a little *green* and doesn't know how to do some things.

✍ Plan / Prepare

line up — arrange, make ready for action

USAGE: They were unable to *line up* a speaker for the ceremony so they had to change the event to another date.

look into — investigate something
USAGE: The police have been *looking into* the series of robberies for several weeks.

look to — attend to; take care of
USAGE: Betty is a very caring nurse and places a high priority *looking to* the needs of her patients.

✎ Quantity

more or less — somewhat; to some extent
USAGE: I like the new color *more or less* but it's not great.

✎ Relationship

in with — in friendship with
USAGE: We always believed the beginning of Roger's problem was that he got *in with* the wrong group of students while in high school.

✎ Satisfaction

kick in the pants — extremely fun and/or humorous
USAGE: We had a real *kick-in-the-pants* time at the reunion party.

kick up one's heels — have a good time, celebrate
USAGE: Kevin and Susan *kicked up their heels* at the New Year's party last night.

labor of love — something done for personal pleasure and not for money
USAGE: David always said his painting was a *labor of love* and a project he doesn't plan to sell.

✎ Service

hand-out — (1) sheet of paper given to students or people who attend a meeting; (2) a gift, usually from the government
USAGE (1): The professor distributed a *hand-out* that was an outline of the lecture.
USAGE (2): The government stopped giving welfare *hand-outs* to people unless they proved they were actively searching for a job.

✍ Similar

real McCoy — the genuine thing
USAGE: John told the others that the new computer was the ***real McCoy*** and will run the latest software.

✍ Superior

one-upmanship — ability to keep ahead of others; trying to keep an advantage
USAGE: Thomas was tired of Bill's ***one-upmanship*** and his constant desire to show he is better than others.

✍ Time

in the long run — the distant future; in the end
USAGE: While it was a tough time for John because of his current unemployment, he was optimistic about his circumstances ***in the long run***.

in time — early enough
USAGE: The teenagers didn't arrive at the theater ***in time*** to hear the concert.

in two shakes of a lamb's tail — quickly; in no time at all
USAGE: The host at the restaurant told customers they would have their food ***in two shakes of a lamb's tail***.

✍ Understand

look at the world through rose-colored glasses — see only the good things about something
USAGE: Joseph advised Mary not to be innocent and only ***look at the world through rose-colored glasses***.

look for — think likely; expect
USAGE: The faculty is ***looking for*** Bill to become a very fine research professor.

look on — be a spectator
USAGE: There were several thousand people who gathered to ***look on*** at the outdoor music festival.

look out — (1) be alert or watchful; keep looking for something; (2) take care; be careful; be on guard
USAGE (1): Angela asked the music store manager to ***look out*** for any early Rock and Roll records that she would like.

USAGE (2): Lawrence advised the group to ***look out*** for pick-pockets as they spend time in large crowds.

✍ Work

keep after — remind someone many times
USAGE: The teacher remarked she has to continually ***keep after*** Johnny to finish his in-class assignments.

✍ Achievement

knock oneself out — make a great effort
USAGE: The teenagers *knocked themselves out* trying to make the graduation party successful.

leave no stone unturned — try in every possible way
USAGE: The police detectives *left no stone unturned* when they were examining evidence from the crime scene.

let it rip — become involved and make the most of something; really try to win
USAGE: Prior to the game, the coach gave the athletes a motivational message and then he yelled, "*Let it rip*."

let loose — release something being held
USAGE: Because the injured bird had regained his strength, the boy *let the bird loose* in the park.

✍ Agree / Approval

right on — indicating approval, agreement, or acknowledgement
USAGE: Are you trying to become part of the Olympic soccer team? *Right on*!

✍ Authority

push (someone) around — make someone do what you want
USAGE: The manager *pushes around* his staff members too much and they resent his behavior.

✍ Bad / Negative

lay hands on someone — do violence to; harm; hurt
USAGE: The teenager angrily told the other boy that if he ever *lays hands on him* again he would call the police.

lay/light into — attack physically or do something with energy
USAGE: He *laid into* completing the project with enthusiasm and finished it
fast.

✍ Business Action

give someone the ax — fire an employee (usually abruptly)
USAGE: The manager *gave the employee the ax* because he was constantly
arriving late to work.

✍ Communication

(a) little thick — too much praise; too many nice statements
USAGE: While I thought the presentation was good, I felt his comments and
praise were a *little thick*.

look a gift horse in the mouth — complain if a gift is not perfect
USAGE: I told Richard he shouldn't complain about the gift and reminded him
that a person doesn't *look a gift horse in the mouth*.

look in on — go to see; make a short visit with; make a call on
USAGE: Robert asked his wife if she would *look in on* the baby and see if she
was sleeping well.

lose touch with — fail to keep in contact or communication with someone
USAGE: After graduation, I *lost touch with* most of my friends at the university.

lose track of — lose contact with someone
USAGE: I've *lost track of* most of my friends from high school.

✍ Completeness

go through with — finish, do as planned or agreed
USAGE: He decided to *go through with* his plans to go back to school.

✍ Consequence

make up for something — compensate for a loss or mistake
USAGE: I have to work hard in order to *make up for the loss* from the poor
sales.

make waves — create a disturbance
USAGE: Charles is very cooperative and doesn't like to *make waves*.

(a) new lease on life — a new expectation; better things to follow
USAGE: The encouraging report from the doctor gave James *a new lease on life*.

✍ Different

out-of-date — no longer current or in style
USAGE: Computers and other technology items become *out-of-date* very quickly.

✍ Disagree

nothing doing — certainly not
USAGE: When asked if he was going out to celebrate after work, Jim said, "*Nothing doing*, I'm tired and want to get home and rest."

out of favor with someone — not have a person's goodwill
USAGE: The group of employees has been *out of favor with* their supervisor for a few months.

✍ Emotion

holy cow — strong feelings of astonishment, pleasure or anger
USAGE: Amazed at the crowd, John said, "*Holy cow*! It's hard to believe there are this many people at the game."

holy mackerel — strong feelings of astonishment, pleasure or anger
USAGE: "*Holy mackerel*," said Henry when he received the cash award from the company president.

holy Moses — strong feelings of astonishment, pleasure or anger
USAGE: *Holy Moses*! It is almost noon and I haven't even started work on the project yet.

hope against hope — continue to hope when things look very bad
USAGE: Even though they had been working for 12 hours straight, the rescue team was *hoping against hope* the mine workers would be found alive.

hopping mad — very angry
USAGE: Rebecca was *hopping mad* when I told her that her car received a dent in the parking lot.

✍ End

put out — extinguish a flame or light
USAGE: The man *put out* his cigarette on the concrete walkway.

✍ Entertainment

paint the town red — go out and party
USAGE: Celebrating their graduation from the university, the students went
   out and *painted the town red*.

✍ Error

make a mistake — make an error
USAGE: Accidentally answering the wrong question, he *made a mistake* on
   the history test.

✍ Failure

give way — collapse; fail
USAGE: The wall *gave way* and the side of the building collapsed to the
   ground.

go back on — not be faithful to
USAGE: Jack pledged to the group he wouldn't *go back on* his word about the
   vacation trip.

✍ Health

out cold — unconscious; in a faint
USAGE: After being hit hard by the door handle, Steven was *out cold*.

✍ Importance

mean business — be very serious; ready to take action
USAGE: She *means business* when insisting she will work to change the
   attitude among the employees at work.

✍ Money

little steep — too expensive
USAGE: Elizabeth believed the price to pay for the new car was a *little steep*.

live from hand to mouth — live on little money

USAGE: Mary's brother is an aspiring writer and has to *live from hand to mouth* because he doesn't have much money.

loaded — has much money
USAGE: His father is really *loaded*.

✍ Movement

keep up with — go at the same speed as a person or thing
USAGE: Steven remarked he couldn't *keep up with* the other students.

kick off — begin; launch; start
USAGE: The soccer team *kicked off* their new season last Saturday morning.

✍ Ownership

off one's hands — no longer in one's care or possession
USAGE: Jason was delighted he finally sold his old car and got it *off his hands*.

✍ Personal Description

green thumb — skill in making plants grow
USAGE: Janet has a real *green thumb* and terrific looking garden.

had a bellyful — had too much
USAGE: Mary *had a bellyful* of complaints from the teenagers and told them to focus instead on their jobs.

hang one on — get very drunk
USAGE: Zach really *hung one on* last night after he heard about his admission to the MBA program.

✍ Plan / Prepare

make up — put on cosmetics
USAGE: Cindy always takes a long time to *make up* her face before she leaves for work.

matter of course — the usual way, habit, rule
USAGE: John approved the request as a *matter of course* and it really wasn't anything special.

might as well — be somewhat preferable
USAGE: Peter told the others they *might as well* leave because no one else would be coming.

✍ Quantity

more the merrier — the more people who join in the better it will be
USAGE: When more people started to arrive at the party, he remarked, "The *more the merrier*."

✍ Relationship

item — a couple in a romantic relationship
USAGE: Didn't you know that Roger and Carol are considered an *item* now?

lay off — stop bothering; leave alone
USAGE: The players were told by the coach to *lay off* teasing the new player so he could relax before the game.

✍ Satisfaction

lady killer — a man who some women find charming
USAGE: Charles is considered a *lady killer* because many girls are attracted to him.

lap up — take in eagerly
USAGE: She *lapped up* the praise her supervisor gave her for the outstanding job done.

leave/let well enough alone — be satisfied with something that is good enough
USAGE: Jack should *let well enough alone* and be satisfied with the existing standards.

✍ Time

jump the gun — start before you should
USAGE: Stanley *jumped the gun* and opened his store before the usual starting time.

just now — this very moment; a minute ago
USAGE: The earthquake was reported *just now* and the emergency officials are responding.

keep at — persist with

USAGE: As a new university student, James made the commitment to *keep at* his studies so he'll earn strong grades.

keep good time — work accurately (a clock)

USAGE: Stanley remarked his wristwatch has not been *keeping good time* recently.

✍ Understand

look over something — inspect; examine

USAGE: Each member of our group was advised to *look over the forms* before we signed them.

lose sight of — forget, fail to see

USAGE: The parents reminded Karen not to *lose sight of* the reason she worked so hard in college.

lowdown — the facts of a matter

USAGE: The managers met with the employees and gave the *lowdown* on the production requirements that would be required for the company.

✍ Achievement

let up — do less or stop working too hard
USAGE: John realized he needed to *let up* on his work schedule so he could manage his stress level.

lock up — to be assured of success
USAGE: Rebecca was informed she had *locked up* the promotion to the new job.

make a dent in — make progress
USAGE: Although the employees worked hard, they weren't able to *make a dent in* the most difficult part of the project.

make a go — succeed; to produce good results
USAGE: Roger was highly frustrated because he couldn't succeed in *making a go* in his new business.

✍ Agree / Approval

see eye to eye — agree, comply or conform
USAGE: Robert and Scott usually don't *see eye to eye* on issues, but they are able to cooperate on completing projects.

see off — go with someone to a point of departure
USAGE: Her parents went to the airport to *see Julie off* on the trip.

✍ Authority

put the screws to someone — try to force someone to do or say what you want
USAGE: Under intense questioning, the police detectives were *putting the screws to the criminal suspects*.

✍ Bad / Negative

lead a dog's life — live a hard life; work hard and be treated unkindly

USAGE: Henry said he's been *leading a dog's life* since he moved to the large city from a small town.

lead on — insincerely encourage
USAGE: It seemed like the salesman was *leading me on* when he described the features of the product.

leave a bad taste in one's mouth — leave a bad impression; make one feel disgusted
USAGE: Because of the argument that broke out at the party, everyone in our group *had a bad taste in their mouth*.

✍ Business Action

grandfather clause — exemption for a rule based on past circumstances
USAGE: Due to a *grandfather clause*, Joseph will be exempted from the rule requiring he has a university degree to become certified.

✍ Communication

loudmouth — a noisy, indiscreet, boastful or foolish talker
USAGE: Jacob has a reputation of being a *loudmouth* because he frequently talks indiscreetly about things.

make a point of — do or say something with a definite intent
USAGE: He *makes a point of* introducing himself to new people he meets.

make fun of — ridicule; mock; laugh at
USAGE: The girls were *making fun of* the boys having a ponytail hair style.

make no bones about something — make no secret of something; openly disclose
USAGE: Jack *made no bones about* how he wanted to someday become president of the company.

make one's hair stand on end — frighten; horrify; terrifying
USAGE: The film was so horrifying to the teenagers that it *made their hair stand on end*.

man to man — frank or direct
USAGE: Peter had a *man-to-man* talk with Stanley about dealing with the problem.

✍ Completeness

head over heels — completely; deeply
USAGE: Susan fell *head over heels* in love with the young man she met on the subway.

honeymoon is over — the first happy period of friendship and cooperation between two groups is over
USAGE: Facing the realities of the budget, the *honeymoon was over* for the general manager of the company.

✍ Consequence

no strings attached — having no conditions or restrictions attached
USAGE: Michael wanted to borrow the money with *no strings attached*.

not a leg to stand on — no good evidence or defense to offer someone
USAGE: Robert realized he *didn't have a leg to stand on* in his attempt to avoid paying taxes.

not lay a finger on someone — not touch someone; not bother to do something (not even a little)
USAGE: During the court session, the judge told the teenager *never to lay a finger on another person*.

off the hook — out of trouble or free from a difficult situation
USAGE: While Thomas was *off the hook* for now, he recognized that budget problems would occur again and he would need to be prepared.

✍ Different

outside of — other than; except for
USAGE: *Outside of* the boring speech during the first session, the conference was very worthwhile.

✍ Disagree

out of tune — not in agreement; not going well together
USAGE: The new faculty member was *out of tune* with the other professors in the department. Other professors believed his research was neither valid nor relevant.

pick a quarrel — start a quarrel with someone on purpose

USAGE: Jack was disliked by the other students because he was always trying to *pick a quarrel*.

✍ Emotion

hot and bothered — agitated and worried, displeased
USAGE: Susan was ***hot and bothered*** about her dispute with co-workers at the office.

hue and cry — an excited public protest or alarm
USAGE: A large crowd gathered to raise a ***hue and cry*** about prisoners being released from confinement before their sentences had been fully served.

hyped-up — have an excess of energy; be excited
USAGE: Martha has been ***hyped up*** all morning because she is giving a presentation to club members this afternoon.

ill at ease — feel nervous; uncomfortable
USAGE: William seems to be ***ill at ease*** when meeting with managers at work.

in cold blood — without feeling or pity, cool and deliberately
USAGE: The police determined the man was murdered ***in cold blood*** by the criminal gang.

✍ End

rub off — remove or be removed by rubbing; erased
USAGE: After continued use, she ***rubbed off*** the serial number on her laptop computer.

✍ Error

on tenterhooks — in suspense or strain because of uncertainty
USAGE: Members of the committee have been ***on tenterhooks*** awaiting the outcome of the decision.

✍ Failure

go from bad to worse — get worse; deteriorate
USAGE: Because of financial difficulties, conditions have ***gone from bad to worse*** at the company.

go haywire — become damaged; stop working properly

USAGE: While the operations at the office were initially going smooth, conditions recently have *gone haywire*.

✍ Health

out like a light — fall asleep very quickly
USAGE: Since he was very tired from the trip, Scott was *out like a light* when he went to sleep last night.

✍ Importance

measure up — be equal; be of high quality
USAGE: The coach was concerned that, in his estimation, the talent of this year's team didn't *measure up* to last year's squad.

✍ Location

make oneself scarce — leave quickly; go away
USAGE: I will *make myself scarce* and go to the beach for the day.

make the scene — be present; go to a certain place or event
USAGE: He decided to *make the scene* and go to the disco for the evening.

✍ Money

lose one's shirt — lose a lot of money
USAGE: Jack *lost his shirt* on a bad investment.

make a bundle — make a lot of money
USAGE: He *made a bundle* through a well planned investment.

make a killing — make a large amount of money
USAGE: Jeffrey *made a killing* on the development of a new software program.

✍ Movement

kick over — a motor begins to work
USAGE: At first the car engine wouldn't start, but after several tries, it *kicked over*.

knock about — travel without a plan; go where one pleases
USAGE: Jack and Ted decided to go to Europe and *knocked about* for three weeks.

✍ Ownership

on hand — available
USAGE: John advised Frank he didn't have any medicine *on hand*.

✍ Personal Description

hard nut to crack — a person who is difficult to deal with
USAGE: Benjamin is a *hard nut to crack* and can be challenging.

hard on (someone/something) — treat something/someone roughly
USAGE: Sometimes knocking it around, Charles can be very *hard on* his laptop computer.

hard-nosed — stubborn in a fight, contest or negotiations
USAGE: Eric has a *hard-nosed* attitude about employees who are not productive on the job.

✍ Plan / Prepare

mind one's P's and Q's — be very careful about what one does or says; socially correct behavior
USAGE: Scott was told to *mind his P's and Q's* and not say anything to offend his manager.

name of the game — the main part of a matter
USAGE: The *name of the game* is for the salesmen to succeed in reaching his sales goals.

off balance — unable to meet the unexpected
USAGE: Jack was caught *off balance* when asked to give a speech at the meeting.

✍ Quantity

out of — have none left
USAGE: The store was *out of* cleaning supplies in its inventory.

✍ Relationship

let alone — certainly not
USAGE: Henry said he didn't have enough money to take an overnight trip *let alone* go on a foreign trip to France.

✍ Satisfaction

life of Riley — a soft easy life; pleasant way of living
USAGE: Enjoying retirement, John has been living the *life of Riley* with many comforts and pleasures.

live high on the hog — live very luxuriously or comfortably
USAGE: Peter has been *living high on the hog* since he began a high paying job last year.

living end — great; fantastic; the ultimate
USAGE: She said last night's concert performance was the *living end*.

look after someone — take care or attend to someone
USAGE: Robert has been *looking after his father* since his heart surgery in September.

✍ Service

have my ears lowered — to have a haircut
USAGE: He said his hair was getting long and that he needed to *have his ears lowered*.

have one on me — to pay the bill for someone
USAGE: Celebrating the completion of the project, John told Bill, "*Have this drink on me!*"

✍ Time

keep on (doing something) — continue
USAGE: While Joe says he wants to stop smoking, he *keeps on* smoking cigarettes at the same rate.

keep time — keep the beat; keep the same rhythm
USAGE: It is a real challenge for Roger to *keep time* with the other members of the band.

keeps good time — show the right time
USAGE: Even though my watch is old, it *keeps good time*.

✍ Understand

luck out — suddenly get lucky when it looks like you won't succeed
USAGE: Vickie *lucked out* in her efforts to get the concert tickets.

make believe — act as if something is true while one knows that it is not; pretend
USAGE: The young children were playing *make believe* and pretending they were parents.

make of something — interpret; think of
USAGE: Stanley asked her, "What do you *make of the new rules* that have been adopted?"

make one's mouth water — want to eat something because of the thought of food
USAGE: Thinking about the delicious food at the restaurant *made his mouth water*.

✎ Work

keep one's nose to the grindstone — work very hard
USAGE: Working hard each day at work, John has been *keeping his nose to the grindstone*.

✍ Achievement

make a hit — considered very successful
USAGE: The cake Susan baked really *made a hit* at the party.

make a name for oneself — become well known or famous
USAGE: Roger has *made a name for himself* in the field of educational technology.

make for — go toward; start in the direction of
USAGE: With the weather forecast predicting a storm, we decided to *make for* a safe and dry place.

make good — do what was promised
USAGE: The manager *made good* on his pledge to increase the number of paid holidays for the employees.

✍ Agree / Approval

side with — support a position in a dispute
USAGE: Wanting to be a supportive husband, John *sided with* his wife on the issue concerning their son.

sit right — to be acceptable
USAGE: The idea to relocate the company headquarters to a different city didn't *sit right* with the employees.

✍ Authority

put the smack down — to regulate, maybe by force
USAGE: The party started to get out of hand, so the police were called to *put the smack down*.

rule the roost — be the dominant one in the family
USAGE: While Jacks says he is the head of the household, everyone knows his wife, Lisa, *rules the roost* in their family.

✍ Bad / Negative

loose ends — without something definite to do
USAGE: Frustrated and with nothing to do, James has been at *loose ends* since
  he lost his job.

make a mountain out of a molehill — make a big problem out of a small one
USAGE: Peter is *making a mountain out of a molehill* by worrying about
  issues relating to his son's admission to the university.

✍ Business Action

hard sell — trying to sell something very aggressively
USAGE: Bill received the *hard sell* approach from the car salesman, so he
  went to another dealership to look for a car.

✍ Communication

mum's the word — do not reveal the secret
USAGE: Susan told him, "Don't worry, *mum's the word* on the surprise party.
  I won't tell anyone."

mumbo jumbo — speech one doesn't understand
USAGE: Louis was frustrated because he couldn't understand any of the
  mumbo jumbo by the scientist.

off one's back — stop from bothering someone
USAGE: Tom said he hoped his boss would get *off his back* so he could get his
  work done.

off one's chest — talk about a problem to someone
USAGE: Frank was relieved by being able to talk to his friend and get some of
  his problems *off his chest*.

on the air — broadcasting or being broadcast on radio or TV
USAGE: The popular radio program has been *on the air* for about five years.

✍ Completeness

hook, line and sinker — without question or doubt, completely
USAGE: Mary had fallen in love with her new boyfriend *hook, line and
  sinker*.

in a way — to a certain extent; a little

USAGE: Joseph suggested that, *in a way*, he wanted to attend the lecture.

inside and out — in every part, completely
USAGE: In searching for the lost keys, they looked *inside and out*.

✍ Consequence

on one's coat-tails — along with someone else, as a result of someone else doing something
USAGE: Benefiting from his famous family, Tim achieved success in the music business *on the coat-tails* of his father.

on one's shoulders — one's responsibility
USAGE: James believed the success of the marriage rested *on his shoulders*.

out of kilter — not balanced right; not in a straight line or lined up right
USAGE: The newly constructed window frame seems to be *out of kilter* and doesn't work well.

✍ Disagree

pocket of resistance — a small group of people resisting
USAGE: The community leaders ran into a *pocket of resistance* when they encountered the group of concerned mothers.

put a damper on — discourage, spoil a person's fun
USAGE: The death of Larry's father last week *put a real damper on* the graduation celebration.

✍ Emotion

in love — liking very much; loving
USAGE: Roger has been *in love* with his girlfriend since he met her in their first year of college.

in seventh heaven — very happy
USAGE: She told her friends she's been *in seventh heaven* since she met her new boyfriend.

in stitches — laughing
USAGE: The men were *in stitches* over the jokes told by Lawrence.

jump at — take or accept quickly and gladly

USAGE: John *jumped at* the chance to be reassigned to the London office.

jump out of one's skin — be badly frightened
USAGE: Carol said she nearly *jumped out of her skin* when she saw the dead animal.

✍ End

rub out — destroy completely; kill; eliminate
USAGE: The troops *rubbed out* the soldiers hiding in the enemy village.

✍ Entertainment

play by ear — play a musical instrument by remembering the tune and not by reading the music
USAGE: Although Barbara can't read music, she can *play by ear* and is a terrific guitar player.

✍ Error

out of order — against the rules; not suitable
USAGE: During the trial, the judge ruled the lawyer's question was *out of order* and was to be taken out of the written record.

✍ Failure

go nowhere fast — unable to advance
USAGE: The professor emphasized that without good study habits, the students would be *going nowhere fast*.

go to pot — deteriorate
USAGE: Many people believe the company has *gone to pot* since he became the chief manager.

✍ Health

out of breath — to be tired and breathing quickly
USAGE: Having just completed a 10K race, James was *out of breath*.

✍ Importance

my goodness / my God — used to express surprise or shock
USAGE: "*My goodness*," Betsy said when she observed a wireless connection to the Internet for the first time.

✍ Location

make way — stand or move aside, so someone can go through
USAGE: All the cars have to move to the side of the road to *make way* for the emergency vehicles.

neck of the woods — an area or part of the country
USAGE: Joe is coming to my *neck of the woods* to see what our town is like.

needle in a haystack — something that is very hard to find
USAGE: Trying to locate her lost contact eye lens is like looking for a *needle in a haystack*.

✍ Money

make a living — earn enough money to live
USAGE: Tim recognized he needed a higher paying job in order to *make a living* in the city.

make ends meet — be able to live on the money one has
USAGE: Bob and Mary realized it's hard to *make ends meet* on his salary alone.

money to burn — to have more money than is needed
USAGE: Some people said Steven is so wealthy that he's got *money to burn* and never has to worry about working.

✍ Movement

knock off one's feet — surprise or shock someone so much that he does not know what to do
USAGE: Robert was *knocked to his feet* when he found out he was awarded the full scholarship.

lead a merry chase — delay or escape capture by someone; make a person work hard
USAGE: Ted *led the police on a merry chase* before they finally caught and jailed him.

let out — (1) make clothes longer or looser; (2) allow to go out or escape; (3) dismiss or be dismissed (from class or practice etc.)
USAGE (1): Because he had gained weight, Joseph had to go to the tailors to have them *let out* his jacket.
USAGE (2): He *let out* the dog this morning and he hasn't come home yet.

USAGE (3): The students were *let out* to attend the inauguration of the new governor.

✍ Personal Description

has the makings — has the potential
USAGE: The captain states John *has the makings* of a good soldier.

hat in hand — to ask in a humble manner
USAGE: After the company went bankrupt under his leadership, Charles came *hat-in-hand* to the bank for a loan.

hatchet man — a person whose job is to say negative things about the opposition; also a person in a company who must fire extra workers or cut other expenses
USAGE: He is acting as a *hatchet man* for the boss but I don't think he really believes what he is saying.

✍ Plan / Prepare

off guard — not alert to the unexpected
USAGE: It caught me *off guard* when she suddenly asked for $800.

off the cuff — without preparing ahead of time what one will say
USAGE: While Jack made some remarks *off the cuff*, he's never really explained in detail his plan.

off the top of one's head — from memory, spontaneously
USAGE: Betty knew many of the statistics relating to the project *off the top of her head*.

✍ Quantity

pour out — come out in great number or quantity; stream out
USAGE: After the championship game, tens of thousands of fans *poured out* of the stadium into the street.

quite a few — many
USAGE: As an avid book collector, John has *quite a few* books at home.

✍ Relationship

like father, like son — a son usually acts like his father

USAGE: When he saw his son playing soccer at the stadium, Jacob said, "*Like father, like son!*"

make a pass at someone — make romantic advances to a member of the opposite sex
USAGE: The staff member was fired because he *made an unwanted pass at a female co-worker* in the office.

✍ Satisfaction

look forward to something — anticipate with pleasure
USAGE: He's been *looking forward to the concert* for a long time.

look up to — think of someone as a good example to copy
USAGE: Tony said he *looked up to* his manager as a guiding force in his career and he hated to see him retire.

(a) lucky break — good luck
USAGE: Susan admitted the opportunity presented itself as a *lucky break*.

✍ Service

have/got to — obliged or forced to; must
USAGE: Richard remarked, he *has to* leave at 3:00 PM to attend a meeting.

✍ Similar

run of the mill — ordinary; usual
USAGE: While the restaurant was located in a *run-of-the-mill* building in the old part of town, it served excellent food.

✍ Superior

royally — very; extremely
USAGE: Kevin told him, "He was *royally* upset when you wrecked his car."

✍ Time

lead off — begin; start; open
USAGE: Charles was the first golfer to *lead off* in the tournament.

long haul — a long period of time during which work continues or something is done

USAGE: Fortunately for the company, William has decided to stay here for the *long haul* and not return to his home province for the foreseeable future.

make a beeline for — hurry directly somewhere
USAGE: When Jonathan visits the restaurant, he always *makes a beeline for* the dessert section.

✍ Understand

make out — (1) distinguish; identify; (2) make someone believe, show, prove; (3) understand; interpret
USAGE (1): Many drivers couldn't *make out* the other cars on the highway because of the fog.
USAGE (2): He *made out* that he was at the library last night but I know he wasn't.
USAGE (3): I can't *make out* what Jack is trying to say when he phones me.

make sense — seem reasonable
USAGE: The manager's report about the project *makes no sense*.

make something out — manage to see or read something
USAGE: I was unable to *make out the map* because the paper was faded and unclear to read.

✍ Work

keep someone on — allow someone to continue working
USAGE: Although many other employees are being laid off at the company, the managers have decided Bill will be *kept on* so the warehouse may remain open.

✍ Achievement

make hay while the sun shines — do something at the right time; not wait too long
USAGE: He felt he needed to *make hay while the sun shines* and start the new business while the interest remained strong.

make it up to someone — do something for someone to compensate for an unfulfilled promise
USAGE: John told his son he couldn't take him to the game today but he would *make it up to him later*.

make one's own way — rely on one's own abilities
USAGE: Graduating with his MBA, Steve was looking forward to *making his own way* in the world rather than depending on his wealthy father.

make short work of something — finish quickly
USAGE: Michael was in a hurry so he *made short work of* finishing the project.

✍ Agree / Approval

sit well — please or find favor with someone
USAGE: Tony's decision to leave early didn't *sit well* with the other employees.

stand by — follow or keep (one's promise); be loyal to or support
USAGE: She always *stands by* her husband when he has a problem.

✍ Authority

run (someone) in — take to jail; arrest
USAGE: The police detectives *ran the two suspects in* for questioning about the robbery.

✍ Bad / Negative

mess around — play around; engage in idle activity

USAGE: The young children were ***messing around*** in the playground before
the television show started.

mess up — cause trouble; spoil something; make a mistake
USAGE: She ***messed up*** her chance to get a promotion by repeated absenteeism
on the job.

✍ Business Action

horse trade — business agreement arrived at after hard negotiations
USAGE: In order to reach a deal, Jim and Fred had to do a lot of ***horse trading***.

✍ Communication

on the Q.T.— secretly; without anyone knowing
USAGE: To keep his plans from becoming public, Scott kept them ***on the Q.T***.

on the tip of one's tongue — not quite able to remember something
USAGE: Trying to recall the name, Charles said it was ***on the tip of his tongue***.

open one's heart — talk about one's feelings honestly; confide in someone
USAGE: Knowing her friend was emotionally upset, Susan ***opened her heart***
to demonstrate her compassion.

out of one's shell — out of one's silence or shyness, into friendly conversation
USAGE: We got her ***out of her shell*** and she decided to join in with the rest of
the group.

over and over — repeated many times
USAGE: I told him ***over and over*** I do not want to go to that restaurant again.

✍ Completeness

into thin air — completely; without anything left
USAGE: The group of hikers vanished ***into thin air*** and was never heard of again.

just about — nearly; almost
USAGE: I waited ***just about*** one hour before the concert started.

✍ Consequence

out of the frying pan and into the fire — out of one trouble and into more
trouble; from something bad to something worse

USAGE: When he changed jobs he went *out of the frying pan and into the fire*. His new job is much worse.

out on a limb — in a dangerous or risky position
USAGE: He really went *out on a limb* to offer his brother the job.

over a barrel — in a helpless or trapped position
USAGE: I think we have them *over a barrel* and should be able to win the contract easily.

✍ Different

set off — decorate through contrast; balance by difference
USAGE: He painted the trim of his house red in order to *set off* the light colors.

✍ Disagree

put down — criticize; make someone look bad
USAGE: He is always *putting down* his girlfriend in front of his friends.

put off — discourage; cause a bad feeling
USAGE: He *put me off* with his complaints about the hotel room I had reserved for him.

✍ Emotion

keel over — fall over and faint
USAGE: Three of the members of the band suddenly *keeled over* because of the heat.

keep a stiff upper lip — be brave; face adversity bravely
USAGE: The firemen work hard in *keeping a stiff upper lip* about their work even though they have an extremely challenging job.

keep one's chin up — be brave; be determined
USAGE: The counselor advised John to try and *keep his chin up* because things would be improving.

keep one's head — stay calm when there is trouble or danger
USAGE: Vincent is a solid leader and does a good job in *keeping his head* during an emergency.

keep one's shirt on — calm down; keep from losing one's temper or getting impatient

USAGE: Brian urged Jim to *keep his shirt on* because there is a solution in sight.

keyed up — excited; nervous
USAGE: Because I was *keyed up* after the exciting game, I had a hard time getting to sleep.

✍ End

run down — crash against and knock down
USAGE: Tragically, my dog was *run down* by a car last week in front of the house.

✍ Entertainment

rain check — a free ticket to an event in place of one cancelled because of rain
USAGE: Because the baseball game was cancelled due to the rain, Roger and I received two *rain checks* to another game.

✍ Error

out of place — in the wrong place or at the wrong time; improper
USAGE: Joe recognized what he said at the meeting was totally *out of place*.

✍ Failure

go up in smoke/flames — burn or be destroyed by fire; fail; not come true (dreams)
USAGE: His hopes to start his own business have *gone up in smoke* because of health problems.

goose is cooked — failed opportunity
USAGE: The players knew if they didn't win this game, their *goose is cooked*.

✍ Health

over the hill — past one's prime; unable to function as one used to
USAGE: Kevin realized he was *over the hill* and shouldn't push himself so hard.

✍ Location

off the beaten track — not well known or often used; unusual

USAGE: Mark and Carol enjoyed a delicious dinner last night at a small restaurant *off the beaten track*.

on a dime — in a very small space
USAGE: Jack's new car has superb handling and can stop *on a dime*.

✏ Money

nest egg — money someone has saved up
USAGE: He has been saving his money a little at a time and has built up quite a *nest egg*.

on a shoestring — with very little money
USAGE: While the company is very large and successful, it was started *on a shoestring*.

✏ Movement

let up — become less or weaker; become slower or stop
USAGE: The stormy weather finally *let up* and the sun came out to shine.

like crazy — very fast, with great energy
USAGE: During the school's recess period, the children were outside running around *like crazy*.

like mad — very fast, with great energy
USAGE: John worked *like mad* to finish the project by the end of the day.

✏ Ownership

on/upon one's head — on one's self
USAGE: Larry brought the difficulty *on his own head* and shouldn't try and blame someone else.

✏ Personal Description

have a head on one's shoulders — be smart or sensible
USAGE: The new manager *has a solid head on his shoulders* and is a very effective leader.

have a screw loose — (1) act in a strange, unconventional way; be foolish; (2) eccentric behavior
USAGE (1): I think he may *have a screw loose* because he can be very peculiar.

USAGE (2): I believe Susan **has a screw loose** because she reports hearing voices at night.

✍ Plan / Prepare

on ice — away for safekeeping or later use; aside
USAGE: The company president decided to put the plans for expansion **on ice** due to budget problems.

on purpose — intentionally
USAGE: It was obvious that Robert dropped the glass container **on purpose**.

on the safe side — take precaution to reduce risk
USAGE: Just to be **on the safe side**, John decided to conduct the meeting inside in case it rained outside.

part and parcel — a necessary or important element
USAGE: Traveling and being on the road is **part and parcel** of Bill's job.

✍ Quantity

rough guess — an approximate estimate
USAGE: Needing an approximate count for the gathering, John made a **rough guess** on the number of people attending.

✍ Relationship

make eyes at — flirt, look at a member of the opposite sex to try and attract them
USAGE: Highly attracted to her, George was **making eyes at** the lady.

make friends — form friendships with people
USAGE: Martha has a wonderful personality and is able to **make friends** easily.

✍ Satisfaction

lucky star — a certain star or planet which is thought to bring a person good luck and success in life
USAGE: You should thank your **lucky star** that you have a wonderful family and job!

make oneself at home — act as if you were at home

USAGE: Kathy was told to *make herself at home* when she was at Mary's house over the weekend.

make out — do; progress
USAGE: Peter asked John how he *made out* on the examination last week.

✍ Service

heaven help us — facing a problem; needing help
USAGE: Perry told his colleague, "*Heaven help us* to overcome the challenge we're facing."

✍ Similar

run off — produce with a printing press or copy machine
USAGE: The students *ran off* one thousand copies of the advertisement for distribution.

✍ Superior

run away with — be much better than others; win easily
USAGE: The school soccer team *ran away with* the city-wide championship.

✍ Time

make a day of it — do something all day
USAGE: Robert decided to *make a day of it* at the art museum.

make time — be successful in arriving at a destination in a short time
USAGE: Driving back from the beach we *made good time* and arrived home before evening.

mark time — move one's feet up and down to music
USAGE: With his headphones and portable music player, Peter was *marking time* to the beat as he rode the subway train.

✍ Understand

make something up — invent, think and say something that is new or not true
USAGE: It was determined that Scott *made up the story* about the robber breaking into the house.

make up one's mind — decide

USAGE: Tom said he hasn't ***made up his mind*** yet about whether to accept the new job.

matter of fact — (1) telling something as an actual fact; (2) something that is really true; something that can be proved
USAGE (1): In a very ***matter-of-fact*** way, Joseph described the circumstances of the crime.
USAGE (2): As a ***matter of fact***, I know he is in town and will be attending the game.

✍ Work

keep tabs on — watch or check; keep under observation
USAGE: Roger's parents have been ***keeping tabs on*** his spending patterns since he's been at college.

✍ Achievement

make the best of — do as well as possible in a bad situation
USAGE: Sharon has really *made the best of* her time since beginning her university studies.

make the grade — make good; succeed; meet a standard; qualify
USAGE: She wasn't able to *make the grade* and earn a satisfactory score on the college admission examination.

make the most of — use to the greatest advantage
USAGE: He *made the most of* his time during his tour of the United States and visited several different cities.

✍ Agree / Approval

stand for — (1) allow to happen or be done; permit; (2) speak in favor of something or show that one supports it
USAGE (1): The professor will not *stand for* students submitting late assignments.
USAGE (2): The new manager gave a speech in which he told the employees he *stands for* increased salaries for all staff members.

✍ Authority

send someone packing — tell someone to leave; dismiss someone
USAGE: The new worker was *sent packing* because of his poor attitude and performance on the job.

send up — sentence someone to prison
USAGE: The convicted thief was *sent up* for ten years for armed robbery of a bank.

✍ Bad / Negative

monkey business — unethical, illegal or objectionable activity; cheating

USAGE: James was suspected of being involved in some *monkey business* with a questionable business enterprise.

nappy — gross; disgusting
USAGE: The other boys said Bill's hair is really *nappy*.

✍ Business Action

house of cards — a weak plan that is in danger of collapse
USAGE: The negotiated agreement between the two companies was like a *house of cards* and did not last because subsequent problems that developed.

✍ Communication

(a) pat answer — a planned or memorized answer
USAGE: He did not give a solid, complete response to the question, only a *pat answer*.

pat on the back — a message or gesture of praise or approval
USAGE: The senior manager gave me a *pat on the back* upon submitting the final details on the budget.

pay attention — look at or listen to with focus and attention
USAGE: Roger sometimes doesn't *pay attention* to what his wife tells him.

pep talk — a speech to encourage people to try harder and not give up
USAGE: Before the championship finals, the coach gave his players a *pep talk* to motivate them for the game.

pick on — do or say bad things to someone
USAGE: The older brother seems to always be *picking on* his little sister.

✍ Completeness

lick and a promise — a quick plan of limited action
USAGE: While Michael said he had cleaned his room, actually he just did a *lick and a promise* at straightening up.

made up — make something by putting things or parts together
USAGE: The professor told the students a successful paper is *made up* of four separate sections.

✍ Consequence

paint oneself into a corner — get oneself into a bad situation that is difficult or impossible to get out of
USAGE: When Benjamin argued with his supervisor about the project, he *painted himself into a corner*.

par for the course — just what was expected; nothing unusual; typical
USAGE: That was *par for the course* for Jack. He always did things that created problems for himself.

play on/upon (something) — cause an effect on; influence
USAGE: They *played on* his feelings of superiority to get him to undertake the project for them.

✍ Different

shoe is on the other foot — opposite is true; places are changed
USAGE: The *shoe is on the other foot* now that the professor himself is taking a government examination for certification.

✍ Disagree

put one's foot down — object strongly; take firm action
USAGE: The teacher *put his foot down* and didn't allow late assignments to be submitted after 5:00 PM.

put someone in his/her place — scold someone for rude or bad behavior
USAGE: After he insulted her, she *put him in his place* over the rude remark.

✍ Emotion

lash out — attack someone physically, verbally or in writing
USAGE: In a bizarre incident, the man on the bus abruptly *lashed out* and hit the passenger sitting beside him.

let down one's hair — relax, act freely and naturally
USAGE: At the graduation party, all the students *let down their hair* and had a good time.

let off steam — get rid of extra energy or strong feelings by doing some activity
USAGE: Phillip was furious when he got the bad news, but he went to the fitness center and *let off a lot of steam*.

light up — suddenly look pleased and happy
USAGE: When I mentioned Kevin's name, Susan's face *lit up* and she started smiling.

like hell — with much effort and energy, not so, untrue
USAGE: He had to work *like hell* this morning to catch-up.

✍ End

shut off — make something like water or electricity stop
USAGE: He always *shuts off* the electricity when he is performing routine maintenance of appliances around the house.

✍ Entertainment

roll out the red carpet — make a big effort to greet and entertain someone
USAGE: When our nephew visited during the holiday, we *rolled out the red carpet*.

✍ Error

out of the question — impossible
USAGE: Steven told his son, "Since you're out of a job and have no money, traveling to the South is *out of the question*."

✍ Failure

gum up — cause not to work; ruin something; make something go wrong
USAGE: The fax machine became *gummed up* just as he was starting to send a fax message.

in a pig's eye — not under any condition
USAGE: Knowing his history, Jim quickly said, "*In a pig's eye* would I ever let him borrow my car."

✍ Health

pass away — to die
USAGE: Vickie's father *passed away* when he was 88 years old.

pass on — to die
USAGE: John's grandmother *passed on* when she was 77 years old.

✍ Importance

never mind — don't worry; don't bother
USAGE: When the repair technician told Roger he wouldn't be able to work on his computer for a few days, he said ***never mind*** because he decided to upgrade to a new computer.

✍ Location

on board — on a ship, plane or similar form of transportation
USAGE: The students were waiting at the airport to get ***on board*** the airplane.

on hand — nearby; within reach
USAGE: The tourists were advised they should always keep their passports ***on hand*** in case it is needed.

✍ Money

on credit — pay for something not in cash
USAGE: Stanley was able to afford the television set through buying it ***on credit***.

on easy street — having enough money to live comfortably
USAGE: Since Paul earned a significant amount of money through his investment, he's ***on easy street***.

✍ Movement

line up — adjust correctly
USAGE: The teacher ***lined up*** the children to participate in the spelling contest.

little by little — gradually
USAGE: Steven hasn't been able to exercise for a couple of weeks because of a knee injury, but ***little by little*** it is getting better.

look (someone) up — seek and find
USAGE: When I was in Shanghai last summer, I ***looked up*** my friend from the university.

✍ Ownership

own up — take the blame; admit one's guilt
USAGE: The suspect finally ***owned up*** to the crime in his confession.

✍ Personal Description

have a way with — be able to lead, persuade or influence others
USAGE: Mark really *has a way with* women because they seem to be attracted
to him.

have an eye for — have good taste in something; be able to judge correctly
USAGE: Betsy *has an eye for* fine art and her job at the museum depends on
her expertise.

have (something) going for one — have ability, talent or good looks
USAGE: Chuck *has a lot going for him* and his future looks very hopeful.

have one's feet on the ground — be practical or sensible
USAGE: John is a very sensible person and *has his feet on the ground*.

✍ Plan / Prepare

pick out — choose or select
USAGE: Bill went to the store to *pick out* a birthday gift for his father.

pick up — make neat and tidy
USAGE: Mary *picked up* in the room before her best friend came to visit.

pipe dream — an unrealistic plan
USAGE: While Scott is a capable person, he has *pipe dreams* about getting
rich.

✍ Quantity

round up — bring together; collect
USAGE: He *rounded up* enough of his friends who wanted to play a round of
golf.

✍ Relationship

make up — become friends again after a quarrel
USAGE: Bob and Mary *made up* after their upsetting argument last week.

mend fences — to improve a poor relationship
USAGE: John had a desire to *mend fences* with his brother concerning a longstanding conflict.

my boy — a friend

USAGE: Lawrence congratulated him by saying, "Good job and thanks for getting the work done. That's *my boy*!"

✍ Satisfaction

(a) man's home is his castle — to be able to relax at home
USAGE: Believing *a man's home is his castle*, Richard enjoys relaxing at his house.

melt in one's mouth — taste very good; be delicious
USAGE: The candy made by Barbara *melted in my mouth*.

mend one's ways — improve one's habits
USAGE: Jack has *mended his ways* and no longer behaves as a child.

✍ Service

how about — will you have something or will you agree to something
USAGE: Tom asked the others, "*How about* some tea before we start work?"

✍ Time

nick of time — at the very last moment
USAGE: Susan boarded the subway train in the *nick of time*.

nip in the bud — prevent at the start
USAGE: The company's quality inspectors identified the problem early and were able to *nip the problem in the bud*.

✍ Understand

mind you — I want you to notice and understand
USAGE: Bill said he really wants to work on the day shift. "*Mind you*," he said, "If you are in an emergency, I would be available to work if needed."

mix up — an error; some confusion
USAGE: A *mix-up* occurred at the store, and I walked out with the wrong package.

✍ Work

knuckle down — begin to work earnestly
USAGE: During the half-time break, the coach stressed to the team it was time to *knuckle down* and play hard.

learn the ropes — learn how to do a job

USAGE: Melinda has been working at the company for only one month and is still *learning the ropes*.

Week 35

✍ Achievement

make up — do or supply something that is lacking; repay
USAGE: Joe had to *make up* the time on Saturday he lost when he was sick.

move heaven and earth — try every way; do everything one can
USAGE: The lawyer emphasized he would *move heaven and earth* to help the parents adopt a child.

on the ball — intelligent; able to do things well
USAGE: Henry is really *on the ball* and can handle a lot of demands in his work.

on top of — knowing all about something; up-to-date
USAGE: Since he reads two newspapers each day, Kevin is always *on top of* the latest news.

✍ Authority

serve someone right — get the punishment or results that one deserves
USAGE: Since Peter rarely studies, it *served him right* to fail his test.

set the pace — decide on a rate of speed that others will follow; to behave in a way that others try to copy
USAGE: Performing at a very high level, John succeeded in *setting the pace* for the employees under him.

✍ Bad / Negative

no bed of roses — difficult or bad situation
USAGE: Robert remarked it was *no bed of roses* to be unemployed in the city.

no picnic — not pleasant; difficult
USAGE: With much frustration, she said it was *no picnic* trying to manage twenty-five students on a field trip.

not for the world — not at any price; not for anything
USAGE: Helen said she *wouldn't* try to climb the mountain *for the world*.

✍ Business Action

lay off (someone) — get rid of workers when business is bad
USAGE: There were three hundred and fifty-five employees *laid off* at the sewing factory.

✍ Communication

pin down — make someone tell the truth or provide information
USAGE: I tried to *pin him down* on why he resigned from his job but he wouldn't give any details.

pipe up — speak louder
USAGE: John asked the speaker to *pipe up* so we could hear him in the back of the room.

play cat and mouse — tease or fool someone
USAGE: Susan was *playing cat and mouse* with the admiring man, flirting and looking at him playfully with her eyes.

play down — make something seem less important
USAGE: The manager *played down* the effect budget cuts at the company would have on the employees.

✍ Completeness

of age — fully developed; mature
USAGE: Paul came *of age* during the Information Revolution in which the Internet changed the lives of many people.

✍ Consequence

play with fire — invite danger or trouble
USAGE: The father cautioned his son he was *playing with fire* if he got involved with those people.

press (push) one's luck — depend too much on luck; expect to continue to be lucky
USAGE: Phillip is *pushing his luck* if he thinks his business will succeed only in serving people who live in the city.

pull through — recover from an illness or misfortune
USAGE: While his condition was doubtful immediately after surgery, James *pulled through* and made a complete recovery from the illness.

✍ Disagree

raise a fuss — make trouble; make a disturbance
USAGE: Stanley *raised a fuss* at the restaurant when his food was cold.

raise Cain — create a disturbance; cause trouble
USAGE: He started to *raise Cain* when he was asked not to smoke on the airplane.

✍ Emotion

long face — a sad look; a disappointed look
USAGE: Fred had a *long face* when he arrived home from his date with Carol.

lose face — be embarrassed or ashamed by an error or failure; lose dignity
USAGE: Joseph *lost face* when his son corrected him in front of the other people.

lose heart — become discouraged
USAGE: She has begun to *lose heart* in her desire to learn ballet dancing.

lose one's marbles — go crazy or act irrationally; illogical
USAGE: With his irrational response, it seems that Timothy may have *lost his marbles*.

lose one's temper — become angry
USAGE: Peter *lost his temper* when his wife wrecked the car.

✍ End

shut up — close the doors and windows of a building for a period of time
USAGE: Bill and Margaret decided to *shut up* the summer house until their return in late Spring.

✍ Entertainment

round robin (tournament/contest) — game or contest in which each player or team plays every other player or team in turn
USAGE: The team participated in a *round robin tournament* to choose the championship team for the province.

✍ Error

pad the bill — add false expenses
USAGE: William was questioned about the expenses because he has been known to ***pad the bill*** on previous business trips.

✍ Failure

in vain — without effect; without success
USAGE: The police tried ***in vain*** to locate the escaped prisoners.

✍ Health

pass out — faint
USAGE: The two university students ***passed out*** at the graduation party.

✍ Location

on the move — moving around from place to place; in motion
USAGE: Having been in Australia and Japan recently, Laura is really ***on the move***.

on the road — traveling (especially as a salesman or performer)
Paul is a traveling salesman and is usually ***on the road*** Monday through Friday.

out of the way — remote, no longer an obstacle
USAGE: Thomas took Mary to an ***out of the way*** place for a romantic dinner.

✍ Money

on the block — to be sold; for sale
USAGE: Wanting to sell their house, it has been ***on the block*** for six months.

on the dole — receiving welfare
USAGE: Because the neighborhood is poor with numerous people out of jobs, there are many people living ***on the dole***.

on the house — provided free by a business, especially a bar or restaurant
USAGE: Our group enjoyed the reception where our company provided us with free drinks ***on the house***.

✍ Movement

make a run for it — walk rapidly or run; make a speedy escape

USAGE: In a hurry to get to the theater, Charles *made a run for it* as soon as he got off work.

make away with — take; carry away
USAGE: The dog *made away with* the piece of meat sitting on top of the table.

meet up with — meet by accident; come upon without planning
USAGE: During his trip to Australia, Bill *met up with* another group from his university.

(not) move a muscle — don't move even a small amount
USAGE: The doctor told him *not to move a muscle* when examining his chest.

✍ Ownership

pass on — give away something you don't use anymore
USAGE: In order to save money, Melinda always *passes on* old clothes to her younger sister.

✍ Personal Description

have rocks in one's head — be stupid; not have good judgment
USAGE: Sharon sometimes acts as though she *has rocks in her head* when talking as she did today.

have something up one's sleeve — something kept secretly ready for the right time
USAGE: James said he's not really worried about the plan submitted by the others because he *has something up his sleeve*.

✍ Plan / Prepare

pull the rug out from under — spoil someone's plans; withdraw support
USAGE: John was frustrated because it was discovered his old boss *pulled the rug out from under* his plans by opening a store in the same location.

put all one's eggs in one basket — place all one's efforts, interests or hopes in a single person or thing
USAGE: The graduating students were cautioned not to *put all their eggs in one basket* by applying to work at only one company.

put down — write a record of something; write down

USAGE: To comply with company policy, John was asked to *put down* his recommendations in writing.

✍ Quantity

run into — add up to; total
USAGE: Steve was advised if changes were implemented, the complaints would *run into* the thousands.

✍ Relationship

name someone after — give someone another's name
USAGE: Frederick was *named after* his mother's uncle.

neck and neck — equal or nearly equal in a race or contest
USAGE: With strong competition between the two runners, they were *neck and neck* all the way to the finish line.

not have anything to do with — end a relationship
USAGE: Angered by the situation, Charles told the others he *didn't want to have anything to do with* the company.

✍ Satisfaction

music to one's ears — good news; something one likes to hear
USAGE: It was *music to my ears* when he told me he applied for admission at the University.

no sweat — (1) to comply with request; (2) easily accomplished; uncomplicated; to be easily done
USAGE (1): When asked if he could help, Michael replied, "*No sweat*. I'll be glad to help."
USAGE (2): Peter said the job was *no sweat* and not at all difficult.

on an even keel — in a well-ordered way or condition
USAGE: The manager was satisfied the customer service department was operating *on an even keel*.

✍ Service

keep the home fires burning — keep things going as usual while someone is away
USAGE: While Robert often traveled in his job, his wife Julie stayed at home and *kept the home fires burning*.

✍ Time

no end to/of — so many or so much of; to seem almost endless; very many or
   very much
USAGE: Jack had *no end to* financial difficulties when he was fired from his
   job.

now and then — occasionally
USAGE: Joel remarked he really enjoys eating at the French restaurant *now
   and then*.

✍ Understand

(get/become) mixed up — become confused; bewildered
USAGE: When trying to calculate statistical problems, Arthur gets *mixed up*
   and frustrated in the process.

nail down — make certain; make sure
USAGE: Since the visiting professor will be on a tight schedule, I'm trying to
   nail down the exact time for our meeting.

no skin off one's nose — not a matter of interest or concern to one
USAGE: It's *no skin off my nose* whether or not he comes to the meeting.

no wonder — not surprising
USAGE: After spending a day observing Jim's work routine, Susan said, "*No
   wonder* he's so tired when he leaves work."

nobody's home — one's attention is somewhere else, having a simple mind
USAGE: When Charles advised Jane that she might lose her job and she
   continued to gaze out the window, he concluded it was a case of *nobody's
   home*.

✍ Work

legman — someone who performs messenger and errand services
USAGE: Scott was working as a *legman* to the manager, running errands
   around the office.

✍ Achievement

out of this world — wonderful; fantastic
USAGE: The dinner prepared by Elizabeth last night was *out of this world*.

pick up — take on passengers; receive
USAGE: The bus *picked up* the tour group directly in front of the hotel.

play into someone's hands — do something that gives someone else an advantage
USAGE: If you allow John to see you crying about it, you will only be *playing into his hands*.

play one's cards right — take advantage of your opportunities
USAGE: George advised him if he *played his cards right* he would be offered the job.

✍ Agree / Approval

stand in awe of — look upon with wonder; feel respectful to
USAGE: Richard told me he *stands in awe of* the former Prime Minister and his service to the Nation.

stand one's ground — maintain and defend one's position
USAGE: Alan *stood his ground* on his decision not to promote Bill to company manager.

✍ Authority

shake up — change the command or leadership of something
USAGE: When he purchased the company, Paul decided to *shake up* top management as a way to bring change into the organization.

shove down one's throat — force someone to do or agree to something not wanted

USAGE: Sharon said she didn't appreciate his manner because he's always trying to *shove his ideas down my throat*.

✍ Bad / Negative

not much of — rather bad
USAGE: When James rented the car at the airport, he said, "It's *not much of* a car, but I guess it will be okay for today."

not on your life — definitely not
USAGE: "May I borrow your car"? "*Not on your life*."

✍ Communication

play it by ear — decide on something according to the situation
USAGE: Kathy suggested to the group they *play it by ear* and decide what to do after dinner.

play on words — a humorous use of a word to suggest a different or a double meaning
USAGE: Comedians are masters at using a *play on words* to make jokes about phrases with double meanings.

play up — call attention to; emphasize
USAGE: During the job interview, Mike *played up* his skills in financial analysis.

point out — explain; call attention to
USAGE: I asked her to coach me by *pointing out* mistakes I made in the presentation.

pointed remark — a remark clearly aimed at a particular person or thing
USAGE: Jim's *pointed remark* about Laura was both inaccurate and inappropriate.

poke fun at — joke about; laugh at; tease
USAGE: She is often *poking fun at* the way her boyfriend plays tennis.

✍ Completeness

on the whole — in general; all things considered
USAGE: Peter said, *on the whole*, it looks like a great idea, yet he wants to look further at the details involved.

on top of — in addition to; along with
USAGE: Vickie said, *on top of* everything else, her supervisor wants her to work late two nights each week.

✍ Consequence

rain cats and dogs — rain very hard
USAGE: Flooding throughout the region, it has been *raining cats and dogs* for two days.

rat out on — desert or betray someone; leave at a critical time
USAGE: Bill's friend *ratted out on* him when he failed to support him in the dispute.

raw deal — unfair treatment
USAGE: We all agreed Jim got a *raw deal* when he was forced to quit his job.

run a risk — unprotected; open to danger or loss
USAGE: Elaine was cautioned she would be *running a risk* if she allowed him to drive if he had been drinking.

✍ Different

shoot up — grow quickly
USAGE: Our son, Michael, *shot up* very quickly during his second year in high school.

✍ Disagree

rake someone over the coals — scold; reprimand
USAGE: His supervisor *raked him over the coals* upon hearing about the store accidentally being left unlocked.

ram (something) down one's throat — force one to do or agree to something not wanted
USAGE: Mary was furious that Ben argued with her and tried to *ram his ideas down her throat*.

✍ Emotion

mad as a hornet — very angry
USAGE: She was *mad as a hornet* after the meeting yesterday.

make merry — have fun; laugh and celebrate
USAGE: Wanting to celebrate his promotion, George and Karen went to an expensive restaurant to *make merry* for the evening.

make one's blood boil — make someone extremely angry
USAGE: She remarked that anytime she sees him it *makes her blood boil*.

nervous Nellie — a timid person who lacks determination and courage
USAGE: Benjamin is a *nervous Nellie* because he is fearful of the other students.

no love lost — bad feelings; ill will
USAGE: Since they are longtime foes, there's *no love lost* between my father and Uncle Ted.

✍ End

six feet under — dead and buried
USAGE: My father has always said he plans to live in this same house until he's *six feet under*.

✍ Error

palm off — deceive someone by a trick or a lie; sell or give by tricking
USAGE: He *palmed off* his old car as one that was reliable and in good working order.

✍ Failure

jacked — broken or ruined
USAGE: Frustrated that his computer had been infected by a virus, John said, "My computer is completely *jacked*!"

kick out — make someone go or leave; get rid of; dismiss
USAGE: Kevin was *kicked out* of school when he was 16 years old because of continual bad behavior and unwillingness to participate in assignments.

✍ Health

(a) pick-me-up — something that gives energy
USAGE: A cold drink during the afternoon on a hot summer day is a real *pick-me-up*!

✍ Importance

no great shakes — mediocre; ordinary; unimportant
USAGE: The restaurant was *no great shakes* and I wouldn't want to recommend it as a place for good food.

✍ Location

out of thin air — out of nothing or from nowhere
USAGE: While we were driving down the highway, the dog seemed to jump *out of thin air* and onto the road directly in front of us.

pick up — pick up something that has fallen
USAGE: Vickie asked John if he would *pick up* the cup on the floor.

✍ Money

on the make — trying to get some advantage with money or sex
USAGE: Betty warned her to be careful of Jim because he has the reputation of being *on the make* with women, taking advantage of them sexually.

on the mend — healing; becoming better
USAGE: The soccer player broke his leg in a game last season but is *on the mend* and is again healthy for this year's season.

✍ Movement

musical chairs — a change in an organization that has no practical effect or significance
USAGE: The senior management played *musical chairs* by moving the supervisors to different areas of the company.

narrow escape — barely succeeding avoiding danger
USAGE: He had a *narrow escape* from the building engulfed in flames.

nose down — head down; bring down the nose of aircraft
USAGE: In its final approach to the airport landing, the pilot began to *nose down* the aircraft.

pick up speed — increase the speed of
USAGE: As Robert drove down the road, he began to *pick up speed*.

✍ Ownership

pick up — (1) catch or receive the sound of a radio or data connection; (2) get; receive; (3) get without trying, accidentally
USAGE (1): Trying to get online to the Internet, Jack was trying to *pick up* a wireless connection through his laptop computer.
USAGE (2): After calling in his take-out order, Jim went by the restaurant to *pick up* the food.
USAGE (3): He *picked up* the ability to create web pages from several of his friends.

✍ Personal Description

head shrinker — psychiatrist
USAGE: The judge demanded the accused suspect be evaluated by a *head shrinker* to determine his psychiatric status.

heart of gold — good natured and kind; generous or forgiving personality
USAGE: Grieving the death of his grandmother, John recalled she had a *heart of gold*.

heart of stone — someone with a cold and unfeeling nature with no pity
USAGE: They said Carol has a *heart of stone* and doesn't care about other people.

✍ Plan / Prepare

put in — to plant flowers, trees, vegetation
USAGE: They *put in* 20 rows of oak trees at the ranch.

put in for something — apply for something
USAGE: Jack *put in for* a job transfer within the company to a different city.

put on — to clothe oneself
USAGE: Kimberly *put on* a new shirt to wear to school.

✍ Quantity

run short — not have enough; insufficient in quantity
USAGE: Robert *ran short* of money during his tour across the countryside.

run up — add to the amount of something; increase
USAGE: Julie *ran up* a fairly large bill at the department store that she had a hard time repaying.

(a) sack of hammers — a heavy weight, object
USAGE: The box of papers was so heavy that it felt like *a sack of hammers*.

✍ Relationship

on behalf of — representing a person or group
USAGE: The teacher attended the education conference *on behalf of* her colleagues.

on one's back — making continual demands of someone; being an annoyance or bother
USAGE: Peter has been *on his back* all week trying to persuade him to change the proposal.

on the rocks — a relationship breaking up
USAGE: Dale and Jean have been married for three years but their marriage is now *on the rocks*.

✍ Satisfaction

on shaky ground — unstable; not secure
USAGE: Bill's job at the company is *on shaky ground* because of low sales.

on the bandwagon — joining something because many others are doing it
USAGE: Roger jumped *on the bandwagon* asking the government to implement policies to preserve the environment.

on the beam — doing well; just right; operating correctly
USAGE: After examining the process, the inspectors concluded it was right *on the beam*.

✍ Service

knuckle under — yield; submit; give in
USAGE: The company's management *knuckled under* and agreed to the requests of the employee group.

✍ Time

off and on — occasionally; intermittently
USAGE: Vincent and Carol have been dating each other *off and on* during the last year.

old as the hills — very old
USAGE: The antique telephone in his home is ***old as the hills***.

on and on — continually; at tedious length; without stopping
USAGE: John's presentation continued ***on and on*** until we finally left the
  meeting.

✍ Understand

nose around/about — look for something kept private or secret
USAGE: Suspecting he had a girlfriend, Jack's wife was ***nosing around*** his
  desk for evidence.

on faith — without question or proof
USAGE: The group took it ***on faith*** they would stop polluting the river.

on guard — watching vigilantly
USAGE: The group was urged to remain ***on guard*** to observe the situation.

out of it — confused; disoriented; off in one's own world
USAGE: After drinking three glasses of wine, James is really ***out of it***.

✍ Work

legwork — physical work; collecting information; research
USAGE: John was traveling around the city doing ***legwork*** for the building
  project.

let go — discharge from a job; fire
USAGE: Because the company experienced a declined in sales, Karen was ***let
  go*** from her job.

✍ Achievement

plow into — (1) to undertake a task vigorously; (2) crash into with force
USAGE (1): The group *plowed into* the project enthusiastically in order to finish the project as soon as possible.
USAGE (2): The out of control car *plowed into* the group of people walking along the street.

prey on/upon — catch for food; kill and eat
USAGE: It is widely known that cats *prey on* mice.

pull a Nancy Drew — to fake something to escape a situation
USAGE: By that time I was so tired I had to *pull a Nancy Drew* and get it all over with.

✍ Agree / Approval

stick one's neck out — take risks; support someone
USAGE: Believing she could help on the project, John decided to *stick his neck out* and recommend she be added to the team.

stick to (a story / the facts) — remain faithful to something
USAGE: The judge demanded he *stick to the facts* when testifying in court.

✍ Authority

show someone the door — ask someone to go away
USAGE: When he created a disturbance by screaming, he was quickly *shown the door* by the security guards.

sign over — give something legally to someone by signing one's name
USAGE: As a wedding gift to his daughter, he *signed over* ownership of the car to her.

✍ Bad / Negative

not so hot — not very good

USAGE: Scott remarked he had a high temperature and *didn't feel so hot*.

not touch something with a ten-foot pole — consider something completely
   undesirable
USAGE: The job may pay a good salary, but I *wouldn't touch it with a ten-
   foot pole*.

✍ Business Action

pass off — sell or give something by false claims; offer something fake as
   authentic
USAGE: The woman *passed off* the diamond ring as genuine and sold it for a
   lot of money.

✍ Communication

pour it on thick — flatter or compliment excessively
USAGE: In his attempt to get a date with her, Jimmy was *pouring it on thick*.

pour oil on troubled waters — calm down a quarrel; say something to lessen
   anger and bring peace to a situation
USAGE: The others tried to *pour oil on troubled waters* concerning the
   dispute between Scott and Bill.

pour out — tell everything about something
USAGE: Nancy *poured out* to her aunt sadness about her troubled
   marriage.

promise the moon — making excessive promises without delivery of
   obligations
USAGE: Before they got married, Kevin *promised the moon* to Betty but after
   the wedding he failed to carry through on his commitments.

pull someone's leg — trick or fool someone playfully
USAGE: Having a good sense of humor, William tried to *pull her leg* about
   winning the money.

put across — explain clearly; make oneself understood
USAGE: John worked hard to *put across* precisely what he wanted to say.

put in — add to what has already been said
USAGE: Kimberly *put in* that she would like to visit the Forbidden City while
   in Beijing.

✍ Completeness

pile up — accumulate, put things on top of each other
USAGE: Stanley *piled up* his collection of music CD's on the table.

✍ Consequence

run for it — dash for safety; make a speedy escape
USAGE: Trying to get away from the thief, he made a *run for it* and tried to get to safety.

save one's neck/skin — save oneself from danger or trouble
USAGE: In an effort to *save his own neck*, he grabbed the cable to pull himself out of the hole.

school of hard knocks — learn through ordinary experiences of life
USAGE: While he didn't have a formal education, Joe was highly educated in the *school of hard knocks*.

✍ Different

shut off — be apart; be separated from
USAGE: His office is *shut off* from the production area of the building.

✍ Disagree

rock the boat — upset the way things are
USAGE: Jacob angered the manager because he was *rocking the boat* by questioning his decision.

rough and tumble — fighting or arguing in a very rough and reckless way
USAGE: Michael had a reputation of conducting meetings in a *rough and tumble* manner. These meetings always involved a lot of conflict and arguing.

✍ Emotion

not give someone the time of day — dislike someone so strongly that you totally ignore them
USAGE: Peter had such strong feelings against her that he said he *wouldn't give her the time of day*.

nurse a grudge — keep a feeling of dislike toward some person
USAGE: Will's old girlfriend is *nursing a grudge* toward him for breaking up and ending their three year relationship.

nuts about — enthusiastic about something
USAGE: Alan has been *nuts about* computers and the Internet since he was a
   young boy.

off one's chest — thoughts or feelings that one needs to share with someone
USAGE: Joe talked at length with Patricia and got many of his problems *off
   his chest*.

off one's high horse — not acting proud and scornful
USAGE: When Joyce confronted him, Bill was forced to admit mistakes had
   been made and he was knocked *off his high horse*.

✍ End

so long — goodbye
USAGE: When he left the building, Mark said, "*So long*, I'll see you later."

✍ Error

pass off — misrepresent oneself; pretend to be someone else
USAGE: Vincent *passed himself off* as a journalist and obtained access to the
   famous entertainer.

✍ Failure

knock one's head against the wall — waste time trying to do something with
   no success
USAGE: He had been *knocking his head against the wall* trying to find the
   answer to the mystery.

knock out — make unconscious, unworkable or unusable
USAGE: The violent criminal suspect *knocked out* the police officer in a
   struggle.

✍ Health

pooped out — worn out; exhausted
USAGE: The volunteers worked hard on the clean up project and were *pooped
   out* by the end of the day.

put on weight — gain weight
USAGE: The man was told by the doctor he had *put on weight* since his last
   visit.

✍ Importance

nothing if not — without doubt; certainly
USAGE: He is *nothing if not* careful. He gives a lot of attention to taking care
of matters in a very detailed manner.

✍ Location

pick up a trail/scent — recognize the trail of a hunted person or animal
USAGE: The police tracking dogs *picked up the trail* of the criminal suspects.

pin down — keep someone from moving; make someone stay in a place or
position
USAGE: The security guard *pinned down* the suspected thief outside the
store.

pitch a tent — put up a tent
USAGE: The campers *pitched their tent* beside the river.

✍ Money

(a) paltry sum — a small amount of money
USAGE: John earned a *paltry sum* of money in his job.

pay dirt — a valuable discovery
USAGE: Steven hit *pay dirt* when he invented the new wireless Internet
equipment.

pay off — pay in full and be free from a debt
USAGE: Barbara worked hard to *pay off* her loan to free up more monthly
income.

✍ Movement

pull up stakes — move to another location; to leave
USAGE: After a long time at their current location, the owners of the company
pulled up stakes and moved.

push off — start; leave
USAGE: The cruise ship *pushed off* from the dock for a five day cruise.

rat race — endless hurried existence; difficult routine
USAGE: Bill's job can be really hectic and he's often said he would like to get
off the *rat race*.

✍ Personal Description

hell-on-wheels — a short-tempered, nagging or crabby person
USAGE: The workers were cautioned the boss was ***hell-on-wheels*** today because his wife had walked out on their marriage.

high and mighty — arrogant; overbearing
USAGE: They believed he is conceited and has a ***high and mighty*** attitude to others.

high maintenance — requires a lot of work in which a person is needy
USAGE: His girlfriend was considered too ***high-maintenance*** because she always needed to be reassured of her beauty.

✍ Plan / Prepare

put one's own house in order — organize one's own private affairs
USAGE: They told him to try ***putting his own house in order*** before he finds fault with others.

put the cart before the horse — do things in the wrong order
USAGE: We all believed he ***put the cart before the horse*** by purchasing the car before he even got the job.

put up at a hotel — stay at a hotel or someone's home
USAGE: Bob and Sarah ***put up at a hotel*** for the night.

✍ Relationship

out in the cold — neglected; not included
USAGE: He was left ***out in the cold*** by not being invited to the party.

out of circulation — not active; not joining in what others are doing
USAGE: John is dating Rebecca steadily, so he will probably be ***out of circulation*** for awhile.

out of one's element — where one does not belong or fit in
USAGE: When Jim spent the day among the scientists, he felt ***out of his element*** because he didn't know much about science.

✍ Satisfaction

on the go — busy running around
USAGE: Richard has been ***on the go*** since yesterday in preparation for the meeting.

on the nose — just right; exactly
USAGE: When Jeffrey said Sally was difficult to work with, he was right *on the nose*.

on top — in the lead
USAGE: He was *on top* of the standings among amateur tennis players.

✍ Service

look out — provide protection and care
USAGE: The mother asked the teacher to *look out* for her daughter while on the field trip.

✍ Time

on the button — exactly on time
USAGE: Stanley arrived for the presentation right *on the button*.

✍ Understand

over one's head — too difficult for someone to understand
USAGE: The theory was difficult for him to comprehend and went *over his head*.

penny for one's thoughts — request to disclose one's thinking
USAGE: Wondering what he was thinking, Kathy asked, "A *penny for your thoughts*?"

(a) perfect stranger — a stranger; someone not recognized
USAGE: Bill said the man was a *perfect stranger* and he had never seen him before.

pick someone's brains — inquire about another's ideas through questioning
USAGE: They were *picking his brains* to find out about his preferences for a vacation site.

✍ Work

let grass grow under one's feet — be idle; be lazy; waste time
USAGE: He isn't the type of person to *let grass grow under his feet* because he works so hard and steadily.

lift a finger/hand — refuse to work or serve to help or do something

USAGE: Jeremy said he would never **lift *a finger*** to help Robert, with whom he used to be a friend.

Week 38

✐ Achievement

pull (something) off — accomplish something remarkable
USAGE: Robert was successful in *pulling off* project in record time and below the expected cost.

pull one's socks up — make a greater effort
USAGE: The boss advised Charles he had better begin to *pull his socks up* or he would be fired.

pull one's weight — do one's fair share of the work
USAGE: If everyone in the group *pulls their weight* we can finish by Noon.

pull out of a hat — produce something instantly; as if by magic
USAGE: We were looking for a tape measure and, as if he *pulled it out of a hat*, Joe found one and gave it to me.

✐ Agree / Approval

stick to one's guns — defend an action or opinion despite an unfavorable reaction
USAGE: Scott is *sticking to his guns* on his decision to fire the office employee.

stick up for — defend; help; support
USAGE: He has a history of *sticking up for* the physically handicapped and their welfare.

✐ Authority

sign up — promise to do something by signing one's name; join
USAGE: She *signed up* to volunteer her service to help the needy.

split ticket — vote for political candidates from multiple parties
USAGE: Unlike some people who vote a *split ticket*, Jeffrey votes for the person and not the party.

✍ Bad / Negative

off color — in bad taste; not polite; dirty
USAGE: Jim was telling some *off-color* jokes which offended many people.

on the spot — in a difficult, humiliating or awkward situation
USAGE: He was really put *on the spot* when his wife asked him about his
   girlfriend in front of the others.

(a) pain in the ass — a person or situation that causes problems
USAGE: The nagging store clerk was *a pain in the ass* to the customer.

✍ Business Action

(a) piece of the action — a share of the profit
USAGE: Since the profit potential was very great, the businessmen wanted *a
   piece of the action*.

✍ Communication

put in one's two cents — give one's opinion
USAGE: Betty always wanted to *put in her two cents* when given the
   opportunity.

put on — fool or joke with someone; tease
USAGE: I think he was *putting me on* when he said he was going to buy a
   horse on which to ride.

put one's cards on the table — be honest and direct; tell everything
USAGE: Being very honest with James, I *put my cards on the table* and told
   him my feelings about the situation.

put our heads together — discuss together; strategize with others
USAGE: After *putting our heads together*, we came up with a good plan for
   everyone.

put someone in the picture — inform someone about the situation
USAGE: After a while, my work group *put me in the picture* about our
   company's new requirements.

put up or shut up — prove something or stop saying it
USAGE: After bragging he could finish the project by himself, the others were
   tired of his arrogance and told him to *put up or shut up*.

✍ Completeness

played out — worn out; drained of energy
USAGE: After staying at the party until 2 AM, I was *played out* and wanted to go to bed.

polish off — finish something completely
USAGE: It felt good knowing we had *polished off* the work for the day.

✍ Consequence

scrape the bottom of the barrel — take whatever is left after the best has been taken
USAGE: Knowing the man had served prison time, Mark said the company was *scraping the bottom of the barrel* if they hired him.

scratch one's back — do something nice for someone in anticipation they will do something for you
USAGE: John said, "You *scratch my back* and I'll scratch yours," in an effort to gain favorable treatment from Henry.

serve time — spend time in jail or prison
USAGE: While James *served time* as a young man, he is now a family man and hard worker.

✍ Different

something else again — a different kind of thing entirely
USAGE: Susan told her friend she didn't mind working until 7 PM, but being required to work all day on Saturday was *something else again*.

✍ Disagree

rule out — decide against; eliminate
USAGE: The police haven't *ruled out* James as a suspect in the robbery.

run up against (something) — encounter
USAGE: In his efforts to start a business, Bill *ran up against* many problems, including government regulations and obtaining financing.

✍ Emotion

on cloud nine — very happy
USAGE: Sharon has been *on cloud nine* since Paul asked her to be his wife.

on edge — to be nervous or irritable
USAGE: He was *on edge* waiting for the results of the championship game.

on pins and needles — excited; nervous
USAGE: She's been *on pins and needles* all day waiting for the results of the admission examination.

on the edge of one's seat — nervously and excitedly waiting
USAGE: I've been *on the edge of my seat* waiting for the championship game to begin.

on the warpath — very angry; looking for trouble
USAGE: Stanley was *on the warpath* when he discovered his partner stole all the money.

✍ End

stamp out — destroy completely and make disappear
USAGE: The police are making a big effort to *stamp out* drug crime in the city.

✍ Error

put one's foot in one's mouth — say something that is the wrong thing to say in a situation
USAGE: Steven *put his foot in his mouth* when he asked the lady if she was pregnant and she said no.

✍ Failure

lay an egg — fail to win the favor of an audience
USAGE: The singer's performance was poor and *laid an egg* with the concert audience.

lay waste — destroy and leave in ruins
USAGE: All through history, armies triumphed by *laying waste* throughout an enemy's territory.

✍ Health

rough up — attack or hurt physically
USAGE: The three men *roughed up* the bartender at the hotel and were arrested by the police.

run down — get into poor health or condition; look bad
USAGE: His health became *run down* when he stopped exercising.

run ragged — be tired or exhausted
USAGE: She has been *run ragged* by her three children.

✍ Importance

nothing to sneeze at — something you should take seriously
USAGE: The new rules of operation at the company are *nothing to sneeze at*.

✍ Location

play hooky — stay away from school or work without permission
USAGE: The student was disciplined by his parents for *playing hooky* from school.

pop up — appear suddenly or unexpectedly
USAGE: While I was eating at the restaurant, John unexpectedly *popped up* and we talked for quite a while.

✍ Money

pay through the nose — pay much money for something
USAGE: Steven *paid through the nose* for the new luxury car.

pick up the tab — pay the bill for someone else
USAGE: John *picked up the tab* for the visiting group at dinner.

✍ Movement

roll in — arrive in great numbers or quantity
USAGE: With the famous attraction in town, tourists *rolled into* the city.

run in — make a brief visit
USAGE: Jeffrey *ran in* to the store to buy a bottle of shampoo.

run into (something) — hit something or crash into something
USAGE: He failed to apply the brakes in time and accidentally *ran the car into the building*.

✍ Personal Description

high spirits — have energy; be cheerful; joyful

USAGE: Each member of the team had *high spirits* after winning the championship finals.

hit the sauce — drinking alcohol heavily and regularly
USAGE: I believe Jane's been *hitting the sauce* recently even though she denies she's been drinking.

hold a candle to — can be compared favorably with
USAGE: Robert suggested that food from the finest restaurant doesn't *hold a candle to* his wife's cooking.

hold all the trump cards — confidence to win due to using key resource at the right time
USAGE: George was very confident of the outcome of the sales negotiation because he *holds al the trump cards*.

✍ Plan / Prepare

red tape — excessive formalities in official transactions
USAGE: Henry was frustrated in dealing with the *red tape* involved in getting approval to start his business.

rhyme or reason — a plan or reason
USAGE: Without *rhyme or reason* Bill decided to sell his house and move to the country.

run through — read or practice from beginning to end without stopping
USAGE: Before his presentation to the board, John did a *run through* to practice his delivery.

✍ Quantity

short of — not have enough of something
USAGE: Becky said she was *short of* sugar and, therefore, would not be able to bake the cake.

so much — a large quantity
USAGE: There was *so much* noise in the subway station that I couldn't hear a word he said.

soup up — changing and adding something to make it more powerful
USAGE: Peter knew how to *soup up* his computer so it could download data from the Internet faster.

✍ Relationship

out of one's hair — get rid of someone who is a nuisance
USAGE: John got the barking dogs *out of his hair* by calling the security staff to notify the dog owners.

patch up — come to agreement after conflict
USAGE: Paul and Jim came together to *patch up* their longstanding differences.

play footsie — secretly flirt with someone
USAGE: William and Susan were *playing footsie* under the table at the restaurant.

✍ Satisfaction

on top of — managing very well; in control of
USAGE: We are able to keep *on top of* our work now that we have someone to help us.

one-track mind — thinking about only one thing
USAGE: Having a *one-track mind*, all Richard thinks about is girls.

one-two — quick or decisive action that takes the opposition by surprise
USAGE: As an expert salesman with great skills, Jim gave the customer the *one-two* and he ended up buying the car.

open secret — a secret that so many people know it is no longer a secret
USAGE: It's an *open secret* that Roger will soon be asking Susan to marry him.

✍ Service

look to — go for help to; depend on
USAGE: He always *looks to* his mother for help when he has a problem.

✍ Time

on the dot — right on time
USAGE: Always punctual, John arrives for meetings *on the dot*.

on the spur of the moment — an impulse decision; suddenly
USAGE: Carol and Betsy decided to visit the museum *on the spur of the moment*.

on time — at the scheduled time
USAGE: The bus arrived right *on time*.

✍ **Understand**

play (someone) for something — treat someone as something; act toward
   someone in certain way
USAGE: While he thought he could *play me for a fool*, I suggested he better
   think again.

put on one's thinking cap — think hard and long about something
USAGE: Susan told her friend she needed a change and would *put on her
   thinking cap* and develop a new plan.

put on the map — make a place well known
USAGE: The local business became so well known that it *put our city on the
   map*.

put (something/someone) out of one's mind — try not to think about something
USAGE: Wanting to move on with his life, Tom has been trying to *put his old
   girlfriend out of his mind*.

✍ **Work**

(a) man of the cloth — a spiritual leader
USAGE: He is *a man of the cloth* and an inspiration to many people.

monkey business — comical, silly, teasing, playful actions
USAGE: The parents demanded the children stop with the *monkey business*
   and start doing the schoolwork.

Week 39

✍ Achievement

put on — produce or arrange a production
USAGE: Elizabeth worked with the other parents to *put on* the children's play.

put out — produce; make; publish
USAGE: Bob and Carol worked together to *put out* a staff newspaper to the employees.

put (something) over on someone — fool; trick; deceive
USAGE: Trying to *put something over on his boss*, John said he had a bad cough and couldn't come to work.

put up a good fight — try hard
USAGE: The students *put up a good fight* to win the contest between the two schools

✍ Agree / Approval

stick with — stay with; not leave
USAGE: Bill urged Susan to *stick with* her job until a new management staff took over control of the company.

stretch a point — agree to something beyond the limit of what is normally allowed
USAGE: John admitted it was *stretching a point* to connect the national economic problems with the low company sales.

✍ Authority

stand up for — defend against attack; fight for
USAGE: The workers wrote letters to the newspaper to *stand up for* their rights.

stand up to someone — be brave in confronting someone
USAGE: Wendy *stood up to her supervisor* when he unjustly denounced the quality of her work.

✍ Bad / Negative

(a) pain in the butt — a person or situation that causes problems
USAGE: The screaming kids across the street were *a pain in the butt* while we were trying to take a nap.

pain in the neck/ass — an annoying thing or person; bothersome
USAGE: Dealing with my neighbor can sometimes be *a pain in the neck*.

✍ Business Action

pig in a poke — buying something without careful evaluation
USAGE: The new laptop computer with wireless capability he bought was a *pig in a poke* because he didn't try it out first.

✍ Communication

put up to — persuade someone to do something
USAGE: George insists it was his friend who *put him up to* stealing the radio from the store.

put words in one's mouth — to speak for someone else
USAGE: Margaret is very angered when her husband tries to *put words in her mouth*.

read the riot act — to give someone a strong warning
USAGE: The classroom teacher *read the riot act* to the disobedient and unruly students.

right out — plainly and directly
USAGE: He told his wife *right out* he no longer loved her.

ring up — to telephone someone
USAGE: Joseph decided he would *ring up* his friend and ask him to lunch.

✍ Completeness

right under one's nose — in an obvious, nearby place
USAGE: After looking all through the house, Kathryn found her eyeglasses *right under her nose*.

rough and ready — rough or crude but ready to use
USAGE: The outline for the speech was *rough and ready* but John decided it was good enough to deliver to the audience.

✍ Consequence

set off — to cause to blow up
USAGE: The earthquake *set off* a series of explosions through the city.

set (someone) up — put someone in a position to be exploited
USAGE: James believed he was *set up* by one of his ex-friends to be cheated by the salesman.

skate on thin ice — intentionally taking a risk
USAGE: He was *skating on thin ice* at work with his frequent absences and failure to submit required reports.

✍ Different

split hairs — make unnecessary distinctions
USAGE: The argument between them involved trivial issues and *splitting of hair* on these points.

✍ Disagree

sail into — scold or criticize intensely
USAGE: When Roger came home from work, his wife *sailed into* him for lying to her on the telephone.

✍ Emotion

out of sorts — in a bad mood; irritable
USAGE: Tim was *out of sorts* when he found out his employer would have a worker lay off.

perk up — become energetic or happy after being sad or tired
USAGE: Vickie *perked up* when her supervisor informed her she had earned a pay raise.

plastered — extremely intoxicated
USAGE: He went out with his friends after work and got *plastered*.

pluck up — make oneself have courage
USAGE: Peter *plucked up* and asked his supervisor for a pay raise.

(a) poker face — a face showing no emotion
USAGE: The jury was *poker-faced* because they showed no emotion in handing down the guilty verdict.

psych out — find out the real motives of someone
USAGE: George tried to *psych out* the competing businessman to discover his plans for expansion.

✍ Entertainment

smash hit — a very successful action or result
USAGE: Jim's first book was a *smash hit* with readers.

✍ Error

screw up — make a failure of an undertaking
USAGE: The restaurant waiter *screwed up* our food order and we were served dishes we didn't order.

✍ Failure

let down — failure to do what is expected
USAGE: Jack *let down* his parents by failing to graduate from high school.

lose out — failure to achieve what is expected
USAGE: By not qualifying for the final round of competition, she *lost out* on an opportunity to travel with other students to Europe.

✍ Health

second wind — regaining energy after being tired
USAGE: After getting a *second wind*, Robert continued on his bicycle expedition through the countryside.

see stars — a person imagining seeing stars as a result of being hit on the head
USAGE: After falling off his bicycle and hitting his head, Paul began to *see stars*.

✍ Importance

off the record — privately; unofficially
USAGE: The detective told the newspaper reporters *off the record* about the criminal suspect search.

✍ Location

pull over — drive to the side of the road and stop
USAGE: The police *pulled over* Kevin because he had been driving recklessly.

✍ Money

piggy bank — a small bank for saving coins
USAGE: The little girl was saving money in her *piggy bank*.

pinch pennies — be careful with money; be thrifty
USAGE: Having a family to support, John has always *pinched pennies* in order to pay his monthly bills.

✍ Movement

run out — force to leave; expel
USAGE: The men who were suspected as drug dealers were *run out* of the neighborhood by the police.

see out — go out the door with someone
USAGE: I escorted our guests to the front door to *see them out* to their car.

set foot — step into; enter
USAGE: Disliking the owner, John remarked he would never *set foot* in the restaurant.

✍ Personal Description

hold court — to be surrounded by others listening and admiring remarks
USAGE: Roger behaves as if he is *holding court* among his admirers and supporters.

hold out — someone who refuses to give something up
USAGE: He was a *hold-out* in the group's effort to obtain a pay raise at the company.

holier-than-thou — acting as if one is better than others in goodness
USAGE: When he acts in that self-righteous way, Bill really seems *holier-than-thou*.

✍ Plan / Prepare

scratch the surface — make only a small effort to accomplish something
USAGE: While the police have indicated they have some information on the crime, they've only *scratched the surface* on all the available details.

see about (something) — look or check into something

USAGE: Kathy said she'll *see about* calling the repairman to work on the refrigerator.

✍ Quantity

take in — make smaller in size
USAGE: He asked the seamstress to *take in* the waist of his pants so they would fit better.

✍ Relationship

play footsie (non romantic) — cooperation and collaboration especially in a political situation
USAGE: The opposing community leaders were *playing footsie* through negotiation in their attempts to come together on the plan.

play off — match opposing persons, forces or interests for one's own gain
USAGE: The supervisor *played off* one employee against another in order to advance his own interests.

✍ Satisfaction

other fish to fry — priorities; have more important things to do
USAGE: While our project is important, I believe the company president has *other fish to fry* that he will work on first.

out of the woods — out of danger; in the clear
USAGE: John came out of surgery successfully and the doctor reported that he is now *out of the woods*.

rest on one's laurels — be satisfied with past accomplishments
USAGE: He is *resting on his laurels* and not willing to work hard on the project.

✍ Time

once and for all — permanently; to finally settle
USAGE: Bill told Karen *once and for all* he didn't want to have any more children.

once in a blue moon — rarely; very infrequently
USAGE: John said he went to the theater only *once in a blue moon*.

once in a while — occasionally; not very often

USAGE: Since I'm somewhat fearful of flying, I travel by airplane only *once in a while*.

✍ Understand

put two and two together — reach conclusions from evidence or existing facts
USAGE: I *put two and two together* and reached the conclusion that she would not return.

(a) quick study — one who learns something quickly
USAGE: James became *a quick study* in the fine points of playing chess.

rack one's brains — try hard to think or remember something
USAGE: Kathy said she has been *racking her brains* trying to remember his name.

read between the lines — find a hidden meaning in something
USAGE: While he didn't say it, I could *read between the lines* that John favors the changes.

red herring — something that draws attention away from the main issue
USAGE: The employee's complaint of unfair treatment was a *red herring* to keep the discussion away from poor production issues.

✍ Work

nine to five — a job
USAGE: Joe was thankful he had a *nine to five* to provide for his family.

off duty — not working; having free time
USAGE: The bus driver was *off duty* after working almost twelve straight hours.

on call — available if called
USAGE: He works as a security guard and is always *on call* when special events are in town.

✍ Achievement

put up with — patiently tolerates; endure
USAGE: The father *put up with* the nagging and complaints of the young children while on vacation.

raise a hand — do something to assist and help
USAGE: Peter didn't *raise a hand* to help finish the project.

ride herd on — watch closely and control
USAGE: The boss was *riding herd on* the employees to finish the project on time.

ride out — survive safely; endure
USAGE: Joe and Sharon decided to *ride out* the snowstorm by staying inside at the hotel.

✍ Agree / Approval

sure thing — of course; certainly
USAGE: When asked if he would help on the project, John replied, "*Sure thing*, I'd be glad to help on the undertaking."

✍ Authority

step up — rise to a higher or more important position; be promoted
USAGE: Carla *stepped up* to the position of supervisor when the company expanded in size.

swear by — to take oath that what is said is truthful
USAGE: When he took the stand to testify in court, Bill was required to *swear by* the truth of his statements.

✍ Bad / Negative

peeping Tom — someone who looks in people's windows

USAGE: The police were looking throughout the area last night for a reported *peeping Tom*.

penny-wise and pound-foolish — wise or careful in small things to the costly neglect of important things
USAGE: He is *penny wise and pound foolish* because he clips coupons for groceries but is wasteful on spending large amounts on luxury items.

people who live in glass houses should not throw stones — do not complain about other people if you are as bad as they are
USAGE: James realized because of his past problems he shouldn't criticize others because *people who live in glass houses should not throw stones*.

✍ Business Action

sell like hotcakes — sell very quickly
USAGE: The tickets for the rock concert were *selling like hotcakes* during the last week.

✍ Communication

rope into — trick; persuade by pressuring someone
USAGE: While I wasn't too interested in assisting with the project, I got *roped into* helping anyway.

round robin (letter) — a letter written by a group of people with each person writing part of the letter
USAGE: The students mailed a *round robin letter* to the university president to request an increase in the number of Internet connections on campus.

round robin (meeting/discussion) — a meeting or discussion in which each person in a group takes part
USAGE: The faculty conducted a *round robin panel discussion* on historical preservation within the province.

rub elbows/shoulders — be in the same place with notable people; meet and mix
USAGE: At the reception, Bob and Carol were able to *rub elbows* with several famous people from the entertainment business.

rub something in — continue to talk about something someone said or did
USAGE: Scott embarrassed Jane by *rubbing in the mistake she made in* class last week.

rumor has it — gossip
USAGE: John reported that a *rumor has it* the company will close next year.

run down — say bad things about someone; to criticize
USAGE: The reason Susan doesn't have many friends is that she sometimes *runs down* others.

✍ Completeness

run out (of something) — use up; come to an end
USAGE: When Jimmy and Bill went camping last week they *ran out of food* and had to return early.

run over — be too full and flow over the edge
USAGE: With so much rain during the last 2 days, the streets were *running over* and flooding at a high rate.

✍ Consequence

skip it — forget about a subject or issue
USAGE: When asked to elaborate on what he said earlier, Kevin said "*Skip it* for now, I can't remember all the details."

smack into — collide; hit
USAGE: Larry ran *smack into* the truck that was directly in front of his car.

smoke out — force something or someone out with smoke
USAGE: The police *smoked out* the concealed criminal suspects by pumping the building full of smoke.

✍ Disagree

settle a score with someone — pay someone back for a past wrong
USAGE: James wanted to *settle a score with Scott*, with whom he's long had a difficult relationship.

shaken up — be bothered or disturbed by
USAGE: Vickie was a little *shaken up* after feeling the building move from the minor earthquake.

✍ Emotion

psyched up — mentally alert; ready to do something

USAGE: Having prepared for several weeks, John was *psyched up* for the admissions examination.

push the panic button — become very frightened when worrying; may include overreacting
USAGE: Bill became very anxious when Susan wasn't home by 10 PM and *pushed the panic button* by calling the police and reporting her missing.

put through the wringer — cause a lot of stress
USAGE: Jacob *put his wife through the wringer* when he told her he had been fired from his job.

put up a good front — pretend to be happy
USAGE: While Alan *put up a good front*, most of his friends could tell he was actually unhappy.

raise eyebrows — cause surprise or disapproval
USAGE: Barbara *raised eyebrows* when she showed up at the party with a different boyfriend.

✍ End

tear down — take down; destroy
USAGE: The committee recommended the building be *torn down* so it could be the site of an Olympic venue.

✍ Failure

(a) lost cause — something that is not succeeding
USAGE: Since the team didn't win a game this year, their season was *a lost cause*.

louse up — throw into confusion; make a mess of; spoil
USAGE: Richard realized afterwards that he *loused up* the admissions interview and probably wouldn't be entering the MBA program.

✍ Health

shake off (an illness) — get rid of (an illness)
USAGE: Continuing to feel bad, Kathy has been unable to *shake off* symptoms of her ailment.

shoot up — take drugs by injecting them

USAGE: It was very upsetting when the children saw the heroin addict *shooting up* drugs behind the building.

✍ Location

put in — stop at an ocean port on a voyage
USAGE: The cruise ship *put in* at several ports along the expedition.

put one's finger on something — locate precisely; remember exactly
USAGE: The police detectives were unable to *put their finger on any evidence* at the crime scene.

✍ Money

pony up — pay money
USAGE: Rick told his friends it was time for everyone to *pony up* their share of the cost.

(as) poor as a church mouse — very poor; destitute
Robert's clothes were so old that the others thought he was probably *poor as a church mouse*!

(a) pretty penny — a large amount of money
USAGE: Tony was delighted that he would be paid *a pretty penny* for his computer consulting duties.

✍ Movement

set forth — start to go somewhere; begin a trip
USAGE: John and Vickie *set forth* on their cross country journey today at Noon.

set in — weather condition begins and will probably continue
USAGE: The snowstorm was predicted to *set in* at about midnight.

shake a leg — go fast; hurry
USAGE: Ted advised Jim that since the group was in a hurry, he would have to *shake a leg* if he wanted to accompany the group.

✍ Personal Description

holy terror — a very disobedient or unruly child
USAGE: The little boy is a *holy terror* and his teachers feel powerless in trying to discipline him.

hopped up — high on a drug or on alcohol
USAGE: It was discovered by police the man who was arrested for robbery
   was *hopped up* on an illegal narcotic.

horse sense — good judgment; wisdom in making decisions
USAGE: Most people believe Susan has a lot of *horse sense* and is practical.

in character — as usual; consistent with the way that a person usually behaves
USAGE: Optimism and a supportive attitude is *in character* with Kathy's
   usual behavior.

✍ Plan / Prepare

see the light of day — be born or begun
USAGE: Because of his lack of cash, I don't believe Frank's plans to start a
   business will ever *see the light of day*.

set about — begin; start
USAGE: Roger *set about* preparing for the implementation of the new
   production process at the company.

set back — cause to put off or get behind schedule; slow up
USAGE: Production was *set back* about two months because of the damaged
   caused by the typhoon.

✍ Quantity

take on — load
USAGE: The cargo ship *took on* most of its freight a few days before it left the
   port.

✍ Relationship

play-off — to continue to compete or play in to establish a winner
USAGE: The two teams competed in a *play-off* match to determine who would
   advance to the championship game.

play the field — date many different people; avoid steady dating with a person
USAGE: Since Joyce is no longer dating Bill, she is *playing the field* by dating
   three different men during the last two months.

✍ Satisfaction

riding high — attracting attention; enjoying great popularity; success

USAGE: The entrepreneur has been *riding high* since the successful start up of his business.

roll out the red carpet — welcome someone with hospitality and warmth
USAGE: The local leaders *rolled out the red carpet* when the provincial governor visited the town.

security blanket — something one holds on to for reassurance or comfort (like a child and a blanket)
USAGE: He carries around his cell phone as a *security blanket* when he travels.

see one's way clear to do something — feel able to do something
USAGE: Susan asked Jim, "When you *see your way clear to start the undertaking* please let me know."

✍ Service

piggyback — being carried on the someone's back; connecting with something larger
USAGE: The father was having fun with his son, carrying him *piggyback* around the house.

pitch in — give help or money for something
USAGE: Nancy *pitched in* and helped him finish the project.

✍ Time

once or twice — a few times
USAGE: Thomas remarked he has visited the restaurant *once or twice* within the last year.

out of the blue — unexpectedly; from nowhere
USAGE: From *out of the blue*, Frank asked Mary if she would consider taking the tour with him.

over the long run — in the end; over a long period of time
USAGE: Larry said *over the long run* he plans to retire and move overseas.

✍ Understand

ring a bell — remind one of something
USAGE: When asked if he had heard of him, James replied the name didn't *ring a bell*.

search one's soul — study one's reasons and actions to see if one has been fair and honest
USAGE: After the divorce, Peter said he had been *searching his soul* to see if there was anything he could have done to save the marriage.

second thought — after thinking about something again
USAGE: On *second thought*, George decided not to attend the meeting.

second-guess — criticize what someone else did or would have done
USAGE: A person shouldn't try to *second guess* decisions made by police officers in a hazardous situation.

see the light — realize a mistake; understand how to proceed with something
USAGE: Stanley *saw the light* and immediately changed his thinking to reflect his new position.

✍ Work

pay off — results of one's work; a bribe
USAGE: James expects the sacrifice made by earning his MBA will *pay off* when he obtains a job in business.

piece of cake — easy
USAGE: Henry remarked the task was a *piece of cake* and not at all difficult.

✍ Achievement

(a) run for your money — strong opponent
USAGE: The other team gave us a *run for our money*.

run the gauntlet — face a hard test or painful experience
USAGE: Jimmy had to *run the gauntlet* of many tasks associated with starting
a business before he began his company.

save the day — prevent something bad from happening
USAGE: They felt Ted *saved the day* when he knew what to say when the
microphone was put in their face.

scare up — find or gather something with some effort
USAGE: John was able to *scare up* some computers to be used by the visitors
during the meeting.

✍ Agree / Approval

swear by — have complete confidence in; be sure of something
USAGE: Henry *swore by* all the money in the world that he was not at the
scene of the crime last Tuesday evening.

swear in — have a person take an official oath to serve
USAGE: The new premier was *sworn in* last night for a full term of service.

✍ Authority

take a back seat — accept a poorer or lower position; be second to something
or someone
USAGE: I *took a back seat* and allowed Larry to conduct the meeting because
he had previously worked with several of the people.

take a stand on something — declare firmly that one is for or against something
USAGE: The Prime Minister and other leaders *took a firm stand on the import
issue*.

✍ Bad / Negative

pull a fast one — to cheat, trick or deceive
USAGE: He attempted to ***pull a fast one*** by changing the accounting cost figures but was detected by the auditors.

pull the plug — expose someone's secret activities
USAGE: Charles decided to ***pull the plug*** on the man's plan to fraudulently charge the company for false expenses.

pull the wool over someone's eyes — deceive or fool someone
USAGE: Tina was advised not to allow him to ***pull the wool over her eyes*** with his elaborate plan.

✍ Business Action

slow down — a form of employee striking without coming to a complete business shutdown
USAGE: The workers implemented a company-wide ***slow down*** at the factory last week.

✍ Communication

run into the ground — dwell upon excessively; belabor an issue
USAGE: He was ***running it into the ground*** about the high score he obtained on the university admission exam.

run over — try to go over something quickly; review briefly
USAGE: Tommy decided to ***run over*** the report before his presentation to the board.

save one's breath — remain silent because talking will do no good
USAGE: He decided to ***save his breath*** and not ask her about it because it would be futile to obtain her help.

say a mouthful — say something of great importance; meaning or length
USAGE: Robert ***said a mouthful*** when he suggested he had experienced distress over the decision.

say one's piece — say openly what one thinks
USAGE: When asked about her opinion, she ***said her piece*** and the room fell quiet.

say the word — give a sign; show a wish

USAGE: John told his wife, "Just *say the word* and I'll be there to drive you home."

(a) score to settle — an argument to settle
USAGE: Michael and Scott were arguing forcefully with each other because they had *a score to settle*.

✍ Completeness

skin of one's teeth — only just; barely
USAGE: It was an extremely close race and Alan won the 10K run by the *skin of his teeth*.

skin deep — only on the surface; not having any deep or honest meaning
USAGE: James said while most men consider only a woman's looks, he knows real beauty is more than *skin deep*.

✍ Consequence

step on one's toes — do something that embarrasses or offends someone else
USAGE: Because of his abrasive style, George ends up *stepping on people's toes* at work and offending them.

stew in one's own juice — suffer from something that one has caused to happen oneself
USAGE: Scott is *stewing in his own juice* after accumulating a large amount of debt.

stick (someone) with — leave someone with something unpleasant
USAGE: He was *stuck with* the bill for taking the business clients out to dinner and the theater.

✍ Different

square peg in a round hole — a person who does not fit into a job or position
USAGE: Feeling like a misfit in the group, William has often said he feels like a *square peg in a round hole*.

✍ Disagree

short shrift — rude treatment
USAGE: Betty received *short shrift* from her colleague when she asked for assistance on a project.

✍ Emotion

riding high — to feel very good
USAGE: John was *riding high* after he received notice he was admitted to the MBA program of his choice.

(a) royal pain — a feeling of irritation or agitation.
USAGE: He always felt it was *a royal pain* to deal with Susan's complaining.

run wild — be or go out of control
USAGE: The excited fans *ran wild* when the musicians began playing at the rock concert.

scare out of one's wits — frighten very much
USAGE: Fred told her he was *scared out of his wits* after watching the film about the murder.

scare the daylights out of someone — frighten very much
USAGE: When he slipped while walking along the edge of the mountain it *scared the daylights out of him*.

✍ End

tear up — tear something up into small pieces
USAGE: Frustrated at hearing the bad news, Ted *tore up* the report he was reading.

✍ Failure

miss out on — lose an opportunity
USAGE: Joseph *missed out on* playing in the game because it had started by the time he arrived.

miss the boat — lose an opportunity
USAGE: He *missed the boat* on enrolling in graduate school because he failed to meet the application deadline.

✍ Health

(as) sick as a dog — very sick; ill
USAGE: Robert didn't attend tonight's meeting because he was *sick as a dog*.

skin and bones — very skinny
USAGE: I am concerned about Karen's health because she's lost so much weight and she looks like *skin and bones*.

✍ Location

rain closet — the shower
USAGE: After coming home from exercising at the gym, Steven hit the *rain closet* to clean up.

run around — go to different places for entertainment or to do things
USAGE: I've been *running around* taking care of errands all day.

✍ Money

prey on/upon — cheat; rob; unscrupulously profit upon
USAGE: The crooked salesman *preyed on* the elderly man and cheated him out of a large amount of money.

put the bite on someone — ask for money or favors
USAGE: George *put the bite on several of his friends* to obtain money for the fund raising event.

put up — provide money or something needed
USAGE: The business partners were searching for interested investors to *put up* money for the start-up company.

✍ Movement

shoot up — arise suddenly
USAGE: The fire unexpectedly *shot up* over the roof of the warehouse.

slow down — go more slowly than usual
USAGE: Fearful he was driving too fast, Rebecca asked Jim to *slow down*.

snail's pace — a very slow movement forward
USAGE: The traffic along the avenue was moving at a *snail's pace* due to the road construction.

traffic jam — vehicles blocking each other along a road or highway
USAGE: They were delayed in arriving at the meeting because of the *traffic jam* near downtown.

✍ Personal Description

in-your-face — a contemptuous and disrespectful manner
USAGE: The teenager was confrontational in his manner and had a real *in-your-face* attitude about the plan.

keep one's nose clean — stay out of trouble
USAGE: After having some behavior problems in class, Richard was working
  hard to *keep his nose clean* at school.

knockout — a very attractive and pretty woman
USAGE: He said the woman on the train was a real *knockout*.

know what's what — to be informed
USAGE: Bill has been through an ownership change before, so he *knows
  what's what*.

lady's man — a man who is popular among women
USAGE: Benjamin likes to think he's a real *lady's man* but I think this exists
  only in his mind.

lame duck — public official who has a short time left to serve and has less
  power than before
USAGE: Since the mayor will not serve again, he is a *lame duck* and will not
  get much accomplished.

✍ Plan / Prepare

set out — (1) decide to attempt; determine to begin; (2) leave on a journey
USAGE (1): John *set out* to learn to how to develop web pages on the Internet.
USAGE (2): The tour group *set out* to travel throughout Asia for three months.

set sail — start sailing; begin a sea voyage
USAGE: The ship was to *set sail* for an excursion to Australia's Gold Coast.

✍ Relationship

play up to someone — flatter or please someone to try and gain some
  advantage
USAGE: Peter was accused of *playing up to his boss* in order to receive the
  promotion.

polish the apple — try to win favor by flattering someone
USAGE: It was obvious he was trying to improve his standing by *polishing
  the apple* with her.

✍ Satisfaction

sell oneself short — underestimate oneself

USAGE: I feel Paul is *selling himself short* if he believes he can't get another girlfriend.

set one's heart on — want very much; to be determined
USAGE: I've *set my heart on* getting a well paying job that allows me to spend time with my family.

set store on/by — like or value; want to keep
USAGE: The University *sets great store on* the ability of its graduates to obtain good jobs after graduation.

settle down — live a stable life
USAGE: After Henry graduated from the University and got married, he wanted to *settle down* and start a family.

✍ Service

play ball with someone — cooperate fairly with someone; to be compliant
USAGE: The new employees at the company refused to *play ball and work with us* to complete the project.

see to it — take the responsibility to do something; make sure
USAGE: Roger asked Stan to *see to it* that the information was posted on the company's website.

✍ Similar

run with the world — to do what is popular; follow the crowd
USAGE: Roger's father reprimanded him for *running with the world* and not making his own choices in life.

✍ Time

over with — at the end of; finished with
USAGE: Jack remarked that when the soccer game is *over with*, he wants me to accompany him to dinner.

pick up — start again after interruption; go on
USAGE: Joe and his work group decided to take a lunch break and *pick up* where they left off in the afternoon.

pressed for time — in a hurry; have barely enough time
USAGE: Since Julie was *pressed for time*, I wasn't able to discuss the issue with her.

put in (time) — spend time
USAGE: Everyone agreed that Vincent *put in a lot of time* working on the project.

✍ Understand

see the world/things through rose colored glasses — see only the good things about something; be too optimistic
USAGE: Vickie tends to *see the world through rose-colored glasses* since she is typically trusting and idealistic.

see things — imagine sights that are not real; think one sees what is not there
USAGE: Frank sometimes describes bizarre situations in which he is *seeing things* which aren't real. Actually, I think he's having hallucinations.

see through — understand someone's true self or motivation
USAGE: Joe indicated he could *see through* her attempt to influence the decision in her favor.

set eyes on — to see
USAGE: Steven said to the other men, "I *set eyes today on* the most beautiful woman in the world."

shady — unclear or purposely misleading; suspicious results
USAGE: Many people believe Alan has been somewhat *shady* in his business operations.

✍ Work

pink slip — dismissal notice from a job
USAGE: Jack was fearful he would be given a *pink slip* and would no longer have a job.

pound the pavement — look for a job
USAGE: While Anthony has been *pounding the pavement* for several months, he still remains unemployed.

Week 42

✍ Achievement

scrape up — find or gather something with some effort
USAGE: The group of university students *scraped up* some money to take a backpacking trip in southwest China.

see out — finish and not quit
USAGE: While John wanted to leave his company and begin work for the small start-up firm, he decided to stay with the company long enough to *see out* the remodeling of the factory.

see to (something) — attend to or do something
USAGE: I will *see to* obtaining tickets for tomorrow night's concert performance.

set the world on fire — do something outstanding or that makes one famous
USAGE: While Paul hasn't *set the world on fire* with his sales record, he is making good progress on improving his selling skills.

✍ Agree / Approval

switched on — in tune with contemporary ideas and fashions
USAGE: Bill's mother is *switched on* to the latest style and keeps abreast of the trends.

take by storm — win the favor of; become popular with a group of people
USAGE: The performing artist *took the city by storm* when he recently appeared in concert.

✍ Authority

take over — take control; take command
USAGE: The business was *taken over* recently by a foreign company and we wonder if changes will be made.

take the Fifth — refers to the U.S. Constitution which states a person can't be required to testify against themselves (incriminate oneself)

USAGE: When testifying in court, he decided to ***take the Fifth*** rather than risk creating more trouble for himself.

✍ Bad / Negative

put (someone) out — inconvenience; bother
USAGE: When planning to visit Michael and his family, Betsy did not want him to ***put him out*** by hosting her.

put (something) past someone (negative) — be surprised by what someone does
USAGE: I wouldn't ***put it past him*** to quit his job and start focusing on his longtime desire of writing poetry.

put out — be inconvenienced or irritated
USAGE: Laura was ***put out*** that he didn't offer to take her to dinner.

✍ Business Action

take someone for a ride — cheat; swindle
USAGE: The salesman misled John with the proposal and ***took him for a ride*** with the business deal.

✍ Communication

search me — "I don't know"; no answer available
USAGE: When asked what he believed the future of the company would be, Tom said, "***Search me***, it all depends on the economy."

send away for something — to place an order
USAGE: I ***sent away for a book*** advertised on the Internet last week but it hasn't arrived yet.

set forth — explain exactly or clearly
USAGE: The professor ***set forth*** the grading criteria for the class.

shoot the breeze/bull — to talk idly
USAGE: We were just ***shooting the breeze*** as we enjoyed the nice weather in the park.

shut up — stop talking
USAGE: Steven angrily told the others, "***Shut up*** and get to work."

sit in — political demonstration where students or workers refuse to leave their classroom or job sites
USAGE: During the 1960s, American students held *sit-ins* to protest the Vietnam War.

✍ Completeness

sort of — almost; similar to; not quite
USAGE: When his parents asked James if he had finished his homework, he replied, "Well, *sort of*, but not all of it."

take down — take apart; pull to pieces
USAGE: We *took down* our camping tent when we saw the storm gathering in the sky.

✍ Consequence

stir up — cause some action to occur, rouse
USAGE: The open hostility exhibited by some people really *stirred up* the crowd with anger.

straw in the wind — a small sign of what may happen
USAGE: When Jim's career advancement began to slow, it was a *straw in the wind* as to what the future held for his career.

straw that breaks the camel's back — a small problem which follows other troubles that contributes to final determination
USAGE: While there had been problems with Kevin and the company, when it was discovered money was missing, it was the *straw that broke the camel's back* and he was fired.

✍ Different

stand in for someone — be a substitute for someone else
USAGE: Since George couldn't attend the meeting, James agreed to *stand in for him*.

✍ Disagree

sick and tired — dislike something; be annoyed with something
USAGE: Charles said he was *sick and tired* of never having enough money.

sick of (someone/something) — bored with; dislike

USAGE: Wendy remarked she was ***sick of*** the food she had to eat while on her low-fat diet.

✍ Emotion

screw around — loaf about; hang around without doing anything
USAGE: He spent the entire morning ***screwing around*** and getting nothing done.

see red — become very angry
USAGE: Becoming highly upset when hearing the news, Robert ***saw red*** and started drinking.

set one's mind at rest — free oneself from worry
USAGE: To ***set his mind at rest***, I assured him we wouldn't drive at night.

seventh heaven — a state of intense delight
USAGE: Jack has been in ***seventh heaven*** since he was offered the job.

shook up — upset; worried
USAGE: Sharon was ***shook up*** after the car accident and prefers not to drive unless it's an essential trip.

(a) shot in the arm — to energize
USAGE: Susan got ***a shot in the arm*** when she heard the news that Robert was released from prison.

✍ End

throw in the towel — surrender; give up
USAGE: Recognizing she liked Jack more than me, I ***threw in the towel*** and didn't continue to pursue Laura.

✍ Error

slip up — make a mistake
USAGE: I ***slipped up*** when I agreed to teach the class for Dr. Smith. I later realized I was scheduled to be out of town.

✍ Failure

no-show — one who reserves attendance for something but neither comes or cancels

USAGE: While initially agreeing to attend, many of the celebrities were ***no-shows*** at the concert last night.

on the blink — not working
USAGE: My computer has been ***on the blink*** and won't connect to the Internet.

✍ Health

sleep a wink — to sleep only a short amount
USAGE: I didn't ***sleep a wink*** last night.

sleep around — to have sex with many people
USAGE: He has a bad reputation because he ***sleeps around*** with different women.

✍ Importance

on one's toes — be alert
USAGE: The professor was known as a teacher who would keep the students ***on their toes***.

✍ Location

run away with — leave location with someone
USAGE: She ***ran away with*** her boyfriend to another city without informing her parents.

run into (someone) — meet by chance
USAGE: Kevin ***ran into*** his old girlfriend while at the market.

run off with (someone) — go away with someone; elope
USAGE: Jane ***ran off to another city with*** her boyfriend, got married and had a baby when she was young.

run over — drive on top of; ride over
USAGE: The car ***ran over*** a small rabbit while traveling on the road.

✍ Money

rake in the money — make a lot of money
USAGE: Jack's new business has been ***raking in the money*** since its first day of operation.

ring up — add and record on a cash register
USAGE: Deciding to buy the new set of clothes, John ask the clerk to *ring up* the purchase.

rip off — cheat; rob
USAGE: The thieves *ripped off* the unsuspecting visitors to the museum.

rob Peter to pay Paul — take from one person or thing to pay another
USAGE: The government's policy of taking money from the rich to assist the poor is like *robbing Peter to pay Paul*.

✍ Movement

step by step — gradually
USAGE: Bill made a commitment to learn more about technology and *step by step* he learned how to use the World Wide Web.

step on it — go faster; hurry
USAGE: When Don asked his son to drive him to the airport, he told him, "*Step on it*, my flight leaves in one hour."

✍ Personal Description

look like a million dollars — look well and prosperous; appear healthy and happy
USAGE: Vickie *looked like a million dollars* when I saw her at the market yesterday.

look like the cat that ate/swallowed the canary — to appear very self-satisfied as if enjoyed some kind of success
USAGE: After reaching a deal that would promise a great deal of profit, Bryan *looked like the cat that ate the canary*.

loopy — unstable or crazy
USAGE: Barbara has the reputation of being somewhat offbeat and *loopy*.

(a) loose cannon — someone who is unpredictable
USAGE: Walter's lawyer was concerned if his client talked to the newspaper reporter, he might be *a loose cannon* and say something inappropriate.

✍ Plan / Prepare

set up — make something ready to use by putting the parts together

USAGE: After we *set up* the printer to the computer, we were able to print the document.

setup — the way something is arranged
USAGE: My father's office is a nice *setup* with a large desk and window looking out to the park.

shop around — go to various stores to look for something
USAGE: Wanting to get a good deal, Jim and Carl *shopped around* for the best deal on a laptop computer.

✎ Quantity

take up — pull and make tight
USAGE: I asked the seamstress to *take up* my pants so they would fit better.

taper off — slowly come to an end
USAGE: The snowstorm began to *taper off* before midnight.

✎ Relationship

pop the question — ask someone to marry you
USAGE: Richard had been planning for some time how he would *pop the question* to Mary.

pot calling the kettle black — a person who is criticizing someone having the same faults
USAGE: When Don criticized Jim for being a poor manager of money, it was like the *pot calling the kettle black* because Don quickly spends any money he makes.

✎ Satisfaction

settle for — be satisfied with less; agree to
USAGE: While Harold *settled for* less salary than he wanted, he realized he needed to accept the job since he was unemployed.

sewed up — to complete successfully
USAGE: Thomas *sewed up* the interview by being offered the job as a result of his responses during the meeting.

shine up to — try to please; try to make friends with

USAGE: James is always trying to **shine up to** the pretty girl who works in his office.

shoot straight — act fairly; deal honestly
USAGE: Having the reputation of being direct and saying what's on his mind, Roger has a reputation of **shooting straight**.

✍ Service

serve one's purpose — be useful to someone for a certain need
USAGE: The increase in company sales should **serve Stanley's purpose** of being named president of the company.

set loose — set free; release something that you are holding
USAGE: The young boy **set loose** the tortoise he had earlier captured.

✍ Superior

sacred cow — something that is never criticized or laughed at even if it deserves to be
USAGE: The government retirement system is regarded by many people as a **sacred cow** and should never be changed.

show off — a person who brags a lot or acts in conspicuous manner
USAGE: Henry is a **show off** and tries to impress people with his knowledge of technology.

✍ Time

rain check — a promise to repeat an invitation at a later date
USAGE: Since I am out of town tomorrow and can't accept the dinner offer, I would like a **rain check**.

red letter day — a day that is special because of some important event
USAGE: Tuesday was a **red letter day** in the town when the team won the basketball provincial championship.

right away — immediately
USAGE: I went **right away** to obtain the emergency supplies to help in the accident.

✍ Understand

shape up — begin to act and look right
USAGE: Jack's performance has begun to *shape up* and he is doing much
  better at the company.

show off — try to attract attention; display
USAGE: Pamela is proud of her new car and enjoys *showing it off* among her
  friends.

sink in — to penetrate; become understood
USAGE: The circumstances of the tragic accident *sunk in* with many of the
  young people.

size up — form an opinion; assess a situation
USAGE: Karen was *sizing up* the situation before deciding whether to participate
  in the event.

✍ Work

pull the plug — quit a job
USAGE: Bill decided to *pull the plug* on his job and quit the company.

roll up one's sleeves — prepare to work hard or seriously
USAGE: The group members each *rolled up their sleeves* and went to work on
  finishing the job.

✍ Achievement

sink one's teeth into — go to work seriously
USAGE: Bill realized it would be a challenging project, yet he was looking forward to *sinking his teeth into* the task.

sink or swim — fail or succeed by your own efforts
USAGE: Betty knows she will have to *sink or swim* when she begins her new job at the company.

(a) snap — an easy task
USAGE: Many of the staff members agreed it was *a snap* to finish the job.

(a) snowball's chance in hell — a small chance to succeed
USAGE: Without taking a flight to Beijing, Robert has a *snowball's chance in hell* in arriving in time for the meeting.

✍ Agree / Approval

take care of — look after or give attention to someone or something
USAGE: The doctor recommended that Mary stop smoking and *take care of* her health.

take for granted — assume something is a certain way or is correct
USAGE: I *took it for granted* that she realized gambling was extremely risky and she could easily lose money.

✍ Authority

throw one's weight around — use one's influence in an aggressive way
USAGE: Janet doesn't appreciate the way James *throws his weight around* since he's been appointed manager.

tie down — keep someone from going somewhere; confine or limit
USAGE: The responsibilities of Richard's new job *tied him down* and didn't allow him to travel.

✍ Bad / Negative

skeleton in one's closet — a secret that involves shame or disgrace for a person
USAGE: Newspaper reports revealed *skeletons in Bill's closet* that were highly damaging to his reputation.

✍ Communication

sit in on — attend or participate in a meeting
USAGE: The newspaper reporter *sat in on* the meeting to find out details on the plan.

slip of the tongue — say the wrong thing at the wrong time by accident
USAGE: In a *slip of the tongue* he asked the lady if she was pregnant when, in fact, she wasn't expecting a baby.

snow job — (1) an attempt to deceive or persuade through untrue or exaggerated talk; (2) the use of technical words to seem like an expert
USAGE (1): William gave us a *snow job* when he said unless the money was provided, it would be a disaster.
USAGE (2): John's presentation was a real *snow job* with his use of jargon and terminology intended to confuse the audience.

sound off — tell what one knows or thinks in a loud voice
USAGE: The students took advantage of the meeting to *sound off* about their desire for the university to install more Internet connections.

sound out — attempt to find out how a person feels about something by asking questions
USAGE: He has been *sounding out* his boss about an opportunity for pay raises among workers at the factory.

✍ Completeness

to a fault — a trait so excessive it is almost bad
USAGE: He is honest *to a fault* in that he says almost anything that comes to mind.

to a T — perfectly; exactly
USAGE: His wife said his new shirt fit *to a T*.

✍ Consequence

sure thing — something sure to happen; something about which there is no doubt

USAGE: She was told the job offer would be a ***sure thing***.

swear off — decide to give up something previously done
USAGE: Kevin decided to *swear off* smoking cigarettes.

✍ Disagree

sing/whistle a different tune — contradict something said before; talk or act in the opposite way
USAGE: While Rick used to say he would never gamble, he is now ***singing a different tune*** since I saw him at the casino last night.

sixes and sevens — in confusion or disagreement
USAGE: Her unexpected response to his question left him feeling at ***sixes and sevens***.

✍ Emotion

simmer down — become calm, quiet
USAGE: While James was furious when told the news, he later ***simmered down*** and tried to understand the situation.

snap out of it — return to normal; stop being afraid
USAGE: She ***snapped out of*** her self-pity and returned to completing the project.

sob story — a story that makes one feel pity or sorrow
USAGE: The student told the teacher a ***sob story*** about her inability to use her hand did not permit her to finish the assignment.

soft spot for someone/something — a feeling of affection toward a person or thing
USAGE: He has a ***soft spot for stray dogs*** in the neighborhood.

somebody up there loves/hates me — an expression that a higher power has been helpful
USAGE: When she found out about her job promotion, Susan said, "***Somebody up there loves me***."

sore loser — someone who gets angry when losing
USAGE: Timothy is a ***sore loser*** when things don't work out his way.

✍ End

to the wall — into a place from which there is no escape

USAGE: His wife finally pushed him *to the wall* and he demanded a divorce.

✍ Failure

on the fritz — to be broken or to not function properly
USAGE: My computer is *on the fritz* and not working right.

out of line — unacceptable; not correct
USAGE: His attempt to kiss me was *out of line*. We just met two hours earlier.

✍ Health

sponged — thirsty
USAGE: Mike told Jim, "I'm *sponged*! Let's go get a drink."

sweet tooth — an attraction to eating sugar, sweets
USAGE: Since Mark has a *sweet tooth*, he loves to eat chocolate whenever possible.

✍ Importance

play second fiddle to someone — be second in importance to someone
USAGE: As assistant manager, Larry has been *playing second fiddle to his boss* at the company.

✍ Location

scatter around — carelessly put in different places
USAGE: Paul was searching among his papers that were *scattered around* his office to find the receipt.

scrounge around — looking around for something
USAGE: While watching the basketball game on television, the men *scrounged around* the kitchen looking for snack food.

shut up — confine
USAGE: We *shut up* the kitten in the other room because Pam was allergic to cats.

sit back — located a distance away (usually from a street)
USAGE: The new office building *sits back* one hundred meters from the road.

✍ Money

run through — to consume rapidly; spend recklessly
USAGE: Steven and Karen *ran through* a lot of money before they had their first child.

salt away — save money
USAGE: He *salted away* as much money as possible for next summer's vacation.

scrape together — gather money a little at a time
USAGE: We tried to *scrape together* enough money to take a cruise during our vacation.

✍ Movement

step on the gas — go faster; hurry
USAGE: Robert needed to *step on the gas* to arrive at the concert on time.

step up — make something go faster
USAGE: Because of increased customer demand, the company had to *step up* production at the automobile factory.

stop dead/cold — stop moving very quickly
USAGE: When Kevin saw the police car in front of his house he *stopped dead*.

✍ Personal Description

(a) lot on the ball — an intelligent person
USAGE: Many people have remarked that Roger is very bright and has *a lot on the ball*.

man on the street — the average or ordinary person
USAGE: The newspaper article reported that, according to the typical *man on the street*, there is great hope for the economy to improve.

mental — an irrational person; mental illness
USAGE: He appeared *mental* when he suggested he would live forever.

name is mud — a person's reputation becomes bad
USAGE: His *name is mud* now that he has been accused of trying to bribe the police.

✍ Plan / Prepare

shore up — add support to something which is weak
USAGE: The workers found it necessary to *shore up* the foundation of the house after the flooding.

shot in the dark — an attempt without much hope or chance of succeeding
USAGE: His attempt to convict the criminal suspect without any solid evidence was a *shot in the dark*.

show one's cards — disclose one's plans
USAGE: Susan has not yet *shown us her cards* so it's hard to predict her plans.

sit up — stay awake instead of going to bed
USAGE: Because the baby was sick, Laura wanted to *sit up* last night and watch over her.

slap together — make in a hurry and without care
USAGE: Bill and Steve *slapped together* a sack lunch to take with them on their backpacking trip.

✍ Quantity

tip the scales — weigh
USAGE: The boxer *tipped the scales* at around 106 kilograms.

to boot — in addition; also
USAGE: He was informed that he will not only need a new computer but a new printer *to boot*.

✍ Relationship

rob the cradle — to have a romance with someone much younger than oneself
USAGE: All of his friends agreed that Fred was *robbing the cradle* when he dated the college student.

✍ Satisfaction

short end (of the stick) — unfair; unequal treatment
USAGE: Susan complained she received the *short end of the stick* because she was female.

shot in the arm — something inspiring or encouraging
USAGE: He got a *shot in the arm* when she accepted his invitation to dinner.

✍ Time

right off the bat — immediately; from the beginning
USAGE: I told Scott *right off the bat* what we needed was someone who could maintain our website.

roll around — return at a regular or usual time; come back
USAGE: Phillip remarked as he gets older his birthday seems to *roll around* faster.

short and sweet — brief and pleasant
USAGE: The poem written by John was *short and sweet*.

shove off — start; leave
USAGE: Walking to his car, Thomas said to his wife, "It is time for us to *shove off* if we want to arrive home before evening."

✍ Understand

sleep on it — think about something; consider; decide later
USAGE: When the salesman asked Ronald if he wanted to buy the car, he replied that he would *sleep on it* and give him the answer tomorrow.

slip one's mind — to forget or overlook
USAGE: Joseph apologized for missing the meeting and said it *slipped his mind*.

smoke out — find out the facts about something
USAGE: The mayor wanted to *smoke out* the real reasons why the company didn't locate the factory in his city.

soak up — take in information like a sponge takes up water
USAGE: The professor urged his students to *soak up* knowledge through listening to his lectures.

spun out — a confused or stressed state of mind
USAGE: George said he was completely *spun out* after the exhausting job interview in which he was asked to respond to simulated job situations.

stand for — be a sign of; to symbolize
USAGE: Roger was confused because he couldn't figure out what the abbreviation *stood for* in the sentence.

stand to reason — make sense; be logical

USAGE: Kathy advised her friend that if her boyfriend was known to mistreat another girl, it ***stands to reason*** he could also abuse her.

✍ Work

run around in circles — act confused; do a lot but accomplish little
USAGE: Vickie remarked that she's been ***running around in circles*** all day and hasn't been able to concentrate on the project.

snow under — to be overwhelmed with something
USAGE: Thomas was complaining that he's been ***snowed under*** with added work demands during the last week.

Week 44

✍ Achievement

sock it to someone — give everything one is capable of
USAGE: The speaker really *socked it to the audience* with his powerful and motivating speech at the conference.

spread oneself too thin — try to do too many things at one time
USAGE: Janet has been *spreading herself way too thin* lately and I'm worried her activity will leave her exhausted.

stand off — score is tied and winner undecided
USAGE: Since it was scoreless and a *stand off* between the two teams, the game went into overtime.

stick it out — endure; continue
USAGE: While Mary doesn't like her current job, she plans to *stick it out* until a new position opens up.

stick with — continue doing; not quit; persist
USAGE: Joe was able to *stick with* his exercise plan, even when the weather was bad.

✍ Agree / Approval

take kindly to — be pleased by; like
USAGE: She doesn't *take kindly to* other people telling her how to discipline her children.

take one's hat off to someone — admire; respect; praise
USAGE: Jack reminded us we should *take our hats off to him* for doing so much to improve our city.

✍ Authority

tie up — limit or prevent the use of
USAGE: Vincent remarked that almost all of his money is *tied up* in the stock market.

to heel — under control
USAGE: The police brought the suspected gang members *to heel* by watching every move they made throughout the city.

✍ Bad / Negative

skip bail — accused person does not show at trial and forfeits money paid to secure appearance
USAGE: Fearful of being convicted and sentenced to prison, the alleged thief *skipped bail* and became a fugitive from the law.

smell a rat — become suspicious
USAGE: Thinking that something didn't seem right when the clerk wasn't at the desk, John said he *smelled a rat* and later discovered the man had been robbed and tied up in the back room.

stick up — rob with a gun
USAGE: A man with a gun tried to *stick up* my wife on the subway.

✍ Communication

speak for — make a request for; reserve something
USAGE: Wanting to obtain the choice seat for the long drive, Steven *spoke for* the front passenger seat.

speak one's piece — say openly what one thinks
USAGE: John believed it was time for him to *speak his piece* concerning his opinion about the project.

speak out — speak in favor of or in support of something
USAGE: The supervisor *spoke out* in support of a pay increase for workers.

speak up — speak in a loud or clear voice
USAGE: Because there was a large crowd in the lecture hall, a student asked the professor to *speak up* so everyone could hear.

spell out — explain something in very simple words; explain very clearly
USAGE: The teacher *spelled out* the objectives for the assignment.

spill the beans — tell a secret; inform
USAGE: Michael pledged not to *spill the beans* about the factory that will be relocating to our town.

✍ Completeness

to the bone — thoroughly; entirely
USAGE: He became chilled *to the bone* when the ice storm hit.

✍ Consequence

take one's own medicine — accept punishment without complaining
USAGE: While Bobby likes to criticize other people, he can't *take his own medicine* when other people find fault with him.

take the rap — receive punishment; be accused and punished
USAGE: The president of the company was forced to *take the rap* for swindling investors out of a significant amount of money.

tan someone's hide — give a beating to; spank hard
USAGE: The boy's father threatened to *tan his hide* if he lied again to his teacher.

✍ Different

stand on one's own two feet — to be independent
USAGE: Even as a young boy, Richard learned to *stand on his own two feet* and to be self-reliant.

✍ Disagree

skin alive — scold angrily; spank or beat
USAGE: Walter said if he ever discovered who threw the rock at his little brother, he would *skin him alive*.

slap in the face — an insult
USAGE: Linda believed her failure to receive a pay raise was a *slap in the face*.

✍ Emotion

spaced out — confused; incoherent; resembling someone who is using drugs
USAGE: As a result of only sleeping two hours last night, Kevin seemed *spaced out* today.

stars in one's eyes — an appearance or feeling of very great happiness
USAGE: Karen had *stars in her eyes* when Paul asked to marry her.

stir up a hornet's nest — make many people angry; do something that many people don't like
USAGE: James *stirred up a hornet's nest* when he suggested that everyone should start showing their photo identification cards when making withdrawals at the bank.

stuck on — very much in love with; crazy about
USAGE: The college student has been *stuck on* a boy in her history class.

swallow one's pride — bring one's pride under control; become humble
USAGE: John decided to *swallow his pride* and admit he was wrong.

✍ End

top off — come or bring to a special or unexpected ending
USAGE: The conference was *topped off* by a luncheon and a keynote address by a distinguished speaker.

✍ Error

song and dance — excuses to justify something
USAGE: The student gave the professor a *song and dance* about being sick and unable to attend class.

✍ Failure

out of order — not working
USAGE: Several of the computers in the Internet cafe were *out of order*.

shut out — prevent the opposite team from scoring
USAGE: The men's soccer team *shut out* the visiting team.

✍ Health

take a leak — to urinate
USAGE: Bill stopped along the road to *take a leak* while driving home.

take ill/sick — become sick
USAGE: Wendy asked Jim's mother, "When was he *taken ill*?"

✍ Importance

small fry — someone or something of little importance; young children

USAGE: Believing the president wouldn't be interested in hearing from a *small fry* like him, Jim said he wouldn't write a letter. However, Karen urged him to write and express his opinion.

✐ Location

sitting duck — an easy target
USAGE: John advised the tourists not to expose cash in their wallets or they would be a *sitting duck* for a thief.

skid row — area of a city where many people live who have no money and drink a lot of alcohol
USAGE: Some people thought since he lost his job and his drinking was getting worse, he could be headed for *skid row*.

speak of the devil — a person appears when someone is talking about them
USAGE: Laura was talking to the group when Jim walked in. She said, "*Speak of the devil*, we were just talking about you!"

stamping/stomping grounds — a place where a person spends much of his time
USAGE: Steven returned to his teenage *stomping grounds* in the city.

✐ Money

set (one) back — to cost
USAGE: Her friends asked Susan how much her new dress *set her back*.

set up — establish; provide the money for something
USAGE: The investors provided the money to *set up* the new business.

shake down — get money by threats
USAGE: The criminals *shook down* the store owners to obtain money.

shell out — pay
USAGE: John *shelled out* a lot of money to buy a powerful laptop computer.

✐ Movement

stop in one's tracks — stop very quickly, possibly by force
USAGE: Paul was walking down the street when he heard a police siren nearby which made him *stop in his tracks*.

take a powder — leave quickly; run away
USAGE: When I turned around she was gone. She must have *taken a powder* immediately after the meeting.

✍ Personal Description

new person — a person who has improved him or herself
USAGE: Peter feels like a *new person* now that he has quit smoking and has begun an exercise program.

nobody's fool — a smart person; one who cannot be easily fooled
USAGE: Brian is a highly intelligent man and *nobody's fool*.

(have one's) nose in something — unwelcome interest in something
USAGE: He seems to be always putting his *nose in other people's* business. He should mind his own business.

nutty as a fruitcake — a crazy person
USAGE: Our neighbor seems *nutty as a fruitcake*.

oddball — a person who doesn't act like everyone else
USAGE: She seems like an *oddball* with her peculiar manner.

✍ Plan / Prepare

spic and span — very clean; very neat
USAGE: Carol was always busy keeping her house *spic and span*.

spoon feed — make something very easy for someone
USAGE: The teacher *spoon feeds* his students mathematics and other faculty members are concerned the students are not developing proficiency in math.

spruce up — clean; redecorate
USAGE: The students and faculty *spruced up* the school for the alumni reunion,

✍ Quantity

to pieces — very much; greatly
USAGE: James loves his family *to pieces*.

to the full/fullest — very much; fully
USAGE: Always full of energy, Timothy enjoys living his life *to the fullest*.

✍ Relationship

(a) roll in the hay — a couple having sex
USAGE: Steve and Mary went to the bedroom and had *a roll in the hay*!

rub off — pass to someone nearby; transmit to someone
USAGE: Francis did not want her husband's bad habit of talking with profanity
to *rub off* on their son.

rub someone the wrong way — irritate others with something one says or
does
USAGE: William's outspokenness has always *rubbed me the wrong way*.

✍ Satisfaction

show up — (1) become visible; (2) appear; arrive; be present
USAGE (1): At first, the writing on the antique vase wasn't visible but after
cleaning it began to *show up*.
USAGE (2): Stanley wanted to know when the professor finally *showed up* for
class.

(a) sight for sore eyes — someone or something pleasant to see
USAGE: The returning soldiers told the crowd that seeing the children was *a
sight for sore eyes*.

sit back — relax; rest; take time out
USAGE: Betsy and I wanted to *sit back* and enjoy the afternoon.

✍ Service

take in — let someone come in; admit
USAGE: Robert and Carol decided to *take in* the homeless person and assist
him in finding a place to live.

✍ Similar

six of one or half-a-dozen of the other — two things the same; no difference
USAGE: It was *six of one or half-a-dozen of the other* as to whether we
should drive our car or take the train.

✍ Superior

stand out — be more noticeable

USAGE: Paul likes to drive a car that makes him ***stand out*** from other people.

✐ Time

sight unseen — before seeing a thing or person
USAGE: Mary criticized Fred for buying the car ***sight unseen***.

sit tight — wait patiently for something
USAGE: She asked him to ***sit tight*** for a few minutes while she went to get her camera.

so far — until now
USAGE: ***So far*** there's been no update on the location of the missing hikers.

so far, so good — until now things have gone well
USAGE: "***So far, so good***," Mark replied when asked how his MBA studies were going.

✐ Understand

take in — grasp with the mind
USAGE: While Jane suggested the material is especially difficult to understand, she is trying to ***take in*** as much as possible.

take it — (1) understand from what is said or done; (2) endure criticism
USAGE (1): I ***take it*** that you will need additional time to complete the assignment.
USAGE (2): John agreed he needs to learn how to ***take it*** when his supervisor gives him constructive criticism on improving his job performance.

take something into account — remember and consider
USAGE: Her parents asked the teacher to ***take into account*** that she has only been studying English for a few weeks.

take something to heart — consider seriously
USAGE: Susan said we shouldn't ***take what he says to heart***. He is really very kind.

take something with a grain of salt — not take seriously something someone has said
USAGE: He cautioned us that we should ***take what Bill says with a grain of salt***.

take stock — assessing or determining a situation or circumstances
USAGE: Bill was taking stock of the possibility of investing his time in completing an MBA degree.

take stock in (usually negative) — have faith in; to believe in
USAGE: William *took no stock in* the idea that computers will be able to improve the lives of most people.

✍ Work

step down — leave an important position
USAGE: The professor *stepped down* from his longtime job of chairman of the chemistry department.

take on — give a job to, hire; employ
USAGE: The company *took on* 200 new employees to meet the increased customer demand.

✍ Achievement

take a crack at — try; attempt
USAGE: He decided to *take a crack at* working on his car rather than taking it to the repair shop.

take by storm — to please, enthrall a crowd
USAGE: The entertainer *took the city by storm* with his concert performance.

take care of — deal with something; do what is necessary to do something
USAGE: Joseph asked his assistant to *take care of* the office demands including mailing letters and printing documents.

take on — begin to handle; commit oneself to
USAGE: Larry's wife was worried he was *taking on* too many obligations at work and it could affect his health.

✍ Agree / Approval

take to — to like at first meeting; be pleased by or attracted to; accept quickly
USAGE: The employees *took to* the new manager and were optimistic about their future at the company.

tie up — enter into an association or partnership
USAGE: Our department *tied up* with a consulting firm to assist in implementing a new software package.

✍ Bad / Negative

stink / stunk — terrible; bad quality
USAGE: When asked if he approved of the vacation policy at the factory, John said he thought it *stunk*.

string along — to deceive or fool
USAGE: He tried to *string us along* with his story about how the investment would make us all rich.

take for a ride — deceive or fool someone; take unfair advantage of someone
USAGE: I was *taken for a ride* when believing the untruthful claims presented by the salesman.

✍ Communication

stand over — watch closely; keep checking all the time
USAGE: The teacher *stood over* the students to make sure they were preparing for their tests.

stand up and be counted — be willing to say what one thinks in public
USAGE: Feeling very strongly about the issues, Roger believed it was time for him to *stand up and be counted*.

steal one's thunder — do or say something that another person had planned to say
USAGE: Stanley *stole my thunder* when he said changes needed to be made at school to help students develop technology skills.

straight from the horse's mouth — directly from the person involved
USAGE: Wanting to hear it *straight from the horse's mouth*, I asked the manager why I wasn't receiving a pay raise.

straight from the shoulder — open and honest way of speaking
USAGE: Jack is straightforward in his manner and always speaks *straight from the shoulder*.

straight up — used as an affirmation that one is being truthful, precise
USAGE: Tom said *straight-up* what happened; the driver fell asleep behind the wheel of his car.

✍ Completeness

to the hilt — to the maximum amount; completely
USAGE: He played the game *to the hilt* and was very passionate about athletics.

✍ Consequence

tar and feather — punish severely
USAGE: The police chief said he would like to *tar and feather* the person committing the crime.

that'll be the day — that will never happen
USAGE: When asked if he will ever be rich, Jack remarked, "Well, *that'll be the day*."

through the mill — experience a difficult situation
USAGE: He has really been *through the mill* with the supervisor's requirement that he work weekend shifts.

✍ Disagree

squawk about — complain about
USAGE: Dale is always *squawking about* not having enough money to pay his expenses.

stab someone in the back — betray someone
USAGE: He is angry because he believes Jim *stabbed him in the back* and betrayed him during the meeting.

swim against the tide/current — do the opposite of what most people want to do
USAGE: Scott tends to *swim against the tide* and makes his own choices, regardless of what other people think.

✍ Emotion

swamped — overwhelmed
USAGE: Peter was *swamped* by work commitments and was unable to take time for himself.

sweat bullets/blood — be nervous; be very worried
USAGE: Susan was *sweating bullets*, worried she would be laid-off from her job.

sweep off one's feet — overcome with strong feelings
USAGE: She was *swept off her feet* over anticipation of the wedding ceremony.

sweet on — in love with; very fond of
USAGE: Bill said he's *sweet on* a girl he met on the subway last month.

sweat out — wait anxiously; worry while waiting
USAGE: He spent the rest of the week *sweating out* the result of his university admissions examination.

swelled head — a feeling that one is more important than one really is
USAGE: Frank seems a little arrogant with a *swelled head* since he became the
  company manager.

✍ End

toss out — force to leave; dismiss
USAGE: He was *tossed out* of the restaurant for being loud and intoxicated.

✍ Failure

(not a) snowball's chance in hell — no chance at all
USAGE: He doesn't have *a snowball's chance in hell* in getting a date with
  her.

✍ Health

throw up — to vomit
USAGE: He *threw up* after getting sick with a stomach virus.

tire out — make very tired
USAGE: Thomas was *tired out* after returning from the backpacking trip.

✍ Location

stand clear of something — keep away from something
USAGE: The crowd was advised to *stand clear of the door* while the judge
  entered the courtroom.

stand off — stay at a distance; stay apart
USAGE: When delivering a lecture, the professor *stands off* from students in
  the classroom.

✍ Money

shoot one's wad — spend all of one's money
USAGE: Paul *shot his wad* on a trip to Australia last week.

shoot the works — spare no expense or effort; to spend all energy, money
USAGE: The committee is planning to *shoot the works* for the celebration of
  the championship.

split the difference — settle a money disagreement by dividing the difference

USAGE: After negotiating with the salesman, I finally agreed to *split the difference* and we settled on a final figure.

splurge on something — spend a lot of money for something
USAGE: She *splurged on herself* by going on shopping outing.

✍ Movement

take off — (1) depart suddenly or quickly run away; (2) leave on a flight
USAGE (1): The students decided to *take off* on their weekend trip after their Friday afternoon class.
USAGE (2): Richard's plane to Paris *took off* on time.

✍ Ownership

run away with — take quickly and secretly especially without permission
USAGE: Louis *ran away with* the only calculator we had around the house.

✍ Personal Description

off one's rocker — crazy
USAGE: Bill told James he was willing to take his word that Jack is *off his rocker*.

on one's high horse — acting as if one is better than others, being very proud and scornful
USAGE: Phillip got *on his high horse* and wouldn't listen to a word they said.

on the level — honest
USAGE: I was *on the level* with him when I told him that he was making a huge mistake.

on the up and up — honest; trustworthy; sincere
USAGE: I quit because I didn't think the company was treating customers *on the up and up*.

out to lunch — crazy; mad
USAGE: While he seems *out to lunch* in his thinking, he is a courteous and nice man.

✍ Plan / Prepare

square away — put right for use or action

USAGE: Betty asked Mary if she had *squared away* her plans for the Chinese New Year celebration.

stack the cards — arrange things (unfairly) for or against a person
USAGE: John would often get depressed by feeling that his business competitors were *stacking the cards* against him.

stand a chance — have a possibility
USAGE: Ralph really believed he *stood a good chance* of getting the job.

✍ Quantity

to the tune of — to the amount or extent of
USAGE: The new jobs at the factory are expected to benefit the annual economy *to the tune of* 50 million US dollars.

travel light — travel with very little luggage or with little to carry
USAGE: Since the trip would be short, I wanted to *travel light*.

✍ Relationship

run in the family/blood — be a common family characteristic
USAGE: The ability to write interesting stories and poetry seems to *run in our family*.

shack up with — live with someone of the opposite sex without marrying them
USAGE: Many people believe that men who *shack up with* women without marriage lack commitment in their relationships.

sit on — be a member of a jury or board
USAGE: Our university president currently *sits on* the board of directors of several large corporations.

✍ Satisfaction

sit idly by — sit and watch or rest while others work
USAGE: Bill remarked if they think he is going to *sit idly by* while his competitors accumulate more of the market share, they are mistaken.

sitting pretty — be in a favorable situation
USAGE: Peter obtained another pay raise so he is *sitting pretty* at his company.

size of it — the way it is
USAGE: After describing the situation at his company, John said, "That's about the *size of it!*"

smooth over something — make better or more pleasant
USAGE: He wanted to *smooth over the disagreement* among his friends by identifying common ground to all involved.

✍ **Service**

tide (someone) over — help someone through a difficult situation
USAGE: Bill assisted her by offering a loan to *tide her over* until she got paid.

✍ **Similar**

spitting image — exact resemblance
USAGE: When she met him, she was surprised to find out he was the *spitting image* of her first boyfriend.

✍ **Superior**

take it on the chin — be badly beaten or hurt; accept trouble calmly
USAGE: The team members *took it on the chin* at the tennis tournament last week and moved on.

✍ **Time**

sooner or later — eventually
USAGE: The doctor advised Tim that *sooner or later* he would learn the importance of taking care of his health.

square one — in the beginning
USAGE: He realized that his group would need to go back to *square one* and start over again.

strike while the iron is hot — take advantage of an opportunity
USAGE: Susan wanted to *strike while the iron was hot* and collect surveys from committee members in the audience.

string out — something extended over a distance or over prolonged time
USAGE: The championship playoffs were *strung out* over ten days during August.

✍ Understand

take stock of — study a situation or a number of possibilities
USAGE: *Taking stock of* the circumstances, James was excited about the opportunities ahead of him.

ten four — I understand you
USAGE: When asked if he was ready to proceed with the plan, George said, *"Ten-four."*

think better of — to reconsider something
USAGE: I would *think better of* participating in the trip if we were able to extend our stay.

think little of — think that something or someone is not important or valuable
USAGE: Walter seems to *think little of* the process of appeals for people convicted of crimes.

think out — think through to the end
USAGE: Joseph took time away from his routine to carefully *think out* the consequences of the decision.

think out loud — say what one is thinking
USAGE: As if he was *thinking out loud*, Robert blurted out his reaction to the idea.

✍ Work

too many irons in the fire — too many things you are trying to do
USAGE: Caroline is extremely busy and has *too many irons in the fire* at work.

Week 46

✍ Achievement

take part in — participate in
USAGE: The professor was invited to *take part in* the conference on world peace.

take the plunge — do something decisive (often used with marriage)
USAGE: She accepted his proposal and will *take the plunge* to get married in
   August.

take to — begin the work or job of, learn easily, do well at
USAGE: Jason really *took to* the role of school teacher and students regard
   him as a wonderful instructor.

take turns — do something alternately with others
USAGE: The students agreed to *take turns* in reading portions from the textbook.

take up — gather together; collect
USAGE: The group of mothers decided to *take up* a collection of clothes to
   help the homeless family.

✍ Agree / Approval

toe the line — obey the rules and do one's duties
USAGE: Bill realized if he failed to *toe the line* he would be in trouble with
   his friends.

✍ Authority

to order — according to directions given
USAGE: The businessman had a suit made *to order* by the tailor.

✍ Bad / Negative

tight spot — a difficult situation
USAGE: The student felt he was in a *tight spot* when the hard drive on his
   computer crashed and he lost the data.

topsy turvy — upside down; in disarray
USAGE: It was a *topsy-turvy* few weeks when Susan first moved to the
city.

touch and go — uncertain, dangerous situation
USAGE: It was *touch and go* with Richard's health after the surgery.

✍ Business Action

turn over — sell
USAGE: Placing many of the items on clearance sale, the store was able to
turn over most of their inventory before year end.

✍ Communication

sum up — put something into a few words; summarize
USAGE: In *summing up* his speech, the professor emphasized the importance
of caring for the environment.

sweet talk — praise or flatter someone to get what you want
USAGE: The more you try to *sweet talk* her, the more she resists.

take down — write or record what is said
USAGE: The students *took down* notes from the visitor's presentation.

take down a notch/peg — make someone less proud or sure of himself
USAGE: Because he was arrogant, I was happy that he was *taken down a
notch*.

take exception to — speak against; find fault with; be angered by
USAGE: She *took exception to* the dirty language the speaker used in his
lecture.

take the words out of someone's mouth — anticipate and agree with what
someone else was going to say
USAGE: You *took the words right out of my mouth* when you said you didn't
trust him.

✍ Completeness

to the nth degree — to the greatest degree possible, extremely
USAGE: Peter took the concept of advertising *to the nth degree* when he
painted his car to advertise the product.

✍ Consequence

through thick and thin — through all difficulties and troubles; through good times and bad times
USAGE: When they married, Dale agreed to support his wife *through thick and thin*.

throw a monkey wrench into — cause something that is going smoothly to stop
USAGE: When he was called to work unexpectedly, it *threw a monkey wrench into* our weekend plans.

throw down the gauntlet — challenge someone to a fight or something similar
USAGE: In a bid to control spending, the budget office *threw down the gauntlet* by offering a bonus to the manager who could identify the most ways to cut spending.

✍ Different

tip the balance — have important or decisive influence, decide
USAGE: Jack believed the action had *tipped the balance* slightly in favor of those wanting change.

✍ Disagree

take a dim view of — be against; disapprove
USAGE: The teacher *takes a dim view of* students who procrastinate in completing class assignments.

thumb one's nose — look with disfavor or dislike
USAGE: Ted has often *thumbed his nose* at the law and finally was arrested for failure to pay taxes.

✍ Emotion

tail between one's legs — feeling ashamed
USAGE: Robert left the meeting with his *tail between his legs* after being scolded by the manager.

take heart — be encouraged; feel brave and want to try something
USAGE: She *took heart* from the cheerful notes she received while training for the Olympic race.

take it easy — (1) relax; (2) to calm down; usually used to avoid a strong disagreement
USAGE (1): Walter had a busy week and decided to *take it easy* over the weekend by reading a book.
USAGE (2): When he noticed that Burt was upset with what he said, Jacob said, "Burt, I was only kidding. *Take it easy*."

take it out on — be unpleasant or unkind to someone because one is angry or upset
USAGE: The counselor advised Jim if he became angry with his wife not to *take it out on* the children.

take leave of one's senses — behave irrationally and senseless
USAGE: It seems as though Vincent has *taken leave of his senses* because of his strange behavior.

take something lying down — suffer without a fight
USAGE: John remarked there are things he won't *take lying down* and stealing is one of them.

✍ End

turn off — shut off; stop
USAGE: Paul requests that Alan *turn off* the lights when he leaves.

✍ Failure

stand (someone) up — fail to keep an appointment or date
USAGE: Cindy felt miserable because he *stood her up* on a date.

✍ Health

toss off — drink rapidly
USAGE: Bill *tossed off* a couple of beers before the game began.

trashed — to be very intoxicated; usually by alcohol
USAGE: Peter became *trashed* by drinking so much wine after dinner.

turn in — go to bed
USAGE: After a night on the town, we decided to *turn in* about 3:00 AM.

✍ Importance

(not to be) sneezed at — worth having; not to be despised

USAGE: The technology expert suggested that high speed Internet access is *not to be sneezed at*.

✍ Location

stay away from — avoid
USAGE: Because he didn't want to see her, Jim *stayed away from* the route she normally walked.

stay put — stay in one place, not leave
USAGE: I decided to *stay put* during the holiday period instead of traveling home.

✍ Money

stone broke — having no money
USAGE: The college student was *stone-broke* after his backpacking trip in the countryside.

strapped for cash — have no money available
USAGE: Robert told the others he wouldn't be joining them for dinner since he was *strapped for cash*.

strike it rich — become rich or successful suddenly
USAGE: He *struck it rich* when he developed a new software program that would accurately translate languages.

✍ Movement

take off (clothes) — remove clothes
Martha politely asked the guests to *take off* their shoes before entering the house.

✍ Personal Description

pip squeak — a small, unimportant person
USAGE: The girl insulted Billy by calling him a *pip-squeak*. Billy's mother was furious and asked her to apologize.

regular guy — a friendly person who everyone gets along with
USAGE: People who know the film star say he is a *regular guy* and ordinary type of person.

road hog — a car driver who takes up more than his share of the road

USAGE: While traveling down the road, she told Jim not to be a ***road hog*** and stay on his side of the highway.

rolling stone — a person who does not live or work in one place
USAGE: Because he travels most of the time in his job, Lawrence is regarded as a ***rolling stone*** by his colleagues.

✍ Plan / Prepare

stand by — be near; waiting to do something when needed
USAGE: During the basketball tournament there was always an ambulance ***standing by*** for any serious injury.

stand on ceremony — be formal
USAGE: The leaders refused to ***stand on ceremony*** and were very casual during the meeting.

start in — begin
USAGE: The retirement ceremony was emotional as James recalled his ***start in*** the business.

start the ball rolling — begin to do something
USAGE: The leader ***started the ball rolling*** by having all participants introduce themselves to everyone.

✍ Relationship

snake in the grass — an enemy who pretends to be a friend
USAGE: Roger told her that Stanley is a ***snake in the grass*** and untrustworthy.

split up — separate; end a romantic relationship
USAGE: After being married for five years, George and Susan surprised their friends by ***splitting up***.

stand (someone) in good stead — be a great advantage to someone
USAGE: The teacher advised us that a good appearance and the ability to speak effectively will ***stand us in good stead*** in the future.

✍ Satisfaction

some sweet sauce — very good; excellent
USAGE: When Alan won the tennis match, his friend remarked, "Nice game! That was ***some sweet sauce***."

something else — so good as to be beyond description
USAGE: They all agreed the concert performance was *something else* and the best they had witnessed in years.

stand pat — be satisfied with things and be against a change
USAGE: Even though interest rates were falling, they agreed to *stand pat* and not take out another loan.

✍ Service

tied down — have family or job responsibilities
USAGE: As long as the children were young, Steve and Carol were *tied down* and didn't have the opportunity to travel.

✍ Time

take effect — become legally right or operative
USAGE: The new laws enacted by the government will *take effect* at midnight.

take off (time) — be absent from work
USAGE: Michael plans to *take a week off* from work when his daughter gives birth to the baby.

take one's time — do something without hurrying
USAGE: Bruce *took his time* in asking the girl for a date.

take place — happen; occur
USAGE: The game was scheduled to *take place* following final examinations.

✍ Understand

think over — consider carefully
USAGE: He deliberately *thought over* his options before announcing the decision.

think twice about something — think very carefully
USAGE: His mother urged him to *think twice about quitting* school and how that would affect his future.

think up — invent; create
USAGE: Tom has *thought up* different options for him to pursue when he retires in three years.

third degree — detailed questioning

USAGE: The police investigators gave him the ***third degree*** since he was near the scene of the crime when the robbery occurred.

throw off — mislead; confuse; fool
USAGE: The criminal suspects ***threw off*** the detectives regarding their location and were thought to be somewhere in the countryside.

trial balloon — a hint about a plan with the purpose of testing other's reaction
USAGE: Stanley sent up a ***trial balloon*** among the other managers to see if any other supervisors might support the plan.

✍ Work

up to one's ears in work — have a lot of work to do
USAGE: When asked if she wanted to go on the trip, Helen said she would love to but she was ***up to her ears in work***.

walk out — go on strike
USAGE: The newspaper reported that most of the low paid workers at the factory were due to ***walk out*** on strike at midnight.

✍ Achievement

take up arms — get ready to fight or make war
USAGE: The history of many nations involves the bravery of citizens having the courage to **take up arms** to defend their country.

throw in — give or put in as an addition
USAGE: When Joseph bought the new computer, the store **threw in** a printer for free.

tooth and nail — fiercely; as hard as possible
USAGE: John said his group would fight **tooth and nail** to get Internet access throughout the nation, including small towns.

tough row to hoe — a challenging pursuit or activity
USAGE: The company leaders will have a **tough row to hoe** now that other businesses are competing.

✍ Agree / Approval

very well — agreed; all right
USAGE: When asked to participate, the professor replied, "**Very well**, I will be glad to take part."

✍ Authority

turn in — give to someone; hand to someone
USAGE: She went to the police to **turn in** the purse she found in the park.

turn over — give to someone for use or care
USAGE: For safekeeping while traveling, I **turned over** my car to my cousin.

✍ Bad / Negative

tough break — unlucky event; misfortune

USAGE: It was a ***tough break*** for Charles when he broke his leg while training for the race.

tunnel out — to defraud, swindle, or cheat and make lots of money
USAGE: He was not trusted because rumor had it that he ***tunneled out*** the company where he used to work.

✍ Business Action

under the counter — secretly bought or sold
USAGE: Public health officials are about to crack down on stores having unregulated medicines sold ***under the counter***.

✍ Communication

talk back — answer rudely
USAGE: Martha is strict and disciplines her children if they ***talk back*** in a rude manner.

talk big — talk boastfully; brag
USAGE: While Henry would ***talk big*** around other young men, few really believed him.

talk down to someone — use words or ideas that are too simple
USAGE: Michael believed that ***talking down to people*** is not a quality of effective leadership.

talk into — get someone to agree; persuade someone to do something
USAGE: Wendy was successful in ***talking her husband into*** buying a new television set.

talk out — discuss until everything is agreed on; settle
USAGE: Victor and Bill met for lunch and ***talked out*** the issues related to the project.

talk out of — persuade not to; decide not to
USAGE: It was important to ***talk him out of*** divorcing his wife.

✍ Completeness

tone down — make less harsh or strong; moderate
USAGE: We urged him to ***tone down*** his comments and avoid further escalation and confrontation with the opposing group.

✍ Consequence

throw the baby out with the bathwater — reject all of something because some of it is faulty
USAGE: While it was clear there were problems with the plan, we wanted to fix what was wrong and not have a "***throw the baby out with the bathwater***" approach to the situation.

throw the book at — punish severely for breaking a rule or the law
USAGE: The judge ***threw the book at*** Jim after he was charged with drunk driving three times in one year.

throw to the wolves — an expression of sending into danger without protection
USAGE: When directed to present the plan to the Committee I was ***thrown to the wolves***. The Committed asked very difficult questions.

✍ Different

toss off — make or say easily without trying or thinking hard
USAGE: Mike was quick to ***toss off*** the answer about how much it would cost.

✍ Disagree

turn one's back on — refuse to help someone in need
USAGE: She ***turned her back on*** the homeless man asking for money.

turn thumbs down — disapprove or reject; say no
USAGE: The boss ***turned thumbs down*** her request to perform some of her work at home.

✍ Emotion

take to task — scold for a fault or error
USAGE: He was ***taken to task*** by his co-worker for not completing his share of the project.

taken aback — unpleasantly surprised; suddenly puzzled or shocked
USAGE: I was ***taken aback*** when he told me he didn't want to hear a word I had to say.

tempest in a teapot — great excitement about something not important
USAGE: The argument was really a ***tempest in a teapot*** and most people forgot about it within a few days.

think nothing of something — not worry about something; forget it
USAGE: Michael *thinks nothing of driving* two hours to try a new restaurant.

three sheets to the wind — unsteady from too much liquor; drunk
USAGE: I told James if he continued to drink he would be *three sheets to the wind* before dinner.

✍ End

turn out — make a light go out
USAGE: Ted always *turns out* the light before he gets into bed each night.

✍ Entertainment

steal the show — act or do so well in a performance that one gets most of the attention
USAGE: Her singing performance *stole the show* at the music competition.

✍ Error

take back — admit to making a wrong statement
USAGE: Susan had to *take back* what she said regarding the quality of products made by the company.

✍ Failure

strike out — be put out of action through one's own errors
USAGE: Because his bad language offended her, Michael *struck out* in his attempt to get a date with the beautiful young woman.

✍ Health

turn one's stomach — make one feel sick
USAGE: It *turned his stomach* to see the carnage from the fatal car accident.

✍ Importance

so help me / so help me God — I promise; I swear
USAGE: Benjamin asked for a loan by pleading, "I promise you, *so help me*, that I'll repay you within one month."

✍ Location

steer clear of someone — avoid

USAGE: Steven has been *steering clear of her* because of a longstanding dispute.

stick around — stay or wait nearby
USAGE: Larry asked Susan to *stick around* after class so he could give her the diskette.

(a) stone's throw — a short distance
USAGE: Their house was only *a stone's throw* from the lake.

✍ Money

take a bath — come to financial ruin
USAGE: He *took a bath* on several risky investments that went bad.

take a beating — lose money
USAGE: James *took a beating* when several stocks he purchased plunged in value.

take in — to receive; to get
USAGE: The social service agency *took in* a significant amount of money through the fund raising event.

✍ Movement

take to the woods — run away and hide
USAGE: Apprehensive of visitors they didn't know, the campers *took to the woods* when they saw the strangers drive up.

throw out — force to leave; dismiss
USAGE: The referee *threw out* the coach for screaming profanity on the field.

thumb a lift/ride — hitchhike
USAGE: His car would not start, so he *thumbed a ride* to the subway station.

✍ Ownership

second hand — not new; used by someone else
USAGE: Peter believed he would get a good deal on a *second hand* car.

✍ Personal Description

save face — save one's good reputation when something has happened to hurt it

USAGE: Instead of terminating Jacob directly, the manager allowed him to *save face* by submitting his resignation.

(a) screw loose — eccentric behavior
USAGE: He has *a screw loose* because he likes to eat dirt.

sell out — be disloyal; sell a secret; be unfaithful
USAGE: He *sold out* by passing confidential information to the competitors.

✍ Plan / Prepare

start up — begin operating; begin to play
USAGE: Having an entrepreneurial orientation, Stan *started up* his business when he graduated from college.

(a) stitch in time saves nine — preventative action now may prevent larger action later
USAGE: Believing *a stitch in time saves nine*, Joe replaced all four tires on his car.

straighten up — put in order; clean up
USAGE: Before his wife returned from an overnight trip, John *straightened up* the house.

✍ Quantity

up to — as far as; as deep or as high as; close to; approaching
USAGE: Flooding from recent rain resulted in the water level being *up to* 2 meters in some places.

✍ Relationship

sugar daddy — a rich, usually older, man who gives money to a younger woman for companionship
USAGE: Because she was jobless, the young woman was forced to rely on her *sugar daddy* to feed her family.

sweetie pie — darling; sweetheart
USAGE: Even after 25 years of marriage, John affectionately calls his wife "*sweetie pie*."

✍ Satisfaction

stand up — strong enough to use for a long time

USAGE: The school headmaster believed the school bus would be able to *stand up* to another year of service.

sunny side up — eggs fried on one side only; satisfied
USAGE: Steven says his favorite breakfast dish is an egg cooked *sunny-side up*.

take a shine to — have or show a quick liking for someone
USAGE: The salesman has *taken a shine to* his colleague and looks forward to going to the office.

✍ Service

treat someone — pay for someone else
USAGE: William *treated his visitors* to a dinner at the fine restaurant.

✍ Similar

take after — resemble or act like a parent or relative
USAGE: Because of his physical appearance and personality, Joseph seems to *take after* his father.

✍ Superior

top drawer — of the best or most important kind
USAGE: When Steven buys a car, he gets a *top-drawer* model equipped with all the options.

✍ Time

take up — (1) begin; start; (2) fill a place or time; occupy; (3) begin an activity or hobby
USAGE (1): The professor *took up* the lecture where he stopped at the previous class session.
USAGE (2): Many of Andy's evenings are *taken up* playing games over the Internet.
USAGE (3): Timothy has decided to *take up* tennis for fitness and health.

✍ Understand

'rump up — make up; fraudulent
SAGE: Peter was arrested on a *trumped up* charge of robbery by a corrupt ▸oliceman.

turn up — (1) find, discover; (2) appear suddenly
USAGE (1): His lost wedding ring *turned up* underneath the car seat.
USAGE (2): Jason and his friends finally *turned up* around midnight.

under one's belt — in a person's experience, memory or possession
USAGE: Marvin decided he wants to get some work experience *under his belt*
   before he works on his MBA degree.

✍ Work

walk the plank — be forced to resign from a job
USAGE: When the company was sold, the general manager was forced to *walk
   the plank* when he was replaced by a new executive.

✍ Achievement

track down — search for
USAGE: Robert has attempted to *track drown* the original prints of certain master artists.

trial and error — trying different possible solutions until finding one that works
USAGE: Many people believe the best way to learn is by *trial and error*.

trick of the trade — a smart, quick or skillful way of doing something
USAGE: Because he has worked so long in the industry, Jack knows many *tricks of the trade* in publishing.

✍ Agree / Approval

with open arms — greet someone with warmth and hospitality
USAGE: Alan's parents greeted him *with open arms* at the train station.

would just as soon — prefer to do one thing rather than another
USAGE: He *would just as soon* send emails rather than write letters.

✍ Authority

twist someone around one's little finger — have control over someone and be able to make them do anything you want
USAGE: Victor's wife admits she always wanted to marry someone she could *twist around her little finger*.

✍ Bad / Negative

turn down — refuse to accept; reject
USAGE: William *turned down* the job offer because it would have required him to relocate to another city.

twiddle one's thumbs — not busy; not working

USAGE: He has been sitting around *twiddling his thumbs* since he lost his job a few months ago.

✍ Business Action

under the hammer — up for sale at an auction
USAGE: The artwork went *under the hammer* and sold for a record amount.

✍ Communication

talk over — discuss thoroughly
USAGE: The teacher wanted me to *talk over* the plans with my parents before doing anything further.

talk shop — talk about things in one's work
USAGE: My wife urged me not to *talk shop* at dinner.

talk through one's hat — make exaggerated or inaccurate statements
USAGE: Bill sometimes *talks through his hat* and the reliability of his remarks is questionable.

talk turkey — discuss seriously; directly
USAGE: The businessman said to Bill, "When you're ready to *talk turkey* about a deal, call me."

talk up — speak in favor of
USAGE: The salesman was *talking up* the advantages of his product.

tear down — say bad things about; criticize
USAGE: The feud between the two men resulted in each *tearing down* the other.

✍ Completeness

turn down — reduce the loudness, brightness or force of something
USAGE: The parents requested their son to *turn down* the loud music in his room.

✍ Consequence

touch off — cause to fire or explode by lighting the fuse
USAGE: The building fire *touched off* an explosion at the neighboring chemical plant.

trip up — make a mistake
USAGE: He was *tripped up* when someone pointed out the date was incorrect.

turn out — result; end; prove to be true
USAGE: The weather *turned out* to be terrific for the cruise.

✍ Different

turn over a new leaf — make a fresh start
USAGE: George decided he was going to *turn over a new leaf* and stop smoking.

✍ Disagree

turn up one's nose at — refuse as not being good enough for one
USAGE: She *turned up her nose at* the idea of dating Robert since he didn't have a job.

twist one's arm — force or threaten someone to do something
USAGE: He didn't have to *twist my arm* to make the trip because I wanted to go.

✍ Emotion

throw cold water on — discourage; forbid
USAGE: His parents *threw cold water on* the plan to travel to Japan.

tickled pink — very happy
USAGE: She was *tickled pink* when she was offered the job.

tie up in knots — make someone very nervous or worried
USAGE: The student teacher was *tied up in knots* before she taught her first lesson at the school.

too bad — worthy of sorrow or regret
USAGE: It is *too bad* that budget cuts forced the community library to be closed.

too big for one's breeches/boots — feeling more important than one really is
USAGE: Since he received the job promotion, Jack has been acting *too big for his breeches.*

torn up — very upset; sad

USAGE: Paul's been ***torn up*** since she broke up with him.

✍ End

wash one's hands of — abandon; refuse responsibility for
USAGE: He ***washed his hands of*** the problem.

✍ Entertainment

tie one on — to get drunk; intoxicated
USAGE: William and Pete went out to the bar and ***tied one on***.

✍ Error

take for — mistake someone for something
USAGE: The police mistakenly ***took the man for*** a robber and brought him in for questioning.

✍ Failure

take its toll — cause loss or damage
USAGE: Steven's demanding job has begun to ***take its toll*** on his health because he's anemic.

✍ Health

under one's belt — in one's stomach
USAGE: Vincent doesn't like to begin work until he has a full breakfast ***under his belt***.

under the weather — feel ill (but not seriously ill)
USAGE: John has been feeling ***under the weather*** so he won't be at work today.

✍ Importance

to be sure — without a doubt; certainly
USAGE: Roger said that, ***to be sure***, it would be best to check with the professor before completing the assignment.

✍ Location

stop by — visit; pass by

USAGE: She asked Bill to *stop by* the store on his way home.

stop off — stop at a place for a short time while going somewhere
USAGE: They wanted to *stop off* in Tokyo on their way to Los Angeles.

stop over — stay at a place for a short time while on a trip
USAGE: The aircraft had a brief *stop over* in London for refueling.

✍ Money

take to the cleaners — win all someone's money
USAGE: On his visit to the casino, Marvin was *taken to the cleaners* by the card dealers.

taken to the cleaners — take a lot of someone's money or cheat someone
USAGE: The man who invented it had no idea of its worth, so he was *taken to the cleaners* by the investors.

tight squeeze — difficult financial situation
USAGE: Roger is in a *tight squeeze* since he lost his job last month.

✍ Movement

tie up — slow or stop the movement or action of
USAGE: The morning traffic *tied up* drivers for several hours today.

to and fro — forward and back again and again
USAGE: The dog paced *to and fro* in the enclosure.

✍ Ownership

snap up — take or accept eagerly
USAGE: Free tickets to the concert performance were *snapped up* by fans within thirty minutes.

✍ Personal Description

(a) shadow of his former self — smaller or weaker than before
USAGE: After struggling with cancer treatment, Joe was *a shadow of his former self*.

show one's (true) colors — show what one is really like or is thinking
USAGE: Robert has *shown his true colors* with his refusal to assist the homeless people with food.

sitting duck — an unsuspecting person; an easy target
USAGE: The young woman was a *sitting duck* for thieves when she waived large amounts of cash for everyone to see.

smart alec — a comic, cocky, sometimes offensive
USAGE: He is a *smart alec* and thinks he knows everything about everyone.

son of a bitch — a bad or mean person, used as an exclamation
USAGE: He remarked that he wanted the *son of a bitch* who stole his camera to return it.

spring chicken — a young person
USAGE: He's no *spring chicken*; he is 87 years old.

✍ Plan / Prepare

take steps — begin to make plans or arrangements; make preparations
USAGE: Charles is *taking steps* to change careers within the next 4 to 5 years.

take the bull by the horns — take some kind of action
USAGE: He *took the bull by the horns* and was successful in avoiding bankruptcy.

throw together — make in a hurry and without care
USAGE: Because they were in a rush to see the movie, they *threw together* a quick lunch and headed out the door.

✍ Quantity

use up — spend or consume completely
USAGE: Because everyone in the office had been doing a lot of printing, the printer toner was *used up* and needed to be replaced.

✍ Relationship

take liberties — behave in too close or friendly a manner; make unwanted advances
USAGE: The student is *taking liberties* that she shouldn't, such as calling her professor by his first name.

take out — escort or go on a date with someone
USAGE: Paul was delighted he was able to *take out* the beautiful woman.

✍ Satisfaction

take advantage of — use for one's own benefit
USAGE: The students ***took advantage of*** the pool and went swimming.

take in — go and see or visit
USAGE: Ted and Mike decided to ***take in*** the new exhibit at the museum yesterday.

take in stride — accept good or bad luck and go on
USAGE: The film star ***took her newly established fame in stride*** and focused on movie acting.

take the edge off — lessen; weaken; soften
USAGE: Bill wanted a glass of wine to ***take the edge off*** the tension of a difficult day.

time of one's life — a wonderful time
USAGE: Connie had the ***time of her life*** when she went to Greece on the school trip.

✍ Service

turn to — go to for help
USAGE: Peter ***turned to*** his uncle for advice about choosing between two job offers.

✍ Similar

take on — begin to have the look of
USAGE: He has begun to ***take on*** the look of a rock musician even though he doesn't play an instrument.

✍ Superior

top notch — excellent; the best
USAGE: They had a ***top-notch*** carpenter construct the frame for the exhibit.

✍ Time

tie up — keep occupied
USAGE: Jimmy was ***tied up*** all morning finishing the project.

time after time — repeatedly

USAGE: Bill has said *time after time* he would never live outside of the city.

time out (in a game) — time when a game or something is temporarily stopped for some reason
USAGE: There was a *time out* called during the game due to a player injury.

to no end — almost without stopping; continually; very much
USAGE: When he said he wanted a divorce, Cathy cried *to no end* and was in much despair.

touch off — start something
USAGE: The news of an employee lay-off *touched off* a concern among the workers.

✍ Understand

under one's nose — in sight of; in an easily seen or noticeable place
USAGE: She found the lost purse *under her nose* by her bed.

under wraps — not allowed to be seen until the right time; in secrecy
USAGE: The highly awaited book was still *under wraps* by the author when the newspaper story appeared.

up in the air — not settled; undecided
USAGE: The plan to construct a new headquarters for the company is still *up in the air*.

use one's head/bean/noodle/noggin — think carefully about
USAGE: John was advised to *use his head* and think about the consequences of the decision.

used to — accustomed to
USAGE: Because he grew up in the countryside, Phillip isn't *used to* living in the city.

✍ Work

walking papers — a statement that one is fired from one's job; dismissal
USAGE: Carl was given his *walking papers* one week after the new manager took over command at the company.

Week 49

✍ Achievement

trump card — something kept back to be used to win success if nothing else works
USAGE: The businessman's ***trump card*** was the marketing research showing consumers were very motivated to buy the new product.

try (something) out — test
USAGE: We were allowed to ***try out*** the car before we decided to buy it.

try out for — planning to join or take part in a team; competing for a place
USAGE: Richard made a decision to ***try out for*** the school soccer team.

✍ Agree / Approval

wrap around one's finger — have complete control over someone and be able to make them do anything you want
USAGE: He admitted she still has him ***wrapped around her finger*** and he wishes he knew how to get free.

✍ Authority

under one's thumb — obedient to someone; controlled by someone
USAGE: The company boss was an aggressive manager who believed he had his staff members ***under his thumb***.

✍ Bad / Negative

under fire — being shot at or attacked
USAGE: The police were ***under fire*** from the criminal suspects concealed behind the wall.

up the creek — in trouble
USAGE: Peter is ***up the creek*** now that he has quit his job and has a family to support.

up the river/creek with no paddle — in trouble and unable to do anything about it
USAGE: James knew he was *up the river with no paddle* when several people abandoned support of his plan.

✍ Business Action

under the table — in secret and usually illegal
USAGE: They paid money *under the table* to get the plan approved faster.

✍ Communication

tell it like it is — be honest; candid; tell the truth
USAGE: Karen has the reputation of being a person who is straightforward and can *tell it like it is*.

tell it to the marines — an unbelievable account
USAGE: You say he has his own television show? *Tell it to the Marines*!

tell (someone) off — speak to angrily
USAGE: Bill *told off* the store owner when he observed him being rude to a customer.

tell on someone — reveal the activities or wrongdoings of someone
USAGE: Bob *told on his sister* for eating all the pie.

through the grapevine — hear from other people
USAGE: I heard it *through the grapevine* that Jim will be appointed by the Prime Minister to a high government position.

throw a curve ball — take someone by surprise in an unpleasant way
USAGE: I thought I was sure of his next move, but then he *threw me a curve ball*.

✍ Completeness

under cover — hidden; concealed
USAGE: Most police departments appoint law enforcement officers to go *under cover* to identify narcotic dealers.

✍ Consequence

up to — depending on

USAGE: It is *up to* him to determine if he will succeed in graduate school.

water under the bridge — something that happened in the past and can't be changed
USAGE: John told the others the conflict is now *water under the bridge* and we should all move on!

way the wind blows — direction or course something may go; what may happen
USAGE: Politicians are always looking to see which *way the wind blows* in terms of what they say.

✍ Different

turn the tables — reverse the situation
USAGE: The opposing team was able to finally *turn the table*s and won the game.

✍ Disagree

under a cloud — under suspicion; not trusted
USAGE: The banker was *under a cloud* concerning rumors that he was misusing bank money.

✍ Emotion

tread on one's toes — do something that offends someone
USAGE: Mary said she was not going to *tread on Susan's toes* or embarrass her since she was her friend.

tune in — get in touch with and be responsive to feelings and thoughts
USAGE: Betsy enjoyed attending the class to help her *tune in* to her inner feelings.

turn (someone) off — disgust; irritate; repel someone
USAGE: It is a *turn off* when someone brags about their accomplishments.

turn (someone) on — become interested in a person, idea or plan
USAGE: She was *turned on* by the possibility of visiting Paris, France.

turn on someone — become suddenly hostile to someone
USAGE: While Michael used to be a good friend, he suddenly *turned on me* when we worked together on the project.

turn over in one's grave — be so angry that if one was dead, they would not rest quietly in the grave
USAGE: Marvin would *turn over in his grave* if he knew that she was changing the plan to assist the children.

✍ End

washed up — no longer successful or needed
USAGE: After a celebrated career, the soccer player was *washed up* and decided to retire.

✍ Failure

throw up one's hands — give up trying; admit that one cannot succeed
USAGE: He *threw up his hands* in exasperation and suggested he didn't know how to solve the problem.

✍ Health

up and about — recovered from an illness
USAGE: Laura has been *up and about* for several days since her surgery.

✍ Importance

to speak of — important; worth talking about
USAGE: Many people believe the noted author hasn't written anything *to speak of* for some time.

✍ Location

swan song — final appearance
USAGE: At his retirement party, Frank was asked to deliver a *swan song* speech.

sweep under the rug — hide or dismiss casually
USAGE: Embarrassed about the high cost of the project, he *swept under the rug* questions about cost overruns.

take a trip — go for a journey
USAGE: Carl mentioned he planned to *take a trip* to Canada during the summer.

throw off — get free from

USAGE: The criminal suspects were successful in ***throwing off*** the police in pursuit.

✍ Money

tighten one's belt — economize; spend less
USAGE: The economist suggested we all had to ***tighten our belts*** since the economy has been slow.

tourist trap — place that is overpriced and attracts tourists
USAGE: Carol regards the town as a ***tourist trap*** and wants to avoid it during the trip.

trade something in — exchange something old or used for something new
USAGE: Since his car was old and had mechanical problems, Jack decided to ***trade it in*** for a new car.

✍ Movement

turn off — leave by turning onto another road or path
USAGE: When approaching the monument, we were advised to ***turn off*** on the dirt road.

✍ Ownership

to one's name — in one's ownership
USAGE: Peter wants to start a business, although he realizes it will be a challenge because he hardly has a penny ***to his name***.

✍ Personal Description

stick in the mud — someone who is old-fashioned
USAGE: His friends say he is a ***stick in the mud*** and never does anything new.

sticky fingers — the habit of stealing things
USAGE: When I worked at the store, I was warned to watch him closely because he has ***sticky fingers*** for things he likes.

straight — honest or loyal
USAGE: Patricia asked her friend, "Can you really trust a guy who isn't being ***straight*** with you?"

straight out — plainly; in a way that hides nothing

USAGE: I was told ***straight out*** that I would never be hired by the company for any job.

stuck up — acting as if other people are not as good as one is
USAGE: From what I hear, he is very ***stuck up*** and full of himself.

✍ Plan / Prepare

thrown together — to be grouped with others
USAGE: The parents were concerned that the younger children were ***thrown together*** with older teenagers on the field trip.

touch up — (1) paint over (small imperfections); (2) improve with small additions or changes
USAGE (1): I asked the painter to ***touch up*** several places on the outside fence.
USAGE (2): The student reported her thesis would be completed as soon as she finished a final ***touch up*** of the project.

✍ Quantity

water down — make weak; dilute
USAGE: The activists agreed, even in its ***watered-down*** version, the new policy would function better.

✍ Relationship

take (someone) under one's wing — protect, teach or guide someone
USAGE: The experienced manager was looking for someone to ***take under his wing*** and teach what it takes to succeed.

✍ Satisfaction

tune up — (1) adjust a car engine so that it will run properly; (2) adjust a musical instrument to the right sound
USAGE (1): Since we were taking a long drive into the country, I asked the mechanic to ***tune up*** the car before taking the trip.
USAGE (2): After she ***tuned up*** the piano, Susan began to play a beautiful melody.

turn the other cheek — let someone do something to you and not try to get revenge
USAGE: Richard is a very humble and non-violent person. If someone slapped him, he would ***turn the other cheek***.

✍ Service

under one's wing — under the care or protection of
USAGE: Charles is a kind man and frequently takes struggling friends **under his wing** to help them get on their feet.

✍ Similar

tie in — to connect with something else
USAGE: The toys were designed to be **tied in** with the marketing of the action film.

✍ Superior

win out — be victorious or successful after hard work or difficulty
USAGE: While there were initial problems, we finally **won out** and she agreed to sign under our conditions.

✍ Time

turn the clock back — return to an earlier period
USAGE: If the new policy took effect, it would **turn the clock back** to the 1950s when women didn't have many roles in society.

unearthly hour — absurdly early or inconvenient
USAGE: The students had to leave the school at an **unearthly hour** to go on the trip.

✍ Understand

wear thin — grow less interesting or believable
USAGE: Sam has admitted the arguments in favor of the project have begun to **wear thin**.

what about — about or concerning something
USAGE: While she recognized Mike would attend the event, she asked, "But **what about** me?"

what's in the bag? — greeting, similar to "What's up?"
USAGE: Joseph greeted Mike by saying, "Good morning, **what's in the bag**?"

✍ Work

work in — slip in; mix in; put in

USAGE: Although it was a busy day, I was able to **work in** time for some
exercise.

✍ **Achievement**

tug of war — a contest in which two sides try to defeat each other; a struggle
USAGE: There has long been a *tug of war* between environmental supporters and promoters of industrial development.

turn out — make; produce
USAGE: The factory is *turning out* over 10,000 computers each day.

turn over — start an engine or motor
USAGE: Fearful the freezing cold would make it hard to start the car, the engine *turned over* on the first try.

under one's own steam — by one's own efforts; without help
USAGE: Feeling much stronger one week after surgery, Bill left the hospital *under his own steam*.

✍ **Agree / Approval**

yes man — a person who tries to be liked by agreeing with everything (especially by a boss)
USAGE: Some people say he was hired by the manager because he is a *yes man*.

✍ **Authority**

upper hand — controlling power; advantage
USAGE: Because of falling prices of computers, consumers have the *upper hand* in negotiating the best prices for technology items.

✍ **Bad / Negative**

walk away/off with — take and go away with; take away; steal
USAGE: We called the police because someone *walked away with* the office copier during the night.

✍ Business Action

wheel and deal — take part in political or commercial scheming
USAGE: It can take a lot of ***wheeling and dealing*** to get a big event such as a festival set up.

✍ Communication

tip (someone) off — warn; inform
USAGE: The police were ***tipped off*** that a robbery would occur tomorrow.

token gesture — a limited recognition of thanks
USAGE: John hoped the gift would not be a ***token gesture*** but rather a meaningful signal that change would occur.

toot (one's) horn — to praise oneself
USAGE: While Jack didn't want to make it sound as if he was ***tooting his horn***, he did want his friends to know about the award.

touch on/upon — speak of or write of briefly
USAGE: During his speech, Scott ***touched on*** the recent developments at the company.

✍ Completeness

vicious circle — unbroken sequence of cause and effect with bad results
USAGE: Unfortunately, the young woman had fallen into a ***vicious circle*** involving illegal drugs and prostitution.

✍ Consequence

wear and tear — damage as a result of ordinary use
USAGE: Peter uses his laptop computer in many different settings, so he puts a lot of ***wear and tear*** on it.

wear down — (1) exhaust or tire someone out; (2) make something smaller or weaker by wearing or aging
USAGE (1): She was ***worn down*** after the 13 hour flight from Los Angeles.
USAGE (2): Millions of years of erosion ***wore down*** the edges of the rocks to a smooth surface.

✍ Different

turn the tide — change what looks like defeat into victory

USAGE: The major offensive by the army finally ***turned the tide*** and brought victory.

✍ Disagree

up against — confronted with
USAGE: John was ***up against*** significant criticism from opponents of the project.

✍ Emotion

under a cloud — depressed; sad
USAGE: It was clear she was ***under a cloud*** of grief and sadness following her father's death.

up in arms — exceedingly upset and angry
USAGE: He was ***up in arms*** over the comments made by their leader.

up to here with — sick of someone's continual bad or irritating behavior
USAGE: I've had it ***up to here with*** his excessive drinking!

ups and downs — alternate good and bad fortune
USAGE: Our son is having a few ***ups and downs*** as he starts at a new school

upset the applecart — ruin or spoil a plan or idea
USAGE: Paul was very careful not to ***upset the applecart*** when he started the new job.

uptight — worried; irritated; excessively eager or anxious
USAGE: He has been ***uptight*** recently waiting to find out if he has been admitted to business school,

✍ End

wind up — end; finish; settle
USAGE: Approaching the end of class, the teacher suggested he would ***wind up*** things and we could go home.

✍ Entertainment

trip the light fantastic — go dancing
USAGE: While Robert said he was not much of a dancer, he enjoys watching his friends ***trip the light fantastic***.

✍ Error

throw away a chance or opportunity — fail to make use of a chance or opportunity
USAGE: Because of breaking the law when he was young, Victor *threw away his chance* to work for the government.

✍ Failure

to pieces — into broken pieces or fragments; destroyed; not working
USAGE: His car fell *to pieces* during his recent trip through the countryside.

✍ Health

wet one's whistle — take a drink, especially alcohol
USAGE: Guests are encouraged to *wet their whistle* at the hotel bar.

✍ Importance

to the eye — as it is seen; apparently
USAGE: *To the eye*, the used car looked like a solid vehicle but when driving it we could tell there were problems.

✍ Location

tie up — docked (a ship)
USAGE: The ship was *tied up* at the pier three days before it was ready to depart.

✍ Money

two bits — twenty-five cents; a quarter of a dollar
USAGE: Stanley purchased some candy for *two bits*.

upper crust — rich, famous or important people
USAGE: Wealthy people usually consider themselves the *upper crust* of the city.

✍ Movement

turn on — open, start, let water or electricity flow
USAGE: Susan asked him to *turn on* his laptop computer so she could check her email.

✍ Ownership

up for grabs — available for anyone to try to get, ready to be competed for
USAGE: With less than two weeks remaining in the season, the top spot in the conference is still *up for grabs*.

✍ Personal Description

stuffed shirt — a person who is too rigid or too formal
USAGE: She said while he may seem like a *stuffed-shirt*, he is a kind man.

sucker list — a list of easily-fooled people who are persuaded to buy something
USAGE: He was alarmed to find out that his name appeared on the *sucker list* used by the marketing company.

to blame — be responsible for something bad or unfortunate
USAGE: Susan's not *to blame* for the breakdown of the bus.

tower of strength — a person who gives strong and reliable support
USAGE: Susan remarked that she was fortunate to have a friend who was *a tower of strength*.

✍ Plan / Prepare

try on — put on clothes to see how they fit and look
USAGE: Benjamin advised him to *try on* the coat before he bought it.

try one's hand — make an inexperienced attempt at something
USAGE: She decided to *try her hand* at creating a website on the Internet.

turn out — turn inside out; empty
USAGE: When John *turned out* his pockets, he saw the usual collection of items such as coins and paperclips.

✍ Quantity

wear off/away — remove or disappear by use, time or weather
USAGE: Because of much use, the serial number located on the bottom of my laptop computer has *worn off*.

✍ Relationship

take sides — support one side against the other

USAGE: Karen was careful not to ***take sides*** in the argument between the two students.

✍ Satisfaction

turn the trick — bring about the desired result; succeed in what one plans to do
USAGE: She felt her study plan would be enough to ***turn the trick*** to pass the test.

up one's alley — something one is good at or enjoys
USAGE: Working with wireless telecommunications is right ***up her alley***.

✍ Service

wait on (someone) hand and foot — serve in every possible way; do everything for someone
USAGE: Tony ***waits on her hand and foot***, flattering her at every opportunity and always willing to serve.

✍ Similar

tit for tat — equal treatment in return; a fair exchange
USAGE: Robert has a ***tit for tat*** attitude when dealing with Susan. If she angers him, he'll do something to frustrate her.

✍ Superior

winning streak — a series of several wins one after the other
USAGE: The national soccer team has been on an eight game ***winning streak***.

✍ Time

up to / till / until — until
USAGE: ***Up to*** his trip to Japan, he had never flown in an airplane.

when hell freezes over — never
USAGE: Paul said he would agree to see her only ***when hell freezes over***.

while away the time — make time go by pleasantly
USAGE: Since she loves the ocean, she likes to ***while away the time*** on the beach.

✍ Understand

what's the big idea — what is the purpose; what do you have in mind
USAGE: When he came home, Bill asked his son, "***What's the big idea***? Why are you going through our financial records?"

what's up / cooking / doing — what is happening; what is planned; what is wrong
USAGE: As he walked into the office, Lawrence asked, "***What's up***?"

what's (up) with — what is happening; how is everything
USAGE: When Susan walked into work, she asked, "***What's up with*** Steven? He seems to be in a tense mood."

✍ Work

work off — make something go away by working
USAGE: Richard has been able to ***work off*** his wife's medical bill by volunteering at the hospital.

Week 51

✍ **Achievement**

up against — challenge with; withstand
USAGE: The team knew they were *up against* serious competition in the soccer match.

up to — doing or planning secretly; ready for mischief
USAGE: It was difficult to know what James was *up to* since his door was closed.

up to it / up to the job — capable of; fit for; equal to
USAGE: We believe that Scott is *up to the job* because of his valuable skills.

up to one's chin — very busy with; deeply involved in something; guilty of
USAGE: I have been *up to my chin* with details surrounding the project.

✍ **Agree / Approval**

you bet / you bet your boots / you bet your life — most certainly; yes; without any doubt
USAGE: When asked if he loved his wife, John said, "*You bet* your life I love her. I adore her more each day."

✍ **Authority**

walk all over someone — take advantage of someone; win a game easily
USAGE: They *walked all over the other team* at the football tournament.

walk (all) over — make someone do whatever one wishes; make selfish use of
USAGE: He tried to *walk all over* me when I began the job.

✍ **Bad / Negative**

wipe out — a disaster; a calamity
USAGE: The earthquake resulted in a *wipe out* of the village. It was a terrible tragedy.

✍ Business Action

white sale — selling at reduced prices of towels, linens
USAGE: My wife rushed to the ***white sale*** as soon as the department store opened.

✍ Communication

turn a deaf ear to — pretend not to hear; refuse to hear
USAGE: The banker ***turned a deaf ear to*** our plea for a short term loan to help our business.

turn in — inform on; report
USAGE: Complying with the university's honor code, James ***turned in*** a fellow student he observed cheating on an examination.

two cents worth — something one wants to say; opinion
USAGE: Feeling very strongly about the issue, I was compelled to put in my ***two cents worth***.

under fire — to be criticized
USAGE: The company president was ***under fire*** for not using acceptable accounting practices.

under one's breath — in a whisper; with a low voice
USAGE: Because William was angry, he called me bad names ***under his breath***.

waste one's breath — speak pointlessly without the desired results
USAGE: Mary was ***wasting her breath*** by asking John to stop smoking.

✍ Completeness

wear thin — become thin from use or the passing of time
USAGE: The blade on his pocket knife had begun to ***wear thin*** after much use.

✍ Consequence

wear out — use or wear something until it becomes useless
USAGE: I did so much walking on my trip that my shoes ***wore out***.

wear out one's welcome — visit somewhere too long or come back too often so that one is not welcome anymore
USAGE: Timothy ***wore out his welcome*** at our house because he would come by without calling and stay very late.

✍ Different

what's what — know the difference of one thing from another
USAGE: She is trying to distinguish between the items and determine *what's what* at the auction.

✍ Disagree

vote down — defeat in a vote
USAGE: The employees *voted down* a proposal for a longer workday in exchange for a shorter work week.

wade into — attack; join in
USAGE: He *waded into* the fight for justice because he knew it was the right thing.

✍ Emotion

vibe — a distinctive feeling
USAGE: Joseph said he felt negative *vibes* on the date with Carol.

walk on air — feel happy and excited
USAGE: Since Kelly found out she performed well on her examination, she's been *walking on air*.

walk the floor — walk back and forth across the floor, pace
USAGE: He was *walking the floor* with great anxiety, waiting to hear the results of the experimental space flight.

warm one's blood/heart — make one feel warm or excited
USAGE: The sight of the sister hugging her little brother after he was rescued *warmed the heart* of all the people.

warm up — become friendly or interested
USAGE: When asked if he wanted to parachute from the plane, he was surprised at first but soon *warmed up* to the idea.

watered — to feel sad; hurt; low
USAGE: He's pretty much *watered* right now because of the news of his uncle's death.

wear on — frustration; anger; annoy; tire
USAGE: Being on the diet and going without chocolate and bread was *wearing on* my nerves.

wear one's heart on one's sleeve — show one's feelings openly through actions
USAGE: John likes *wearing his heart on his sleeve* because he is spontaneous in the sharing of his feelings.

✍ End

wipe out — remove, kill or destroy completely
USAGE: There are proven ways that insects and mice may be *wiped out* around a house.

✍ Error

turn over — roll over; upset
USAGE: During an intense storm at sea, the boat *turned over*.

✍ Failure

(as) useless as a fifth wheel — not very useful; not relevant
USAGE: The professor's latest invention was *useless as a fifth wheel*.

wash out — failure; to be eliminated
USAGE: Phillip *washed out* of the police training program after two weeks.

✍ Health

with child — pregnant; going to have a baby
USAGE: The young woman is *with child* and is about to give birth.

✍ Importance

two cents — something not important or very small; almost nothing
USAGE: I wouldn't give him *two cents* for the car because it was old and broken-down.

✍ Location

turn out — (1) come or go out to see or do something; (2) make someone leave or go away
USAGE (1): A record crowd *turned out* for the soccer championship game.
USAGE (2): She could never convince the father to *turn out* his son.

✍ Money

well heeled — rich
USAGE: He seems *well-heeled* and above the crowd.

well off — wealthy; comfortable; prosperous
USAGE: Since they were considered *well off* and affluent, they didn't need to
  worry about finances.

well to do — wealthy; comfortable; prosperous
USAGE: Robert was raised in an affluent, *well to do* family.

✍ Movement

turn on one's heel — turn around suddenly
USAGE: He *turned on his heel* and walked away to his car.

✍ Ownership

up one's sleeve — kept secretly ready for the right time or when needed
USAGE: I've known Mike long enough to believe he has something *up his
  sleeve* when he says a new plan is needed.

✍ Personal Description

ugly duckling — an ugly or plain child who grows up to be pretty and
  attractive
USAGE: Karen grew up as an *ugly duckling* but has developed into a beautiful
  young woman.

wasted — extremely inebriated, maybe vomiting or passing out from
  intoxication
USAGE: At the party last night, Thomas was *wasted* and later fainted.

wet behind the ears — inexperienced; immature
USAGE: While intelligent, it was clear that Karen was a little *wet behind the
  ears* and didn't understand how business deals are reached.

wet blanket — person who discourages others from having fun
USAGE: Tom can be a *wet blanket* when the rest of us are having a great time.

✍ Plan / Prepare

up front — honest and direct

USAGE: She was *up front* and told me the facts of the case.

warm up — get ready for an event by practicing or exercising
USAGE: The players were on the field one hour before the game *warming up* for the match.

✍ Quantity

weed out — remove what is unwanted; get rid of
USAGE: Sometimes teachers *weed out* students who are not motivated to learn the lesson material.

✍ Relationship

tell apart — distinguish between two things or people
USAGE: It is difficult to *tell* the twin sisters *apart*.

throw in one's lot with — join, take part in something
USAGE: He chose to *throw in his lot with* the group finishing up the project.

✍ Satisfaction

up to par/scratch/snuff/the mark — equal to the usual level or quality
USAGE: The computer experts agreed the software was not *up to par*.

walk of life — way of living; manner in which people live
USAGE: There were people from every *walk of life* participating in the volunteer project.

well and good — good; satisfactory
USAGE: William said, "All this is *well and good*, but how can this help our company?"

✍ Service

wait table — serve food
USAGE: The college student earned money by *waiting tables* at night.

✍ Similar

to the letter — exactly; precisely
USAGE: Steven is very careful in his approach and follows the law *to the letter*.

✍ Superior

with flying colors — with great or total success
USAGE: He was commended by the professor for passing the examination *with flying colors*.

✍ Time

while back — several weeks or months in the past
USAGE: I saw Kevin a *while back* but haven't seen him lately.

year round — operating all year
USAGE: Their apartment building has an indoor pool that allows them to go swimming *year round*.

✍ Understand

wise up to — finally understand what is going on after a period of ignorance
USAGE: Fred finally *wised up to* the fact that his wife was less than faithful.

within reason — sensible; reasonable
USAGE: Alan believed that, *within reason*, the students should be able to explore on their own during the trip.

✍ Work

work on/upon — have an effect on; try to influence
USAGE: I am *working on* convincing my wife we should purchase a new computer.

✍ Achievement

up to someone to do something — be responsible to take care of something
USAGE: It is ***up to him to determine*** the schedule of the event.

whale of a game — an enjoyable and exciting game
USAGE: After winning the game, the coach told the newspaper reporter, "It was a ***whale of a game*** played by our team."

whip up — (1) make active; stir to action; (2) make or do quickly or easily
USAGE (1): The pop singer ***whipped up*** the crowd into a chant.
USAGE (2): Jim and Mary ***whipped up*** a quick snack.

window of opportunity — an extraordinary opportunity or chance
USAGE: The development of the popular new product was a ***window of opportunity*** for the company.

work in —rub in
USAGE: The custodian ***worked in*** the cleaning solution to the dirty carpet.

world is one's oyster — everything is possible for one; one can get anything
USAGE: Benjamin thought the ***world was his oyster*** until his girlfriend broke up with him.

✍ Agree / Approval

you said it / you can say that again — used to show strong agreement with what another person has said
USAGE: "***You can say that again***," Ben replied when Jack said it was freezing outside.

you're telling me — used to show that a thing is so clear that it need not be said
USAGE: When Tom remarked the food at the restaurant was too expensive, John said, "***You're telling me***!"

✍ Authority

watch it — be careful (usually used as a command)
USAGE: Kathy warned her son as he rode his bicycle, "*Watch it* or a car may hit you!"

wear the pants in a family — be the boss in a family
USAGE: Mary is a headstrong woman and, unlike most women, *wears the pants in her family*.

✍ Bad / Negative

write off — accept a loss or trouble and not worry any more about it
USAGE: He regarded the poor investment as both a *write off* and learning experience.

✍ Business Action

wildcat strike — a labor strike occurring spontaneously by a group of workers
USAGE: Leaders among the workers called for a *wildcat strike* over a dispute about paid holidays.

✍ Communication

weigh one's words — be careful of what one says
USAGE: William realized it was important to *weigh his words* carefully before speaking to the group.

wisecrack — funny; witting or sarcastic remark
USAGE: John is funny with the hilarious *wisecracks* he makes during our meetings.

word for word — in exactly the same words
USAGE: She needed to know *word for word* exactly what happened.

word of mouth — passing information from one person to another
USAGE: The reputation of the restaurant's good food spread by *word of mouth*.

write up — write or describe in writing; give a full account of
USAGE: John took time to *write up* a summary of the discussion.

you go girl — phrase of affirmation or encouragement
USAGE: When I told Kathy I did it, she said "*You go girl!*"

✍ Completeness

what with — because; as a result of
USAGE: We wanted to go on a vacation, but ***what with*** our financial trouble, we decided to put off the trip.

work into — force into little by little
USAGE: He struggled to ***work the piece of metal into*** the small open slot.

✍ Consequence

wear thin — weakened personal quality
USAGE: My tolerance of his continual lying was ***wearing thin*** and I told him it had to stop.

when the chips are down — when a circumstance is urgent and crucial
USAGE: ***When the chips are down***, Thomas is decisive and takes effective action.

worse for wear — not as good as new; worn out
USAGE: The soccer stadium has long been in busy use and is beginning to look the ***worse for wear***.

✍ Different

whistle a different tune — change one's attitude; contradict previous ideas
USAGE: Now that Bill is a parent, he is ***whistling a different tune*** about drinking than when he was younger.

✍ Disagree

wide of the mark — far from the target or the thing aimed at; incorrect
USAGE: His strategy for growth was ***wide of the mark*** from what the board previously emphasized.

yeah right — an expression of doubt or disbelief
USAGE: In disbelief to what he described, I responded, "***Yeah right!***"

✍ Emotion

weigh on/upon — be a weight or pressure on someone or something
USAGE: The strain of job obligations has begun to ***weigh on*** Stanley.

wind up — make very excited, nervous or upset

USAGE: He was really *wound up* this morning when he found out he was admitted to the MBA program.

work up — stir up; arouse; excite
USAGE: Jimmy *works up* a sweat when he walks rapidly on the treadmill.

worked up — feeling excited, angry, worried
USAGE: She was *worked up* when Peter failed to let her know he was leaving.

you don't say — used to show surprise at what is said
USAGE: When I told her I had front row tickets to the concert, she replied, *"You don't say!"*

✍ Entertainment

tune in — adjust a radio or television to pick up a certain station
USAGE: We were looking forward to *tuning in* and watching the championship game on television.

✍ Error

white lie — a harmless lie told for the sake of politeness
USAGE: I told her a *white lie* when I said her new dress was pretty.

✍ Failure

wild goose chase — absurd or hopeless search
USAGE: For whatever reason, she sent us on a *wild goose chase* looking for their house.

will not hear of — will not allow or consider
USAGE: My grandmother said she *will not hear of* us staying with anyone else when visiting her city.

✍ Health

within an inch of one's life — until one is almost dead
USAGE: The attacker assaulted the victim to *within an inch of his life*.

work out — exercise
USAGE: Jason regularly *works out* at the stadium.

✍ Location

wrong side of the tracks — the poor side of town
USAGE: Michael was attracted to a girl whom his parents said was from the *wrong side of the tracks*.

zero in on — adjust a gun so it will hit a target; aim at
USAGE: The shooter *zeroed in on* the target.

✍ Money

worth a cent — worth anything; of any value
USAGE: The outdated computer is very obsolete and not *worth a cent*.

worth one's salt — worth what one is paid
USAGE: Anyone *worth his salt* should have noticed the mistake.

write off — remove (an amount) from a business record as a loss
USAGE: The businessman decided it was necessary to *write off* the bad investment in the accounting report.

✍ Ownership

waltz off with — to take, get or win easily
USAGE: The film actor *waltzed off with* three awards for his acclaimed acting performance.

✍ Personal Description

what it takes — ability for a job; courage
USAGE: Because she is a great researcher, Kelly has *what it takes* to be an outstanding professor.

will power — strength of mind
USAGE: A person needs a strong *will power* to maintain a daily exercise and fitness routine.

wise guy — a person who acts as if he or she is smarter than other people; obnoxious; sarcastic
USAGE: Billy acts like a *wise guy* when we have a substitute teacher.

wolf in sheep's clothing — a person who pretends to be good but really is bad
USAGE: He was a *wolf in sheep's clothing* in his deception toward our group.

yellow streak — cowardice in a person's character
USAGE: He has a *yellow streak* and isn't a person you can expect support from when facing difficulty.

✍ Plan / Prepare

wing it — act without preparation
USAGE: Because of a technology malfunction, Kathryn was not able to use the computer presentation so she had to *wing it*.

work out — devise or arrange a plan
USAGE: Kevin and Scott *worked out* a schedule for filing the production reports.

✍ Quantity

whole show — everything
USAGE: When Karen is at the office, she tries to run the *whole show*.

✍ Relationship

tie the knot — to get married
USAGE: After dating for eighteen months, Robert and Susan decided to *tie the knot*.

two faced — disloyal; untrustworthy; double-dealing
USAGE: Since Jack says one thing and does another, I think he is *two faced* and deceitful.

✍ Satisfaction

what have you — whatever is leftover or available
USAGE: She said, "I'll have a dark roasted coffee brew or *what have you*."

work out — end successfully; be efficient
USAGE: He said, "Just do your best and everything will *work out*."

wrap up — put on warm clothes; dress warmly
USAGE: Since it was very cold outside, he *wrapped up* himself in a heavy jacket.

you tell'em — to agree, affirm someone in what they are saying
USAGE: To acknowledge and affirm the speaker, Charles said, "*You tell'em*!"

✍ Service

wait up for — not go to bed until someone arrives or something happens
USAGE: Joyce's mother *waited up for* her to come home.

wind up — tighten the spring of a machine to make it work or run
USAGE: My grandfather *winds up* the wall clock each night before bed.

✍ Similar

with the best of them — as well as anyone
USAGE: Henry proved he can still play basketball *with the best of them*.

✍ Superior

work over — to hurt someone in order to intimidate them or get money
USAGE: The lawless young people *worked over* the man while committing the robbery.

✍ Time

zero hour — the time when something is scheduled to start
USAGE: At *zero hour* the unmanned rocket was scheduled to blast off into orbit.

✍ Understand

work out — solve, find an answer to
USAGE: Scott consulted with the teacher in an effort to *work out* the mathematics problem.

wrapped up in — thinking only of; interested only in
USAGE: Like most teenagers, she is entirely *wrapped up in* her own activities.

zero in on — give one's full attention to
USAGE: The manager *zeroed in on* a proposed strategy to increase profits for the company.

✍ Work

work one's fingers to the bone — work very hard
USAGE: John has been *working his fingers to the bone* to complete the project.

- Each entry is listed alphabetically according to the first word which forms an integral part of them.
- Words in parentheses are disregarded in determining the order of entries.
- Each entry is followed by its category in abbreviations:
  ACH — Achievement; **AG** — Agree / Approval; **AUTH** — Authority; **BAD** — Bad / Negative; **BUS** — Business Action; **COMM** — Communication; **COMP** — Completeness; **CONS** — Consequence; **DIFF** — Different; **DIS** — Disagree; **EMO** — Emotion; **END** — End; **ENTE** — Entertainment; **ERR** — Error; **FAIL** — Failure; **HEAL** — Health; **IMPO** — Importance; **LOC** — Location; **MON** — Money; **MOVE** — Movement; **OWN** — Ownership; **PER** — Personal Description; **PLAN** — Plan / Prepare; **QUAN** — Quantity; **REL** — Relationship; **SAT** — Satisfaction; **SER** — Service; **SIM** — Similar; **SUP** — Superior; **TIME** — Time; **UND** — Understand; **WORK** — Work

A

a barnburner (ENTE) 4
a barrel of laughs (ENTE) 12
a big shot (PER) 6
a big wheel (PER) 6
a big wig (PER) 6
a bimbo (PER) 13
a bite to eat (SAT) 7
a blank look (PER) 13
a bum rap (CONS) 3
a bun in the oven (HEAL) 5
a cheap drunk (PER) 14
a chicken in every pot (SAT) 7
a crush on (REL) 6
a go-getter (PER) 14
a going concern (ACH) 1
a level playing field (SIM) 7
a lot of bunk (ERR) 4
a month of Sundays (TIME) 7
a nail-biter (ENTE) 12

a picture is worth a thousand words (COMM) 2
a piece of my mind (COMM) 2
about that (AG) 1
about time (TIME) 7
about to do something (TIME) 7
above and beyond the call of duty (ACH) 1
above board (AUTH) 1
absence makes the heart grow fonder (REL) 6
absent-minded (PER) 21
according to Hoyle (BUS) 2
ace (REL) 7
ace in the hole (SUP) 7
Achilles' heel (PER) 21
across the board (SIM) 15
actions speak louder than words (COMM) 2
add fuel to the fire (COMM) 2

I